A Soldier's Life

THE BLACK SOLDIER IN WAR AND SOCIETY

New Narratives and Critical Perspectives

LE'TRICE DONALDSON AND GEORGE WHITE JR., EDITORS

A Soldier's Life

**A BLACK WOMAN'S RISE
FROM ARMY BRAT TO
SIX TRIPLE EIGHT CHAMPION**

Edna W. Cummings
Colonel, US Army, Retired

UNIVERSITY OF VIRGINIA PRESS
Charlottesville and London

University of Virginia Press
© 2025 by Edna W. Cummings
All rights reserved
Printed in the United States of America on acid-free paper

First published 2025

9 8 7 6 5 4 3 2 1

LIBRARY OF CONGRESS CATALOGING-IN-PUBLICATION DATA

Names: Cummings, Edna W., author.
Title: A soldier's life : a Black woman's rise from Army brat to Six Triple
    Eight champion / Edna W. Cummings, Colonel, US Army, Retired.
Description: Charlottesville : University of Virginia Press, 2025. |
    Series: The Black soldier in war and society | Includes bibliographical
    references and index.
Identifiers: LCCN 2024045142 (print) | LCCN 2024045143 (ebook) | ISBN
    9780813953144 (hardcover) | ISBN 9780813953151 (paperback) | ISBN
    9780813953168 (ebook)
Subjects: LCSH: Cummings, Edna W., 1956– | United States. Army—African
    American officers—Biography. | Women soldiers—United States—
    Biography. | Families of military personnel—United States—Biography.
    | Women soldiers—United States—History—20th century. | African
    American soldiers—History—20th century. | Military spouses—United
    States—Biography. | United States. Six Triple Eight Congressional Gold
    Medal Act of 2021. | 6888th Central Postal Directory Battalion Monument
    (Fort Leavenworth, Kansas)
Classification: LCC UB418.A47 C86 2025 (print) | LCC UB418.A47 (ebook) |
    DDC 355.0089/96073—dc23/eng/20241129
LC record available at https://lccn.loc.gov/2024045142
LCCN ebook record available at https://lccn.loc.gov/2024045143

All photos are from the author's collection unless otherwise noted.

Cover photos: Front, members of the 6888th Central Postal Directory
Battalion in parade and ceremony, May 27, 1945, in honor of Joan of Arc
at the marketplace where she was burned at the stake, Rouen, France
(Army/National Archives ID 17539237); back, the author, as First Lieutenant
Cummings, Uijongbu, South Korea

Cover design: Cecilia Sorochin

To my parents, Retired US Army Sgt. 1st Class Willie R. Cummings, and Jessie N. Cummings; my children, Walter and Nisa; and my late husband, Retired US Army Maj. Walter C. Cummings Jr.

CONTENTS

PART IV. UNRECOGNIZED CIVIL RIGHTS PIONEERS

Illustrations follow page 96

ABBREVIATIONS

AGR	Active Guard and Reserve
ATC	Air Traffic Control
CGSC	Command and General Staff College
COSCOM	Corps Support Command
DMZ	Demilitarized Zone
DOD	Department of Defense
DSCA	Defense Support to Civilian Authorities
ETO	European Theater of Operations
JSF	Joint Security Force
KATUSA	Korean Augmentation to the United States Army
KPA	Korean People's Army (North Korea)
LD	Legislative Director
MEDEVAC	Medical Evacuation
MSCA	Military Support to Civilian Authorities
OBC	Officers' Basic Course
ODS	Operation Desert Shield
OOTW	Operations Other Than War
ROTC	Reserve Officers' Training Corps
2LT	Second Lieutenant
SES	Senior Executive Service
STD	Sexually Transmitted Diseases
UNCMAC	United Nations Military Armistice Command

USO   United Services Organization
WAAC   Women's Army Auxiliary Corps
WAC   Women's Army Corps

FOREWORD

The story of this heretofore unknown unit from World War II, the 6888th Central Postal Directory Battalion, remained largely untold for over a half century. It is the story of perseverance, dedication, and service, how young American women of color signed up, volunteering to defend their country—a country that often didn't recognize their value or respect their service. They served anyway. But in 1945, the war ended, and, like many units, their unit in particular ceased to exist. Against all odds they had met the moment, achieving their mission—organizing, sorting, and moving out massive backlogs of mail from storage units in England to troops in forward areas on the continent, improving morale, maintaining family connections, and exceeding every expectation the United States Army had for their success. Afterward, they went home forgotten and without awards or recognition for their service.

Twenty years on, they began to hold reunions, enjoying one another's company again. A few articles were written about them. Then another woman, a Black Army veteran of causes and conflicts from the twentieth into the twenty-first century, found them. Retired US Army Col. Edna Cummings has served since the mid-1970s, in active and reserve capacities, as an officer, Army wife, mother, widow, and then retiree. Edna calls herself a "6888 Advocate." But she was and is much more than that. She planned, organized, mobilized, and led thousands of other volunteers and supporters to turn the story of this forgotten World War II battalion—the only all-Black, all-female unit to deploy overseas in the war—into an icon. This shining light now is held up for future generations to admire, to learn from, and to respect.

The 6888th Central Postal Directory Battalion was led by the indomitable Charity Adams. Perhaps the universe was speaking when Edna Cummings met Charity Adams—because Charity went by her middle name of Edna. Although Lieutenant Colonel Adams passed away in 2002, her legacy resonated with Colonel Cummings on every level. They had many similar experiences in the Army—and faced the same issues of racism, misogyny, and undisguised prejudice in a variety of official settings. Edna found much to admire in the career of Charity Adams. And I found much to admire in them both. Reading Charity Adams's autobiography, I learned exactly how she prepared herself for every challenge: reading, studying, and volunteering for experiences that would make her a better soldier, officer, and leader. She never once backed down or compromised her principles.

Reading this book, I learned the same about Edna Cummings. She too never backed down from a challenge, even if she felt unprepared or unsuited to the task at hand. But I say this to anyone who wonders what they can learn from reading about the remarkable women of the 6888th Central Postal Directory Battalion and their fierce champion, Edna Cummings:

Here is the story of struggle, resilience, and achievement. And in Edna Cummings's telling of the story, there are numerous lessons of leadership and a strength of will—for that is what it takes to never give up. As Edna says, "Sometimes your calling calls you."

May God bless the women of the 6888th, their families, and all their champions.

MARI K. EDER
Maj. Gen. US Army (Ret.)

A Soldier's Life

INTRODUCTION

ON MARCH 3, 2022, at approximately 12:00 p.m. Eastern time, I stood in the office of Speaker of the House, Rep. Nancy Pelosi, at the US Capitol. On that day, she held a signing ceremony for Public Law 11797, awarding the Six Triple Eight the Congressional Gold Medal to honor the all-Black 855-member 6888th Central Postal Directory Battalion of the Women's Army Corps (WAC). A few days earlier, on February 28, 2022, if just for a moment, the Six Triple Eight—as this unit is also known—brought opposing factions of Congress together. With the help of a robust network that I helped to build, the bipartisan legislation to honor the 6888th passed in a polarized political environment with a unanimous vote of 422–0.

Staff members from the office of the sponsor of the House of Representatives Congressional Gold Medal, Rep. Gwen Moore, District 4, Wisconsin, escorted a handful of 6888th family members and me into the building. We walked into the US Capitol's foyer where, a year and two months ago, on January 6, 2021,[1] rioters stormed this same area. Soon after we walked through the security desk and obtained our badges, I recognized the African American retired Army officer who walked past our group. He was Retired US Army Maj. Gen. William J. Walker, selected by Speaker Pelosi to be the first African American sergeant at arms.[2] Being a veteran and an Army officer, I wanted to break from the crowd, shake his hand, and congratulate him. But I didn't. I either believed that action would have been inappropriate, or I was just afraid of being scolded by some security official lurking in a corner waiting for a visitor to step out of line. I'd only seen Walker's face on television, but his voice commanded everyone's attention in Congress when he announced at the State of the Union address, "Ladies and Gentlemen, the President of the United States!" As we moved down the corridor in awe of the Capitol, another imposing figure lingered near Speaker Pelosi's door, a six-foot, seven-inch Capitol police officer named Harry Dunn. Dunn testified to Congress about the visceral hate he experienced on January 6.[3] "Get it together, Cummings!" I whispered to myself. "This is not the time to be starstruck."

Within minutes after we entered Pelosi's office, three Black congresswomen—Representatives Moore; Joyce Beatty, District 3, Ohio; and Barbara Lee, District 12, California—arrived. I was awed by these poised and powerful Black women at the highest level of our government. My initial emotions were mixed with wonderment and uneasiness. I was standing in the space that had been filled with visceral hate and ransacked on January 6. Though I was somewhat unnerved by shadows of the disrespect that previously occupied that space, the warmth and excitement of the day dissipated the images from January 6 that were broadcast throughout the world. The Speaker's regal office was now a place of respect, dignity, and legislative action. Her signature would be the first of three required to enact this legislation. The second signature would be the vice president's, and the final signature—that of the president of the United States. Pelosi's signature was the beginning of an action to bestow the nation's highest civilian honor, the Congressional Gold Medal, upon a group of overlooked World War II Black military women, the 6888th. These Black military women helped us win the war, but, until now, no one seemed to really care.

During World War II, members of the Six Triple Eight faced sexism, racism, and fascism, but they never faced the US Congress. Seven decades later, as their advocate and champion, I did it for them. The result was their receiving the nation's highest civilian honor, the Congressional Gold Medal, awarded to the unit for solving the Army's mail and morale problems in the European Theater of Operations (ETO). With fewer than two hundred of these awards given since General George Washington was designated as the first recipient in 1776, the 6888th was the first of two women's military units to receive this distinction.

The 6888th was the only Black WAC unit that served overseas during World War II. These 855 Black women were predominately African American members of the WAC. I write "predominately" because some of the 6888th members were from the Black diaspora, Mexican American, Puerto Rican, and from the West Indies or Caribbean. Just as my father did when he enlisted in 1946, 6888th members could check only one of three boxes on the military's entrance documents: Negro/Negroid, White, or Other.[4] Some of the Black WACs either chose to join a segregated (Negro) unit or were assigned to one based on their skin tone. However, the term "predominately African American" can be used to describe any Black unit that served during World Wars I and II. Eighteen members of the Harlem Hellfighters were recruited from Puerto Rico.[5] Black men from the Virgin Islands served with the Tuskegee Airmen.[6] Regardless of the ethnicity, skin color also determined whether or not troops were assigned to a segregated unit. National Defense University indicates that "the prevailing attitude was that White men made the best Soldiers and should provide the preponderance of combat forces. . . . The Army had no issue with enlisting Blacks, Filipinos, or Puerto Ricans if they were in separate units."[7] With a few exceptions for Latino and Native Americans, units were either Black or White.[8] The Armed Forces did not authorize desegregation until July 26, 1948, when President Truman's issued Executive Order 9981, "The Desegregation of the Armed Forces."

While the nation recovered from the Great Depression, the United States mobilized for World War II against the Axis powers of Germany, Japan, and Italy. Newspapers and ad campaigns requested women to help America fight the looming threat to democracy. Although the Armed Forces recruited from the masses, a 1925 Army War College study surmised that the "Negro or colored"[9] soldier was fit for only menial tasks. Both male and female troops of color endured hostility and humiliation from society and the military. But society's prejudice did not deter Black women from volunteering to join the military ranks.

With more than one million African Americans serving in the Armed Forces during World War II, the war became a two-pronged battle against racism at home and fascism abroad.[10] The *Pittsburgh Courier* labeled it the "Double Victory" campaign, and the battle extended to Black women in the military. If not for the efforts of First Lady Eleanor Roosevelt and Dr. Mary McLeod Bethune, Black women's military history would have had a different outcome. Roosevelt and Bethune were powerful advocates for the approximately seven thousand Black women who served in the United States and abroad.[11]

One decade and a year after the end of World War II, I was born into a military environment with a shield, albeit flawed, against Jim Crow segregation. Little did I know that I would follow a trail blazed by Black military women and would one day reignite those flames into another trail of advocacy and action.

My autobiography shares the pivotal events that shaped my life, recounting how I, as a Black woman born in the 1950s, forged a successful path in the military and society with the odds stacked against me, and how I, fifteen years after my Army retirement, became an international champion for the 6888th. It's also about my multiple roles and experiences as a military family member, a soldier, a mother, a wife, a widow, and, ultimately, an advocate. I share my life's highs, lows, and pivotal moments about how my journey provided a platform to advocate for the 6888th and other Black women who served in the military during World War II. More than seven decades later, their country finally honors their service and remembers them as heroes and role models. My story serves as a reflection of events and their impact, all of which got me to this point—an advocate for my fallen World War II sisters in arms who pioneered my service. I also hope individuals and organizations who wish to elevate their voices gain useful information about the advocacy process. Most of all, I want my story to inspire and motivate others to at least try to tackle difficult situations.

I've had a military identification card since the day I was born. The ID card provided access to medical care, stable housing, and educational opportunities. Growing up as a military brat, or a child of a parent who served in the military, provided me insights to a community engulfed in war, death, diversity, and civic duty. I embraced these lessons that ignited a passion to travel, problem-solve, and make meaningful contributions to my slice of society and the world.

Now, as a veteran, I embrace a lifestyle experienced by less than 7 percent of the US adult population.[12] Furthermore, less than 2 percent of women in the United States in my age range are veterans.[13] Living my life first as a military child, then as a family member of someone who served, and as a soldier myself, I know firsthand that the military is neither a job nor a career. The military is a lifestyle with its own culture and jargon. I've always believed that if I survived the military, I could make it anywhere because nothing would ever be as hard. While stationed at assignments such as the Pentagon and stressing about PowerPoint slides, a few of us staff officers would chant, *"We are above ground, we are not sleeping in a tent, and no one is shooting at us."* These chants helped us to put our current situation in perspective and reminded us that others are sacrificing their lives and livelihoods in far worse conditions.

While growing up in Fayetteville, North Carolina, I saw several Black WACs, including a neighbor who recruited me to be a child model at one of the United Services Organization (USO) events that she organized. She and the other WACs seemed confident, no-nonsense, and almost intimidating. They appeared to be fearless and unflappable. My main reason for attending college and joining the Army Reserve Officers' Training Corps (ROTC) was to become one of these incredible WACs. I didn't have a long-term career goal for my service. I only wanted to earn the right to wear the uniform. I could not wait to wear the gold second lieutenant bar on my collar and sign my name as 2LT Edna W. Cummings.

I achieved my goal, and soon I decided that I was done with the Army, or so I thought. However, after the death of my husband, I decided to return to what was familiar—the Army. A fellow officer and friend convinced me that the Army wouldn't be as bad the second time around.

He was wise and right about me rejoining the military. It wasn't easy, just better. My promotions and seniority placed me in positions to make impactful decisions and mentor other military personnel.

After retiring from the Army in 2003, I worked as a defense contractor and then decided to launch my own consulting company in 2008. A little more than a decade after my military retirement, in 2016, I stumbled upon an online story about the 855 women who had served in the 6888th Central Postal Directory Battalion overseas. Throughout my military career, other than a few nurses, I seldom read anything about Black military women in World War II.

I was more than fascinated by the story of Maj. Charity "Edna" Adams, a Black female battalion commander. Her middle name, "Edna," drew me to the story of the 6888th. I was in awe of how, with limited training and exposure to military mail operations, at only twenty-six years old, she led a battalion of 855 Black women overseas. Adams implemented a system to clear a multiyear backlog of multimillion pieces of mail and packages in Birmingham, England. The 6888th broke all records for sorting mail and improving troop morale. Yet they returned to the United States unheralded.

In today's military, a battalion command position is held by someone at the rank of lieutenant colonel with approximately sixteen to eighteen years in the Army. Until I learned about the 6888th, I was also unaware of the 6,520 non-nurse Black WAACs (Women's Army Auxiliary Corps) and WACs who served on active duty during World War II. After reading about the 6888th and their impact, Major Adams's journey reminded me of my frustrations at my first duty assignment. I related to some of the other indignities she encountered as a Black female officer. Major Adams and the 6888th deserved some type of recognition and honor for their service. I parked the quest for their recognition in my brain and was determined to find a way to honor Major Adams and the 6888th.

In 2018, I was searching the Rocks, Inc., website to obtain information about an annual scholarship fundraising event. The Rocks, Inc., is a professional development organization for military officers and senior civilians.[14] They asked for donations to raise funds for a monument to honor the 6888th. I donated online and called the project director,

Carlton Philpot, a retired US Navy commander. I asked, "How can I help?" During the early 1990s I had bought an artist's print from him to raise funds for the Buffalo Soldier Monument at Fort Leavenworth, Kansas.[15] He did not remember our almost three-decade-old encounter. But we spoke for at least an hour, and I offered to assist him with fund-raising the approximately $50,000 needed to complete the monument.

Little did I know that Retired US Army Master Sgt. Elizabeth "Lizz" Helm-Frazier had made the same call. Coincidentally, Lizz lives about fifteen minutes from my home in Laurel, Maryland. Obviously, the universe and its divine forces were at work directing our paths for this monument. Lizz and I met for lunch, prayed for guidance, and mapped out a plan to raise funds. During the next four to five months, we contacted our friends and families and asked them to contribute to the monument. Donors submitted money from my social media posts and raised the remaining funds of approximately $50,000. The monument was dedicated in a ceremony at Fort Leavenworth in November 2018.

My research into World War II history and the 6888th provided me with context about the approximately 150,000 WAACs and WACs who served in the Army during that era. I now better understood my father's objections to me joining the Army after high school unless I became an officer. According to *The Women's Army Corps,* a publication of the Center of Military History (CMH):

In early 1943 the number of women joining the Women's Army Auxiliary Corps (WAAC) dropped drastically due to a sudden backlash of public opinion against the employment of women in the Armed Forces. Unfortunately, a variety of social factors had combined to produce a negative public image of the female soldier. Letters home from enlisted men contained a great deal of criticism of female soldiers. When the Office of Censorship ran a sample tabulation, it discovered that 84 percent of soldiers' letters mentioning the WAAC were unfavorable. . . . It was import-ant that the family and community remain unchanged. Women in the military represented change. . . . Many soldiers believed that the WAACs' duties included keeping up morale and "keeping the men happy." It was rumored that 90 percent of the WAACs were prostitutes and that 40 percent of all WAACs were pregnant.[16]

Researching the 6888th connected the dots for me regarding attitudes toward all women in the military, but I still noticed the omission of Black military women's history. Furthermore, I could not recall seeing Black military women represented in World War II movies, documentaries, or other media. These oversights either deleted Black women's contributions to World War II or made them irrelevant. This warped history fueled my passion to not only raise funds for the monument but to bring the 6888th's story of resilience and courage to the forefront of the nation's memory. With an elevated narrative, I believed that the 6888th's history would inspire service members of all races and genders. And it did. Their Congressional Gold Medal attests to that.

Recognition for this once-forgotten unit continues to grow. What started out in November 2018 with the 6888th Monument at Fort Leavenworth, Kansas, transformed into a movement to honor their story with the 2022 Congressional Gold Medal award. Additional recognitions followed. Along with the 2023 redesignation of Fort Lee as Fort Gregg-Adams, an exhibit about the 6888th opened at the Army Women's Museum located at that installation. A Broadway-bound musical and a movie based on the 6888th are in development. My success ensuring these incredible women receive their due recognition happened because of my own career in the US Army. What my experiences taught me about persistence and what it didn't teach me about leveling the playing field were both instrumental in getting me here today as a champion of the 6888th.

The 6888th changed history—and I helped to elevate their story.

PART I

A 10 PERCENT CHANCE

She ain't gonna make it 'round them White folks.
They gone run her off that mountain.

—Unnamed acquaintance of my mother

1

THEM "COTTON PICKING" WARS

ON APRIL 27, 2023, I attended an outdoor Army ceremony with immense pomp and circumstance and with enough military brass and stars to form a constellation. This particular occasion was considered the main event of dethroning the Confederacy's patron saint—redesignating the Fort Lee Army installation as Fort Gregg-Adams.[1] The previous name, Fort Lee, commemorated the iconic Confederate Gen. Robert E. Lee, who led forces against the Union army during the Civil War.[2] The new name honors Retired US Army Lt. Gen. Arthur S. Gregg, a prominent logistics officer who was the first African American to rise to the rank of a three-star general within the Army. The name also honors Lt. Col. Charity Edna Adams Earley, the first Black woman commissioned as a military officer in the Women's Army Auxiliary Corps (WAAC) and who commanded the now historic segregated Women's Army Corps (WAC) 855-member unit, the 6888th Central Postal Directory Battalion (Six Triple Eight), which served overseas during World War II.[3]

During World War I, Army military bases were named for Confederate officers to gain support from southerners. The Army's role in World War II was larger than its role in World War I and required more installations to support the war. The War Department's policy allowed camps in the South to receive southern names, resulting in eight major camps or military installations with Confederate names.[4] Retired US Navy Adm. Michelle Howard, a Black woman, led the 2021 Department of Defense commission to rename assets honoring the Confederacy. The commission's charter tasked them with "modifying or removing anything that commemorates the Confederate States of America or any person who served voluntarily with the Confederacy."[5] The catalyst for the renaming of military bases was the May 25, 2020, murder of George Floyd, who died while in custody of a White police officer who positioned his knee on Mr. Floyd's neck for approximately eight minutes. As a result of public outcry over Floyd's death, Confederate statues and military bases named for Confederate generals became recognized nationally as the symbols of institutionalized racism that they were; renaming these bases was a first step for the nation to reject this legacy.[6]

Since I am a retired Army logistics officer, I knew about Lieutenant General Gregg, but I didn't learn about Lieutenant Colonel Adams until 2016–17.[7] Her leadership in the United States and overseas has now made Black women's World War II military history relevant and impacted my life in ways that I never imagined. My attempts to remain stoic during the redesignation ceremony were unsuccessful. I dabbed a few drops of fluid that trickled constantly from my eyes and nose. I blamed the body moisture on the humidity and sauna-like conditions from the plastic outdoor event tent filled with more than six hundred people attending the ceremony. I used the program as a personal fan to dry the sweat dripping from my face and neck. People thanked me for making this event happen. I graciously accepted the praise, but I felt numb. I asked myself two questions: "Why are you here? How did you arrive at this moment?"

In 1947, two years after World War II ended, and a year after Adams left the Army, my father's military duty required him to be stationed in Italy as a member of the Army's European Occupation Force. Then, one year after his return from the Korean War in 1955, I was born. My excitement and recollections about the Army began around the age of four, in 1960. Our family lived on an Army base where my father was stationed at Fort Gordon, Georgia, outside of his hometown of Augusta. (In October 2023, Fort Gordon was renamed Fort Eisenhower.)

I associate Fort Gordon with Kiki, a blond, wide-eyed German American boy with a bowl haircut, maybe my age. If he wasn't my age, he was at least my height. Almost daily, Kiki sat by our front screen door and waited for me to come outside and play while my mom combed and braided my hair. His voice has vanished from my memory, and his facial features are now invisible. I only see the angle of his body braced against the screen door with his legs crossed and head slightly bowed.

Perhaps Kiki's mom wanted his playtime with me accelerated. Or maybe she wanted to relieve my mom's daily styling struggle with my hair. Regardless, his German mother advised my mom to use the Army-issue stainless steel fork from Dad's mess kit to untangle my hair, especially when it was wet. I cringed and sniffled with the occasional "Oww!" while Mom perfected her "pick, comb, brush, braid, and secure" rhythm. Pick out the kinks with the fork, comb, smooth with a brush, braid, and secure the braid's end with a plastic barrette. The moms didn't know that they were ahead of a styling trend, with the Army's mess fork as a prelude to the 1970s Afro pick. The routine lasted about fifteen minutes, but it left a lasting impression on me and future hairstyling techniques.

When wet, my hair shrank and coiled to approximately four to five times less than its original length. At that time, Prell shampoo and Royal Crown hair grease were the standards for Black hair grooming: Prell to wash, and Royal Crown to smooth the tight coils. To untangle my hair after washing it, Mom separated the frizzy and coily mane into sections with hairpins and allowed it to air-dry for a few hours. We didn't have a hair dryer, and my hair dried naturally just like our clothes did on the clothesline outside. Except I stayed inside and waited for Mom's "It's dry!" announcement. After my hair dried, Mom applied the hair grease and used the straightening comb heated on an electric stove burner to smooth it out. However, Mom's arsenal of styling tools could not combat Georgia's year-round heat and humidity.

But the daily hair rituals didn't matter to Kiki. He was patient. He sat and waited until we could play. I don't think he hung around for the hair-washing ritual. I lost track of Kiki, but he had to be one of the nicest friends I ever had. Wherever he is, I hope he never lost his commitment to friendship. My dad's next military assignment broke that friendship bond, but I soon made friends at his next duty station.

In April 1960, Dad received an assignment as a signal section chief with Headquarters, Company A, 82nd Airborne Maintenance Battalion, Fort Bragg, North Carolina. (In June 2023, Fort Bragg was redesignated as Fort Liberty.) We moved to a townhouse with hardwood floors at Fort Bragg, 102 Ganahl Place. The great room, or living room area, had a 36- to 40-inch round beige wooden coffee table with a T-shape divider with four sections to store magazines and knickknacks beneath the glass tabletop. A neighbor's son later broke the glass when he did a forward roll too close to the table. I don't think he received any cuts, but his mom did yell at him for breaking our glass tabletop. I'm certain he got mad at me for telling her how he broke our table.

Our kitchen was at the rear of the home and faced a sliding board and swing set nested on gray dirt surrounded by a well-manicured common area. I'm confident that the playground awaited my post-breakfast arrival. Some days, Mom and I caught a cab to Fort Bragg's hospital, Womack, for my routine checkup or to receive vaccinations. We sat in the waiting room lined with black hard plastic chairs. Mom entertained me with writing and spelling games from the names on the doors, "A-d-m-i-n-i-s-t-r-a-t-i-o-n" or "P-r-i-v-a-t-e." When I became bored with spelling, she switched to reading the paper customer service ticket numbers and asking me to count until our number was called. Mom said she was amazed when I threw a tantrum when our number was called for a vaccination. My counting skills impressed her—I really knew how to count. Womack Army Hospital had to be the foundation of my elementary education along with the development of "white coat syndrome." I didn't like doctor's visits then, and I don't like them now. My worst visit to Womack was when I soared too high on the swing and landed too hard in the gray dirt beneath the swing set. After a couple of days of home remedies, my knee was leaking green pus, so a Womack nurse cleaned the wound. My right knee still bears the scar from the Fort Bragg playground.

While living on Fort Bragg, Dad required me to follow some basic rules. The most important rule was to remember my home address and his name, rank, and serial number. He gave me routine drills to ensure I remembered this vital information. The second rule was to never throw paper or anything on the ground. The third rule was not to walk on the grass. Fort Bragg had "Keep Off the Grass" signs all over the place. I never questioned why we couldn't walk on the grass. I just didn't do it. To this day, I still remember my dad's serial number, I do not litter, and I try hard not to walk on grass in public places.

Fort Bragg soldiers greeted each other with a loud "Airborne!" The response to this was always, "All the Way!" For the longest time I thought that the soldiers were yelling, "Air-Bone." I'm not sure when I learned that the greeting was "Airborne" and not "Air-Bone." I had no clue that these men jumped out of aircraft into war zones.

During that time at Fort Bragg, I truly believed that my mom was a magician. I now refer to her hard work in our home as "Military Mom Magic," or M3. Her M3 powers seemed effortless. Her coffee magic trick was absolutely the best one. Whenever she poured hot water from the tin coffee pot into a coffee cup, the water turned brown. It took me about a year to figure out that magic trick. Tears welled into my eyes whenever I poured clear water into my dolls' tea set cup. No matter how hard I tried, I could never make the water turn brown. Years later when I grew taller, I realized that instant coffee was in the bottom of the cup. It wasn't magic—just instant coffee. Occasionally, the brown liquid would fill the glass knob on the tin coffeepot on the stove. I didn't know how that happened either; my mom just made it happen. It had to be magic. That magic also became reality when I learned the difference between instant and ground coffee. To this day, I prefer instant coffee; it's easier to make.

Along with her coffee magic, the M3 happened during the week before sunrise. When Dad left for work around 5:00 a.m., Mom prepared a hearty breakfast. When he returned home in the evenings or at night, Mom always had a hot dinner ready for him. Not just hot, but "piping hot," and the steam rose, or "piped," from the food when served. She said that the least she could do was ensure that her husband had a comfortable home and hot meals. My mom never said, "The way to a man's heart is through his stomach," but she must have believed it because my breakfast was Dad's leftovers. My standard morning fare was two slices of crispy fried bacon, one scrambled egg, one slice of evenly browned oven toast with a melted butter circle, a bowl of grits with a melted butter square, and a glass of milk. I'd like to think that Dad left bacon slices just for me.

Mom's M3 extended to his military uniform, or fatigues, consisting of a long-sleeved dark-green shirt and pants. Instead of sending clothes to the cleaners, Mom perfected her own cost-saving methods to launder Dad's uniforms. She washed and sprayed his fatigues with starch to have razor-sharp creases in the pants and alongside the arm of the shirt. The cardboard-hard pants and shirt made a cracking and scratching sound when he put them on after they'd been ironed. I'm sure the term "breaking starch" must have come from those sounds. Breaking starch is no longer required in the military; the uniforms are now what was then called wash-and-wear. My dad broke starch every day.

Polished jump boots were another vital accessory to my dad's starched uniform. Using a torn white T-shirt, he applied a shiny black paste from a round can to his bubble-toed, black-laced jump boots. The black paste—Kiwi shoe polish. To maintain the shine, he applied the polish on his boots and paid special attention to the bubble toe and heel area of the shoe. After applying shoe polish, he waited until it dried to a dull finish. With an approximately six-inch flat shoe brush, he brushed the entire boot. After brushing, he dipped the tip of a white T-shirt into the shoe-polished lid half-filled with water. He then rubbed the tip and heel area of the boot, alternating the polish and water until the boots had a mirrorlike quality. This was a spit shine. But I never saw my dad spit on his boots; he only used the water from the shoe polish lid.

Polished and shined shoes became my mom's dating and marriage tips. But I didn't hear these tips until I was about twenty-four years old. Mom advised me to always look at a man's shoes to see if they were polished to a shine: "Pay special attention to scuff marks on the heel of a man's shoe. If the heels of his shoes run down or had an angle, he is not the man for you. If a man can take good care of his shoes, there's a good chance that he will take care of his family." I never told her that I disproved her theory. Unfortunately, I've met many well-heeled people throughout my life who were incapable of focusing on anything but themselves and their accoutrements.

Besides "Air-Bone," another phrase permeated our home, "inspection." To prepare for inspection, Dad polished these round, gold metal-like, quarter-sized circles or insignia. Inspection uniforms were either a full green wool blazer or khaki shirt and pants adorned with insignia on the lapels, military ribbons and medals above the chest pocket, and the pants tucked into the boots. He explained to me that inspection meant that everything on his uniform had to shine without any spots. To achieve the shine, he first rubbed a bile-yellow liquid called Brasso onto his insignia until it dried into a gray powder. Second, he removed the gray powder with a piece of a torn white T-shirt and rubbed the insignia. The final step was to remove the gray residue stuck in the insignia crevices with a toothpick tip covered with a torn T-shirt strip.

Fort Bragg was also the birthplace of my new legal name. One day when I was around six years old, a lady visited our home. She came upstairs to my room and asked me a bunch of questions. I don't know if she was a social worker or someone from the court system. To me she was just someone asking questions. I later learned that my birth mother had died when I was fifteen months old, and my parents began the process of adopting me. That meant changing my name from Edna Wannis Dixon to Edna Wannis Cummings.

I was the fifth of six children. At thirty-two years old, our mother, also named Edna, died at Womack Army Hospital at Fort Bragg from childbirth eclampsia and cerebral hermorrhage. She was pregnant with her sixth child, who also died. My current mom, Jessie Cummings, is my birth father's sister. She had an ectopic pregnancy and could not have children. Edna, my birth mother, had been married previously. She left two teenage girls, fifteen and thirteen, by her first marriage and three children, including me, by her second marriage. After our mother's death I lived with my new mom and her husband, my dad, now Retired US Army Sgt. 1st Class Willie R. Cummings. My birth father became my uncle. Until then I had no idea that I was adopted.

My adoption and new legal name as Edna Wannis Cummings were finalized in 1962. The legalization really didn't matter to me; I never knew the difference. For as long as I can remember, my name was Edna Cummings, but with the adoption I was legally an only child. Decades later while I underwent the Army's security background investigation, my mom reminded me that I was born as Edna Dixon. Even now, I get a kick out of seeing my name online as a.k.a. "Edna Wannis Dixon." Weird thing is that I never wrote my name as Edna Dixon. Cummings has been my last name for as long as I can remember.

Even now, people get confused when my sisters refer to my mom as "Aunt Jessie" and I call her mom. We only explain our relationship when people ask or if we notice the obvious confusion. Besides, the names didn't matter. We all grew up together in Fayetteville. My sister Jackie, who is three years older than me, began living with us when she was twelve years old.

Sometime in 1962, other phrases became part of my vernacular, "alert" and "orders." "Alert" meant that my dad might have to go somewhere without Mom and me. One day he came home from work repeating the phrase, "I got orders, I got orders." His orders sent him to Vietnam in late March 1962. A few weeks later my mom and I were on a bus headed to her home in Utica, Mississippi. During that time, military families had to move out of military housing if the service member got deployed to a combat location. My mom's childhood home in rural Mississippi was the only place available for us to live.

My mother Jessie grew up on a farm in Utica, about thirty miles southwest of the state's capital, Jackson. My grandparents lived in a wooden three-bedroom farmhouse next to a cotton field with a water well in the front and a barn and an outdoor toilet in the rear. Somehow, my grandparents raised eleven children in that same home, and my mom was one of the younger girls. When we returned to Utica, my grandparents slept in one bedroom, and my mom and I slept in the front room, or living room, that doubled as a bedroom. My two uncles and an aunt slept in another room. My grandparents raised chickens, hogs, and cows and had a garden filled with every edible plant imaginable. I loved the sugarcane, strawberries, corn, and peanuts. My grandfather was an incredible farmer who dried peanuts on the roof of the barn and cut sugarcane into bite-sized sticks and placed them in a cup for me to savor. He taught me how to sew clothes from scrap fabric for the corn husk dolls he made for me. I regarded my occasional trips to the cotton field as playtime. I found great delight in picking the white fuzzy flowers and dropping them into somebody's tan burlap bag. That experience in the cotton field made me appreciate the saying "living in tall cotton." This means that you don't have to bend over too far to pick the cotton, thereby reducing back strain.

My cotton picking teachers were other family members and neighbors who taught me how not to include the dried brown outer parts of the cotton flower and the stalks as I picked the cotton. Too much trash mixed with the cotton reduced the yield. Another egregious error was to pick the green cotton buds that had not yet blossomed. Picking those meant that you prevent a full cotton harvest and degrade the quality of cotton for sale.

Sometimes my grandmother rewarded me with ten or twenty cents for just going to the cotton fields and mimicking work. I used the money to visit the store down the street run by a White family. Years later, an investigation revealed the store owners had family members who were members of the Ku Klux Klan (KKK). The store owners weren't implicated, but their family member was later indicted as a KKK Grand Dragon. During my many visits to the store, I never suspected anything suspicious. I was never warned about going to the store or felt uncomfortable there. In retrospect, my interactions were simply transactional. I gave them a penny or two for cookies, candy, or whatever goodies I could afford.

Living on the farm also taught me about recycling and organic foods. Leftover food and dishwater went into a white plastic bucket for hog slop (food), paper went into the fireplace. Glass soda bottles were returned to the store for a refund. My grandmother milked cows, churned butter, and made fresh biscuits daily. Food was cooled in an icebox with ice purchased from the "ice man," who sold blocks of ice from a truck. She canned vegetables from the garden and sold a cow or sacks of cotton. Living on my grandparents' farm in 1962 was a lesson in self-sustainment, or "living off the land."

In mid-June 1962, a short, thin-framed White lady wearing cat-eyed glasses appeared at my grandparents' house. She was from the Red Cross. She said a few words and handed Mom an envelope. The next item she gave Mom was a small yellow, white, and brown square tin containing Bayer aspirin. Red Cross workers must have been taught to give the bad news (envelope), wait for a response, and then give the aspirin. Mom sat on the wooden porch steps with the Red Cross lady and opened the envelope. The envelope contained a US government Western Union telegram typed in all capital letters:

"THE SECRETARY OF THE ARMY ASKED ME TO ADVISE YOU THAT YOUR, HUSBAND, SGT. WILLIE. R. CUMMINGS WAS INJURED IN VIETNAM ON JUNE 13. EXTENT OF THE INJURY UNKNOWN. UPON RECEIPT OF FURTHER INFORMATION, YOU WILL BE ADVISED IMMEDIATELY." MR. JOHN CUMMINGS, FATHER IS ALSO BEING NOTIFIED.
    J.C. LAMBERT, MAJOR GENERAL, U.S. ARMY
    THE ADJUTANT GENERAL

After sitting on the porch with my mom for a few minutes, the lady drove away.

Mom's tears flowed freely, and her shoulders shook while she whimpered with angst and sorrow. She and I gathered around a ten-inch black-and-white television with my grandparents and a few other relatives who were in the home. The television was to the left of the wood-burning fireplace and set atop a light oak-colored dresser about five feet tall. Chances are we moved the television antenna to get the best reception. We listened to hear something else about the Vietnam War. We hoped to hear Dad's name. We did not.

Three days later, Mom received another telegram:

ADDITIONAL INFORMATION RECEIVED CONCERNING YOUR HUSBAND, SGT. WILLIE R. CUMMINGS. HIS PRESENT CONDITION AND PROGNOSIS IS GOOD. ESTIMEATE [sic] LENGTH OF FURTHER HOSPITILIZATION IS FOUR MORE WEEKS. UPON

RECEIPT OF FURTHER INFORMATION, YOU WILL BE ADVISED
IMMEDIATELY.

Dad recuperated in a hospital in Manila, the Philippines. His good
prognosis meant that he was well enough to return to Vietnam when
he was discharged from the hospital. He returned to the battlefront
with shrapnel still lodged in his neck and chest and additional scars on
his arms and back. Many years later, I located his Military Assistance
Training Advisory Course Certificate from the US Army Special Warfare
School, Fort Bragg, dated March 23, 1962. He left for Vietnam on March 26
and was wounded in less than ninety days.

Years later, he finally talked about his injuries. Dad recounted to me
that he had been part of Advisory Team #4 Infantry, 1st Infantry Division.
The Viet Cong had ambushed his squad and shot him in the chest, arm,
and neck. A sergeant who wore ill-fitting glasses that frequently fell off
his face had been killed. Dad recalled seeing his death: when the sergeant
was shot, his glasses remained on his face. While I was stationed at Fort
Rucker, Alabama, in 1978, Dad pointed out the type of helicopter that had
airlifted him when he was wounded. He recalled hearing the aircraft approach, and then he heard it leave because of the intense ground fighting.
Luckily, the pilot believed that there were soldiers still alive on the ground
and returned to airlift them to a treatment facility. Dad remains grateful
to a mean Army nurse who administered painful breathing exercises and
refused to let him die. His lungs had collapsed from the bullet wounds.

He was assigned to the 1st Infantry Division, 11th Tactical Area, and
the Republic of Vietnam commander sent my dad's senior advisor, a
lieutenant colonel, a letter citing the incident (excerpt):

Captain H. E. Anderson and Sergeant W. R. Cummings Advisors of
the 1st Battalion, 1st Infantry Regiment, were wounded together
with a number of 1st Division soldiers in a fire attack made by
the Viet-Cong on 13 June 1962. . . . [T]hey have won the love of the
Vietnamese unit and clearly demonstrated the will as well as the
spirit of an American soldier who fights with the ARVN for the
common ideal of freedom.

In the fall of 1962, I began school in the one-room schoolhouse of Burley-Hamilton Elementary School in Utica. Thanks to Womack Army Hospital's waiting room school lessons, I excelled at math and spelling. I could count to one hundred on the three-foot-tall upright abacus. My grandmother and mom packed incredible lunches with ham biscuit sandwiches spread with homemade jam in a brown paper lunch bag.

Mom looked forward to Dad's letters from Vietnam. In October 1962, she received a letter from Dad expressing expectations for our future in a new home in Fayetteville. Reading this sixty-year-old letter sheds light on how military personnel find hope while deployed overseas. Dad's letters made us feel connected to him; we knew that he was still alive:

My Dearest Darling,

I have just finished writing a letter to you. I thought I would write you another to let you know how I was feeling tonight after I found out that Floyd Patterson had lost the fight.[8] It made me feel even lower. I was already feeling low enough just thinking about how much I would like to be there with you, but the fight added to this. You can't win them all. Though better luck next time. Well Darling, hope you feel well tonight and also hope you have a good night's rest. Tonight is Wednesday night 26. Jessie, when you go to Fayetteville I want you to see if that lot I wanted is still open. I still want it and I will love for you to pick out the house that you want. If [it] would be all right with you I would like to get that place. The road is probably paved. Now I think it would make a fine place to live. [punctuation added for clarity]

In May 1963, Dad returned from Vietnam with a new assignment to Fort Bragg as a senior radar repairman, member of Company A, 82nd Airborne Signal Battalion. Mom and I returned to Fayetteville. My parents and I lived with a family near Murchison Road behind Melvin's Cleaners until our new residence in Fayetteville was ready. Dad used his GI Bill to buy us a three-bedroom brick house with a carport on a corner lot in a new housing development called Eccles Park. I'm sure this was the housing lot mentioned in his letters, but the streets were not paved as he had hoped. In the fall of 1963, we moved to our new home. Eccles Park was an idyllic community of brick houses with unpaved red clay streets and green lawns filled with African American professionals and military families. Some were schoolteachers (male and female), military officers, military enlisted, and stay-at-home moms. The wives built a close network to ensure that no one went without when money was tight. Neighbors borrowed butter, milk, bread, and occasionally a few dollars. Military families seemed to have frequent pay or salary problems.

Although I didn't have access to a swing set, the red clay in the streets and empty lots provided another type of playground. I drew hopscotch squares and badminton and dodgeball lines in the street. The red clay dirt provided ample supplies to make bombs for simulated warfare against the "Commies" whom our fathers fought overseas. I developed gunfire and artillery voice sounds to mimic incoming attacks whenever my team launched a direct target hit on the opposition.

Mom and Dad made sure I attended Sunday school, and we all attended the local church, Parks Chapel. We were truly blessed. My dad was alive and home from Vietnam.

Life was good. I didn't have to pick cotton, and I had my own bedroom.

2

HIPPIE MURDERERS AND STRAWBERRY MILKSHAKES

MY TWO BEST FRIENDS FROM the first grade are now deceased. But in the early 1960s, the three of us were competitive handwriters. We worked hard to print perfect alphabets and to stay within the horizontal dotted-line guides of the writing paper. Mom told me that I practiced writing like one of my friends because she had received praise from our first-grade teacher, Mrs. Parker. Ferguson Elementary No. 12 grouped students by academic ability, and along with Mrs. Parker's praise, we wanted to maintain our academic spot for the next school year. Without realizing what we were doing, we engaged in academic competition. I was fortunate enough to maintain my academic placement (11, 21, 31, etc.) for the six years of elementary school with most of the same classmates. The first number indicated the grade level, the second number indicated the academic level.

Like our neighborhood, Ferguson also had mixed-race children. Several families had adopted military children from German and Korean orphanages or married interracially. A few of our teachers also appeared to be White, but we later learned that they identified as African American. In the big scheme of things, no one cared about mixed-race families during that time. My friends and I put our energies into not getting disciplined or losing our academic spot in the next school year. A few of us maintain contact on social media and share information about mutual acquaintances from our elementary and junior high school years.

On the afternoon of November 22, 1963, our second-grade teacher, Mrs. Butler, suddenly started crying. She was a thin, tall lady with short, brown, wavy hair who could have passed for White. Another teacher had probably stopped by the room and shared the horrific news. Ms. Butler's skin became flushed, her eyes filled with water, and her nose turned rose pink. As she wiped away the tears and blew her nose, the class became very quiet. She managed to say, "Someone killed President Kennedy," or words to that effect. Silence mixed with grief enveloped the class of second graders. Many of us also started crying. We rushed home after school to watch television to make sense of this catastrophic event. Somehow, we knew that our parents wouldn't have the answers about why someone would kill the president. The president was dead. We were confused and afraid. I believe we knew that our world was changing.

Ann was my best friend in elementary school. Ann was three months younger than me, but one grade behind me in school because of her November birthday. She lived two houses down the street, and her father was also in the Army. Every day, we walked to school together. In the summer, we played school and formed a "Plans for the Future" club. I believe that we were the only two members in the club. Our main activity was turning the pages of department store catalogues and picking out clothes and household items that we hoped to have one day.

In May 1965, our fathers took us to a special event at Fort Bragg. Sen. Robert F. Kennedy was visiting to dedicate the headquarters and buildings at John F. Kennedy Special Operations and Warfare Center.[1] I don't remember his speech. The speech didn't matter. Ann and I were excited to see the former president's brother in person. After his speech, our fathers led us through a stairwell to get to our car. Amazingly, we were in the same stairwell as Senator Kennedy and saw his family! They smiled and said, "Hello." We were in awe and giddy with excitement. When we exited the building, Ann and I were in front of the crowd, standing beside Senator Kennedy's car. We wiped our hands on his car and removed the dust and vowed never to wash our hands again. I think that's when I started collecting Kennedy half dollars, many of which I still have. His kids waved goodbye as their car drove away.[2]

Ann and I broke that vow and washed the Kennedy car dust from our hands. We've maintained contact through college, life's joys, and grief. We were bridesmaids at each other's weddings. Every year we exchange birthday cards. We now discuss how we can best help our aging parents. In June 2024, while I was completing this manuscript, Ann's mom died.

About a month after our exhilarating Senator Kennedy encounter, Dad was off to "Dom Rep," as he called it. The 82nd Airborne deployed in the Dominican Republic in support of Operation Power Pack to stabilize the region after leftist forces overthrew the Dominican leader. Since we were in our own home and not living on a military base, we did not have to move. He never told me what his job was in the "Dom Rep." Thankfully, he returned home with no injuries.[3]

Throughout my elementary school years, I relished the military lifestyle. Food and clothes cost less when we shopped at Fort Bragg, and we didn't pay sales tax. Unlike Fayetteville's retail stores that closed because of the blue law, Fort Bragg's Post Exchange clothing store was open on Sundays.[4] A trip to the food store or commissary yielded at least ten brown grocery bags full of food and treats to last for at least a month. Those excursions represented pride and progress: pride in having a military identification card, and progress because we could shop in the safe and welcoming environment of the military installation. Military police were always around, and we didn't worry as much about racial tensions while shopping.

I also looked forward to scrumptious treats from Dad's leftover C-rations or canned food used during field training. My favorites were white candy-coated chewing gum squares and two-inch round, dusty milk chocolate candy. On some holidays, Mom and I accompanied him to mess halls (now called dining facilities) for Thanksgiving and Christmas dinners. For those meals, we ate with the soldiers from hard copper-brown plastic trays with food compartments for the entrée, side dishes, and dessert. We attended his company cookouts, and I rode in a helicopter for one of my birthdays. Life seemed simple, basic, and fun. Our biggest fear was the death of friends or family members not returning from Vietnam. Then the killing of our nation's leaders started again.

After Dr. Martin Luther King's death in 1968, Sen. Robert Kennedy was assassinated in 1969. His death was another heartbreaking moment for me. I felt a personal connection to the Kennedys. After all, Senator Kennedy and his family saw me in the stairwell and said "Hello" and smiled. His children remembered Ann and me when they got into the car, and we waved goodbye to each other. I also shared a birthday with one of the late President Kennedy's children: Arabella, who was stillborn.[5] For me, these assassinations robbed me of a haven. These deaths were unnerving, probably because I was getting older and better understood the meaning of death. Dying in a war was for the nation and freedom. Assassinations meant murder for no reason other than hatred.

After completing the sixth grade, some friends and I decided to be radical and attend a White junior high school, Alexander Graham, or AG, located in downtown Fayetteville. About five of us opted to ride the city bus instead of a school bus. Apparently, we could attend any school we wanted to if we could arrange our own transportation. By attending AG, I would have the chance to be in the downtown area of Fayetteville, see what the White people did in school, and just do something different from my other classmates.

After a few weeks at AG, I saw that it wasn't that different from a Black school. AG had a few Black students, and other than having more White people, AG didn't seem too impressive. I made a few White friends and discussed race occasionally. When least expected, racial discussions occurred. Two of them stuck with me.

One day, my White friend Rosemary came to school angry at her sister. Rosemary was upset because her sister would not allow her to talk to me when I called her at home. I was proud that she argued with her sister about me. The second event occurred while I was standing in the cafeteria line. A strawberry-haired White girl with freckles mentioned that she didn't like collards. One of my Black friends thought she said "coloreds." They exchanged a few words, and the almost racial event ended with a clear understanding of the differences between the words "collard" and "colored."

Everything was going well at home and at school until the winter of 1969. Dad received orders to go to Vietnam for a second time. In February 1969, he left home for another tour with an assignment to the 173rd Airborne Brigade. Since I was older, I better understood the meaning of the Vietnam War and how many soldiers were being killed. I'd lost a cousin, and a friend in our neighborhood had lost her father. The National Archives indicates that 11,780 Americans died in Vietnam in 1969.[6] I remember hugging Dad and crying intensely as he left. I knew that this would be the last time that I would see him. Dad still had shrapnel, or metal fragments, in his body with scars on his neck, back, and arms from being wounded in 1962. I knew that the odds of him returning home alive were slim or nonexistent. I refused to stay home from school, but I cried most of the day. Mom's advice as I walked out of the door for school was, "Tell your teachers that your dad left for Vietnam." I only told my gym teacher. I don't know what sport we were playing in class, but I felt numb and sad about my dad and did not participate.

Several days after Dad's departure, I had several dreams about a black limousine-style car pulling into our driveway. No one ever got out of the car, and the car just sat at the top of the driveway. That was the extent of the dream. I never talked about it. Eventually, after several months, the dreams stopped. The military didn't have the family support programs like they have now. Our families dealt with our grief the best way we knew how. We were happy to receive letters and packages and offered comfort to families who experienced tragedy. Since Dad was in the Signal Corps (that is, communications specialty), we received occasional telephone calls on a military radio from Vietnam. Our short conversations were laced with radio telephone operator language—Roger, Over, and Out. Those few minutes of hearing his voice were better than any letter. At that moment, we knew that he was alive.

With Dad's telephone calls, a wonderful neighborhood, and new friends, my life was stable. Mom was still working her magic, maintaining the home, and ensuring that I had a morning breakfast of grits, toast, and bacon. However, the round butter circles disappeared from the toast, and we now had a toaster. Butter came in small plastic tubs instead of squares, and Mom spread the butter on the bread after it was toasted. Occasionally, Mom substituted smoked link sausage instead of bacon and offered cold cereal and milk sometimes instead of hot grits. Nonetheless, I still had a daily dose of her breakfast and the Military Mom Magic.

In February 1970, my sister Jackie, Mom, and I were unnerved and terrified by a report of three hippies who allegedly had killed a family at Fort Bragg. A Special Forces doctor, Capt. Jeffrey MacDonald, found his wife and two children murdered viciously in their home. Somehow, he had survived the attack. To protect us from these hippies, Mom located a baseball bat and placed it near the bed. The three of us slept together in her bed for several days just in case the hippies attacked. MacDonald remains in prison convicted of his family's murder.[7] I often wondered why he singled out hippies to cover up his crime since they were known for peace and not violence.

Other than Dad going to Vietnam and surviving the Tet '69 counter-offensive, MacDonald's contrived hippie murderers roaming Fayette-ville, and the almost racial incidents at school, my seventh-grade year was unremarkable. In May 1970, Dad returned home with no additional physical injuries from Vietnam, and I prepared to start eighth grade. In the eighth grade, district rules required me to attend the predom-inately Black school, Washington Drive Junior High. Those of us who returned to Washington Drive were placed in the 81 class taught by Mrs. Ruby Murchison, which caused several other students to move to the 82 class. We 81 AG transfers encountered some mean-girl taunting for their displacement. Physical violence never occurred, only verbal outrage. During those times, walking away from a verbal encounter usually ended the dispute. Besides, I didn't want my parents to get a call from school or disappoint my teacher—that encounter would have been far worse than a student argument. I am proud that my eighth-grade teacher, Mrs. Murchison, won the 1976 National Teacher of the Year and received the gold apple from President Gerald Ford.[8]

I made it through the two years of junior high school without incident and celebrated a relaxing of the dress code that allowed girls to wear pants to school. I was also a rover guard on the intramural six-person girls' basketball team. Apparently, the basketball rule makers didn't believe girls were strong enough to run full court. Only two girls could rover, or run the full court. I was one of those two.

In the ninth grade, Washington Drive became more racially integrated, and I also managed to secure a spot on the coveted cheerleading squad. My primary reason for cheerleading was to attend the football and basketball games for free. Our family was on a tight budget with even tighter household rules. I also knew that the best way to have a social life was to participate in extracurricular events such as intramurals and cheerleading. In those days, the cheerleading teams were not as competitive. A basic cartwheel, partial split, and a good herkie jump with a smile, strong voice, and good grades landed you a spot.

I devised a plan to graduate from high school early and go to college at sixteen. I mapped out my plan, took an algebra II course in the summer after ninth grade, and signed up for geometry in the tenth grade. With my plan in motion, I was all set for high school and early graduation. However, my life changed dramatically when I entered E. E. Smith High School as a tenth grader. E. E. Smith is a legendary high school in Fayetteville. Located less than a mile from Fayetteville State University, E. E. Smith has produced several professional athletes, coaches, national business owners,[9] and Army generals.[10] Even now, E. E. Smith has its annual reunion on Memorial Day.[11] Alumni from throughout the United States attend the event each year. In 2024, I attended the fiftieth reunion, which included several classmates from elementary school. Some of us recalled our competitive academic classes and our determination to make our parents proud of us.

E. E. Smith also had an amazing marching band with a fantastic drum major and a golf club. For some reason, as a tenth grader, I wanted to giggle all the time, because everything just struck me as funny. My grades slipped a little, with a few more Bs instead of As. I also got a D in conduct in one class for talking too much and not paying attention. But I still loved math, especially geometry. As a tenth-grader, I wanted to hang out with my friends and go to house parties and football games. I still planned to graduate early, but E. E. Smith had an energy that made me happy to attend school. I don't know if it was because there were popular eleventh and twelfth graders in my math class, or because of the excitement of meeting kids from other neighborhoods including Fort Bragg. My world became larger and filled with new friendships and social activities and more clothing choices that included wearing pants to school and elsewhere.

Since my sister Jackie was now driving, she replaced Mom as the chauffeur. A few years earlier, Dad had bought us a sewing machine and a pale powder-blue Plymouth Valiant with a push-button transmission and rust spots on the door handle. We nicknamed the car the *Slanthead 6*. I have no idea why we called it that, but the *Slanthead 6* was always filled with my giggly girlfriends and patience from my sister, the chauffeur. Each week I wore a new outfit to school. I sewed fabulous clothes from McCall's and Singer patterns. For a quick skirt I cut the tops from my mom's old dresses and sewed elastic in the waist of the bottom half. To complete the look, I made matching cloth neck chokers from seam tape with appliqués. My favorite choker was one with a peace sign, which gave the outfits a counterculture look, or "hippie" vibe. Since fabric was only about a dollar a yard or less, I could craft a miniskirt with a yard of scrap fabric and a matching peasant blouse. I was on a teenager's glory ride, with transportation and with ample couture designs from my own special clothing creations.

Due to mandatory busing, I left E. E. Smith and attended Reid Ross High School in the eleventh grade, graduating in 1974. In my senior year of high school, girls' athletics were introduced into the city school system that included Reid Ross. Since I was enjoying high school, I relinquished my plan to graduate early. I had completed all my high school graduation requirements except for English. I now had ample time to participate in extracurricular activities—pom-pom squad, basketball, softball, and more. Amid my high school fun, I needed to finalize my college plans. Attending college was non-negotiable with my parents. My goal was to become a teacher like my hero Marva Collins, whom I saw on a television show. Collins was a Chicago schoolteacher who motivated students to learn. She used her personal funds to create Westside Preparatory School, where low-income students excelled.[12]

Reid Ross had a Junior Army Reserve Officers' Training Corps (JROTC) program, but I never thought about joining. The JROTC students appeared too rigid and intense. A couple of the guys in JROTC planned to attend the US Military Academy at West Point. But an article in the *Fayetteville Observer* newspaper about women being allowed to join college ROTC and becoming a military officer caught my attention. I saved the article and discussed joining the Army with my parents. The women in the newspaper ads seemed self-assured and confident. One WAC lived in our neighborhood, and she seemed happy and enjoyed her job. I'd modeled for one of her events at a fashion show she organized at the Fort Bragg United Services Organization. I heard Dad talk about the officers and how they were in charge. Besides, joining Army ROTC guaranteed a management-level job after college, and I could make more money in the Army than being a schoolteacher. That settled it. I set my plan in motion to join the Army as an officer.

My dad's response to my WAC plans included shaking his head—"No. Absolutely not!" He did not want me to become a WAC. I had to go to college. He did not consider the possibility of me becoming an officer. He never told me why; he just didn't like the idea of me joining the Army. He refused to listen to anything I said about my post–high school plans unless I was going to college. He didn't care where I went; I just had to go. He acquiesced when I told him that I could do both—join the Army *and* go to college. I would become an officer. Finally, with his blessing, I practiced writing my name in cursive. I could not wait to write my signature as *2LT Edna W. Cummings.*

Dad was now a college student himself. After twenty-six years of service, he retired from the Army in 1972 as a sergeant first class. He was tired of the racism, slow promotions, and combat deployments. He just wanted out. After he submitted his retirement papers, he learned that his name was on the master sergeant, or E-8, promotion list. He retired anyway.[13]

I applied and was accepted at three North Carolina colleges with Army ROTC programs. I visited one of the colleges and did not like the partying atmosphere or the look of the dormitories. The college was one of the largest in the state, but something about the environment did not make me feel safe—it was too big, loud, and gritty-looking. The other college was too close to home. Based solely on the pictures, the

Army ROTC program, and the black and gold colors of my favorite football team, the Pittsburgh Steelers, I chose Appalachian State University (ASU) in Boone. I did not know anyone who had ever attended this school. ASU was about three and a half hours away from Fayetteville. Located in the North Carolina mountains, ASU was in one of the most picturesque, yet coldest places in the state, but it was not ethnically diverse, During the 1970s, the population of Boone was 8,754.[14] Although I was unaware of the specific the demographic data, my mom's friends sensed that the community did not welcome Black people, and one told her that the "White folks" were going to "run her off that mountain." Forty-eight years later, the 2022 census data states that the city of Boone had 19,368 people, of whom 494 were Black or African American (non-Hispanic).[15] In retrospect, I don't think the White residents of Boone cared enough about Black people to be bothered. There were so few Blacks in the city and on campus that, as a race, we were probably viewed as insignificant.

After graduating from high school in May 1974, I spent that summer working as a cashier at a walk-up Hardee's fast-food restaurant. Hardee's was located at the corner of Hay Street and Bragg Boulevard in Fayetteville's downtown area. Friday and Saturday nights were the busiest because of the nightlife. Fayetteville was still widely known as "Fayetnam." The name, a mix of "Fayetteville" and "Vietnam," was meant to suggest the violence of a war zone but in an urban environment.[16] Some people blamed the crime on the Hay Street clubs, the troops returning from Vietnam with "shell shock," and high unemployment.

At Hardee's, the cashiers wrote orders on paper notepads and totaled them manually. The cash registers also operated manually, meaning that I had to count the change to the customers. If a cashier's drawer was short, the difference came out of the cashier's pay. Hardee's did not accept credit cards. The menu was basic—hamburgers, cheeseburgers, fish sandwiches, fries, apple turnovers, and three types of milkshakes: vanilla, chocolate, and strawberry.

The absolute worst part of my job was making strawberry milkshakes. The vanilla and chocolate milkshakes came directly from the machine. But the friggin' strawberry milkshakes required me to place the strawberry syrup in the bottom of the cup, add vanilla milkshake, place the cup underneath a spinner and pull it out real fast. If I pulled the cup out at the wrong angle, strawberry milkshake went everywhere. I can honestly say that I panicked every time I had to make a strawberry milkshake. And yes, I often left a trail of strawberry milkshake around the machines and on the floor.

Sometime between 2021 and 2022, I visited Hardee's in Fayetteville and ordered a vanilla milkshake and observed the process. The server added flavoring to the milkshake and mixed it in a machine and added a whipped topping. She covered the cup with a bubble lid. Oddly enough, Hardee's milkshake process is basically the same as it was in 1974, but now with a special blender to add flavoring. Fortunately, someone in management realized that the mixing machine needed a safeguard in place to prevent milkshake disasters. The server glanced at me side-eyed as I stared at her making the milkshake. She had no idea that I was reliving my days as a Hardee's cashier and admiring her milkshake-making technique.

In August 1974, my mom, one of my sisters, and a neighbor drove me to ASU. I moved into Cannon dormitory with my belongings in one of my dad's olive-drab metal footlockers. To give it a modern vibe, I covered it with blue-and-white flowered contact paper. I was now a college freshman, but on a no-fail two-part mission: (1) to graduate from college, and (2) to become a 2LT in the Women's Army Corps. Anything less than accomplishing these two objectives was unacceptable. To prepare me for the latter, I am pretty sure that I had a can of black Kiwi shoe polish and a torn white T-shirt in my multipurpose flowered footlocker. I needed to perfect my spit shine. I was ready to meet the challenges that lay ahead.

3

FROM A STUDENT ON THE MOUNTAINTOP TO A SOLDIER IN LOWER ALABAMA

ASU'S FRESHMAN ORIENTATION WAS UNREMARKABLE. I was nervous but refused to show fear about being alone and without friends in a new place. Using the map in my new student packet, I located my first academic meeting place. It was a basic classroom filled with other Black students. A White female faculty member or faculty advisor walked around and stopped at each student's desk. She approached my desk, leaned toward me, and asked, "Can you handle a college algebra class?" I responded in a firm, yet indignant tone, "I've had algebra I, II, and geometry. I *think* I can handle this class." She walked away.[1]

Freshman and sophomore women resided in Cannon dormitory. Cannon sat at the bottom of a 30- to 45-degree-angle hill from Plemmons Student Union. A sidewalk climb to the hill's apex revealed the reward of reaching Plemmons, the gathering spot for campus updates, socializing, and the ice cream parlor. A gas station, theater, and a family-style house converted into a restaurant sat to the left of Cannon. Across the street was a movie theater to lure curious students with XYZ-rated movies on the weekends. The room had two twin beds, one on either side, with storage bins and desks. I'm sure I experienced relief to be away from home, and yet sadness. I had to share this tiny living space with a stranger.

In a matter of days after moving into Cannon, my White roommate approached me with a smile and southern drawl. She had some exciting news: "There's a gurl [girl] down the hawl [hall] you can move in with." I knew exactly what she meant. Girl meant Black female. Apparently, my roommate had sought out a remedy for our uncomfortable situation. Without discussing her discomfort with me, she had located someone else who did not want to room with her Black female roommate. It had never occurred to me that my White roommate would not want to live with me. I should have realized there was a possible racial rooming situation during a summer letter exchange. My assigned roommate and I shared pictures through mail. She sent me a nice letter and a picture of herself, and I did the same. I never heard from her again.

I was now faced with another roommate rejection, but this time in person. My new White roommate didn't want me either. I now no longer cared about whether she wanted me as a roommate. I switched rooms and moved in with the other girl, another Black student whose roommate didn't want her either. Besides, I had other pressing concerns—to become a 2LT, not to flunk out of college, and not embarrass my parents by leaving because of unfortunate situations that befall college students, especially women. Although being an unwed mother or hurried into matrimony weren't the worst things that could have happened, I knew that I did not want to be in that situation. I wanted my mother to hold her head up high around the people who had predicted my failure at ASU. I also didn't want those prophecies of being "run off the mountain" by White folks to come true. I could not allow this girl's prejudice to interfere with my college life. I was not oblivious to the possibility of racism, but I hadn't expected it so soon. Although I was neither uncomfortable nor afraid of attending a predominately White school, I was uncertain about my ability to make it in Army ROTC. I had to figure out how to navigate this unique environment—an environment that laid the foundation for one of many lessons in resilience and putting forth the extra effort to ensure success. My mom later shared that on one of her trips to Boone, a neighbor rode along and brought a small pistol—just in case.

Dad didn't like to visit Boone. The mountains reminded him of the Montagnards, Vietnamese tribesmen who fought alongside American Special Forces. The indigenous Montagnard fighters lived in Vietnam's highlands. During one trip to Boone, while looking out of the car window, he repeated "Montagnards." The Montagnards' name is derived from the French word for mountaineers.[2] He never talked about his encounters with the Montagnards. I presume that he trained with them during his first tour as an advisor. Coincidentally, the ASU community and athletic teams refer to themselves as Mountaineers.[3]

Joining the Appalachian Black Cultural Organization (ABCO) provided a respite from the feeling of being a novelty on campus or isolated as the only Black student in a class. Black students met in a designated room between classes and socialized and vented about college life and racism. Of the 8,014 full-time students enrolled at ASU in 1974, 1,822 were freshman, including 956 freshman women. In 2023, ASU has more than 20,000 full-time students and 590 Black undergraduate students.[4] In August 1974, however, I was one of only nine Black freshmen women. Like me, other Black students faced racism from roommates or racist attitudes from students. I didn't know anyone at the school but soon met a few other people from Fayetteville. Together, my new Black roommate and I explored the campus. She became my first college friend.

The uphill trek on the sidewalk from Cannon to Plemmons during the peak of the autumn leaf color change was exhilarating. I was mesmerized by the trees transitioning into fall hues of sunshine and appearing like red flames on a stick bursting into the atmosphere. The onset of autumn provided a chance for me to pause and gaze at the trees. I grasped a moment of solace as I stood in disbelief. I was in the midst of the fall foliage spectrum and on this campus as a college student. Fortunately, the trees' splendor never failed to inspire as they lost their leaves. The winters turned the evergreen trees into snow-covered upright triangles. While walking to Plemmons and my classes, I focused most of my energies on remaining upright and navigating the treacherous ice-laden sidewalks and building-high snowdrifts.

Entering my freshman year in August 1974, I was the only Black woman in ASU's ROTC program. This was my first time being the only

Black female anywhere. I was accustomed to being one of few, but I'd never been the "only." Army ROTC introduced me to the Army as a future soldier. ROTC classes turned those hills and that foliage into identifiable terrain features. I began to see the world through a soldier's eyes. As an ROTC student, I learned how to use a compass and rappel off cliffs and a university building. Rappelling was almost like a superpower—I could actually leap a tall building in two or three bounds. ROTC classes taught me how to tie special knots beyond shoelaces and sashes. I've secured many items in my lifetime beyond the military by using square knots, slip knots, and half hitches.

ROTC classes also included physical training (PT) with swimming, leadership exercises, and an opportunity to join one of the ROTC clubs. Fortunately, other women were in ROTC, and the male students accepted us and worked to make us feel welcome. In my sophomore year, I was crowned Miss ROTC and was also a member of ASU's homecoming court. The upper classmen became our mentors. However, I was not prepared for the mockery by some of the professors when I wore my uniform to class. I expected some taunting about race in a predominately White environment but not about wearing the Army uniform. Yet the Vietnam War was still at the forefront of people's minds as an example of Western imperialism. I was surprised to be challenged on campus about supporting the military and planning to serve.

My worst antimilitary and racist college encounter occurred in a political science class. Looking directly at me, the professor made a snide remark about the military. He alluded to a "SOB" he met with several stripes on his uniform jacket. After that remark, he quoted an opinion about a public figure. He smirked and repeated the statement, "the Public Figure said that (XXX) should swim across the Atlantic with a N—r under one arm and a Jew under the other." My reaction was as inappropriate as the professor's remark. At the time, I was pledging to join the military sorority, Co-ed Affiliate to the Pershing Rifles (CAPERs). Part of my pledging required me to carry a white wooden rifle around the clock for a few weeks. After the professor made his comments, I picked up the wooden rifle beside my desk. I lifted it off the floor as if I were going to aim it at him. The encounter lasted for a few seconds. The class and the instructor laughed, and he continued the lecture. If that event were to happen during this era, it's highly probable that I would be arrested for a symbolic threatening gesture and the professor may have been disciplined for hate speech. I now realize my ROTC enrollment provided lessons in resilience—remaining focused on the purpose and ignoring ignorance.

As with any college campus, the parties were lively and provided relief from the stresses of academic pressures. I joined my fellow students in frequenting bars in neighboring Blowing Rock, also known as "The Rock," or at concerts at Historically Black Colleges and Universities (HBCUs) located in Winston-Salem or Greensboro. Boone is in Watauga County and was at the time a dry county, meaning alcohol was neither served nor sold. But it was at ASU that I had my first and *last* taste of "moonshine," or homemade alcohol, at a party. The pale-yellow milky or cloudy substance was in a half-quart mason jar with raisins floating on the top. It had a smooth, yet heavy texture. "Ugh!" With one sip, I knew that it was a beverage that would not become a staple in my diet or my libation of choice.

Between my sophomore and junior years, ROTC required attendance at a six-week summer camp. The purpose was to test military and leadership skills. I looked forward to summer camp because it was located at Fort Bragg, near my home in Fayetteville. During summer camp, I visited my parents on weekends and brought a few friends with me for a home-cooked meal or to do laundry. Although I was confident about my ability to graduate from college, summer camp proved to be one of the most challenging events in ROTC. During the week I lived with the other ROTC cadets in dilapidated World War II barracks. This site was referred to as the old 82nd area. Beginning in the summer of 1972, women entered ROTC, and the summer of 1976 was only the second time that ROTC summer camp was co-ed. We lived with women and trained alongside the men. In December 1976, the WAC Center and School at Fort McClellan, Alabama, closed, and in 1978, the WAC was disbanded.[5] I was living and navigating through the early stages of the military's gender integration.

Summer camp was intense, jam-packed with field training exercises designed to simulate combat scenarios, nighttime navigation courses, and a slide for life (the commercial equivalent to a zipline) with a murky lake landing. At the end of each day, we checked ourselves for ticks that had embedded themselves deep into our skin. I'm unsure who pulled out the blood-sucking creature that managed to work its way into my uniform one day. But I am grateful that the only remnant of that tick is a permanent dark pimple on the back of my upper thigh and not Lyme disease or some other malady.

The leadership reaction courses taught teamwork through problem-solving situations, none of which I remember. The summer of 1976 was the first and only time that I threw a grenade and rode in a tank. I had a near accident when I dropped mortar artillery into a muzzle to load the mortar weapon for discharge. Instead of my hands sliding down the mortar's tube on release, one of my hands crossed over the top of the tube. "Good thing you are young and fast," the instructor commented when the artillery left the mortar and exploded in the field. He explained that since my hand crossed the opening, I would have lost a hand when the artillery fired if my hand had lingered over the opening when I dropped the artillery into the tube. The training continued with me as an example of how not to drop artillery into a mortar tube. I breathed a sigh of relief when I passed military stakes, or the final exam, especially after I'd assembled an M16 rifle and M60 machine gun within the allocated time. Not graduating summer camp could result in ROTC termination and would have decimated my dreams of becoming a 2LT.

In the fall of 1976, I returned to the ASU campus as a college junior who had passed ROTC summer camp. Because of my uncertainty about any military career plans, I turned down an ROTC scholarship in my sophomore year. The scholarship students seemed to have extra work in the battalion. But even without the scholarship, I was under a military contract. After signing the paperwork to receive one hundred dollars a month, there was no turning back. If I dropped out of college or didn't receive my commission, I would have to join the Army, but not as an officer. I was undecided about whether I wanted active or reserve duty. The Army offered me an opportunity to travel, but the State Department sounded attractive. Their brochure had convincing pictures about traveling and working for the nation. With the State Department, I wouldn't have to wear combat boots and a uniform or pull my hair back every day and pin it above my collar. I registered to take a test to join the State Department in Charlotte, but in the end, I did not go to the testing site. I decided to stay with the Army.

After summer camp, I must have shared the news with my fellow students in the ABCO about my hundred-dollar-a-month ROTC stipend. I probably bragged about completing summer camp and my guaranteed job after graduation to some of the football players. ASU's football program had not developed to a nationally recognized program wherein the National Football league recruited its players. At least five African Americans members of the football team joined ROTC.

May 1978 finally arrived. On May 21, 1978, I graduated from college *and* was commissioned as a 2LT. That morning, with a raised my right hand, I repeated my name and the oath of office: "I do solemnly swear to support and defend the Constitution against all enemies, foreign and domestic." The professor of military science and my dad pinned the brass bar on the shoulder of my uniform. In the afternoon I donned my robe and marched with my classmates to receive a college diploma.

I did it! I was a college graduate, an Army officer, and a 2LT in the Women's Army Corps. The US Census Bureau cites that in 1978, 10 percent of college students were Black.[6] I was one of the ones who graduated. My mom was also proud of my father, who had used the GI Bill to attend Fayetteville State University and graduated the previous year, in 1977. At the time, I did not know that I was the first and only Black woman to receive a commission from ASU's Army ROTC program.[7] I learned about my mark in history at a 2008 homecoming event, the year after ASU's team had upended college football sports and beat the University of Michigan in Ann Arbor at their season opener.[8] ASU was the underdog team against Michigan, which ranked fifth in the national polls.[9]

Making history at ASU ROTC inspired me to accept a volunteer "Special Government Employee" position in 2021 with the Army Reserve as an ambassador[10] to nominate high school and college students for Army ROTC scholarships. These scholarships pay full tuition or room and board, and students must join the Army Reserve after graduation. As June 2024, I've nominated over fifty students.

Armed with a bachelor of science degree in social studies and the 2LT rank, I began my Army career. With military specialties and jobs for women limited to combat service support, or noncombat roles, I was detailed to the Quartermaster Corps, one of the three logistics branches, along with Ordnance and Transportation. Every newly commissioned 2LT attended an Officers' Basic Course (OBC) to learn a technical specialty. The Quartermaster OBC school was located at Fort Lee, Virginia, where I arrived in June 1978. The WACs in the course wore a uniform called cords. Cords were a two-piece skirt-and-shirt ensemble made of green-and-white striped polyester and cotton corduroy material. We wore fatigues for field exercises and attended academic classes with the men.[11]

The WACs had separate formations and inspections with nonstudent WACs assigned to OBC. The WACs ensured our hair was styled correctly and our uniforms fit to comply with military standards. One of the most important topics the WACs emphasized was the "career killer" sin of fraternization. Their goal was to teach us how to date safely in the Army. Female officers could only date someone below their rank if it didn't undermine order and discipline. The man had to be in another unit and not in the woman's command structure.

Fort Lee had three specialty management tracks—warehouse, food, and petroleum. My track was the warehouse management course for managing ten types or classes of supplies: I—Food, Rations, Water; II—Clothing; III—Fuel; IV—Construction Materials; V—Ammunition; VI—Personal Items (including alcohol); VII—Major End Items (i.e., vehicles, tanks, etc.); VIII—Medical; IX—Repair Parts; and X—Miscellaneous.[12]

Midway through OBC, I received orders to report to my first duty station, Fort Polk, Louisiana. Most likely due to the personnel needs of the Army, I later received orders to Fort Rucker, Alabama, home of the Army's Aviation School for helicopter pilots. Fort Rucker is in "Lower Alabama," outside of Enterprise, the home of the Boll Weevil Monument. (Fort Rucker is now Fort Novesel.) In the early 1900s, the boll weevil destroyed cotton crops, and farmers planted other crops such as peanuts to have a harvest. The town honors the boll weevil and not George Washington Carver, who advised farmers to rotate crops and developed hundreds of products from peanuts and sweet potatoes. Even though Carver was instrumental in restoring the economy, the boll weevil got the statue.[13]

In September 1978, I drove my brand-new, 1978 white Audi Fox with a sunroof and camel-colored leather interior to Fort Rucker, or Fort "Mother Rucker," the training location for Army helicopter pilots. I knew with every ounce of my being that the faceless Army assignment officers were sabotaging my career and wanted me to fail. My training at Fort Lee was in warehouse management, not managing Class III fuel operations. I could not understand why I was going to this assignment without the skills to perform this crucial task. I believed that I was not technically trained for my assignment to the 108th Quartermaster Petroleum Company of about two hundred soldiers. I felt queasy as I drove toward Fort Rucker.

The 108th's mission was to hot refuel the Army's helicopter pilots in training at the aviation school. The pilots landed the helicopters at one of three locations that simulated combat. The pilots could not turn off the aircraft, and my soldiers had to pump explosive jet propellant level-four fuel (JP4) into helicopters that were still running—or "hot refuel." This daily mission was like pumping fuel into a car that was still running at a gas station on a landing pad in a remote area. The 108th was attached to the 69th Engineer Battalion (Combat Heavy) with an Emergency Deployment Readiness Exercise (EDRE) mission to support the XVIIIth Airborne Corps, Fort Bragg. This meant that when the XVIIIth Airborne Corps needed training or combat support, the 108th had to be ready. I didn't have to pump the fuel into the helicopter myself but was tasked with supervising the estimated thirty to forty soldiers in the platoon who worked at three refueling sites. I was the platoon leader who barely knew the location of my Audi's gas tank, let alone what it took to hot refuel a helicopter. I was the only and perhaps the first female officer in this combat battalion of about eight hundred soldiers. I sensed the intense pressure. I could not fail at this assignment. The magnifying glass of constant observation and scrutiny would be focused on me. Once again I was the only one—the only female, and the only Black officer in the battalion.

Every two weeks a new flight school class started with a different color hat. Each class had at least one or two Black officers. I became friends with the Black pilots going through flight school. I listened to their stories of insults from instructor pilots, the difficulties of the instrument classes, and their hopes that they didn't get set back a class for failing a "check ride," or final test. I laughed whenever one of the pilots mentioned seeing me from their helicopters while I inspected the JP4 fuel bags.

The petroleum specialty soldiers had some of the lowest General Technical (GT) scores in the Army. They were considered Category Vs, or CAT5s, because of their Armed Services Vocational Aptitude Battery test. One of the Black sergeants told me that I was assigned to the "Coon Platoon" because most of the soldiers were Black. I believed my soldiers labeled themselves with a self-deprecating epithet to deflect the pain of racism and classism. As Black men, the underdog label provided camaraderie and probably minimized the impact of other names they'd been called. A few soldiers thought that I was from another country because I didn't "talk Black." My challenge was to figure out how to motivate them and restore their dignity. One of the sergeants called the platoon the Third Herd in formation, a less deprecating moniker.

Motivating the Third Herd proved to be antithetical to anything that I learned in the ROTC and OBC leadership classes. The Third Herd appeared browbeaten and wanted to be anywhere else but in this unit. To advise my sergeants of my expectations and standards, I typed a document for them to read and sign. I typed what I thought was a clear and concise memorandum. I made copies (probably with carbon paper), and I called everyone in for a meeting in the white shack where my office sat—in the motor pool, a fenced area with olive-drab vehicles (for example, fuel tankers, trucks, and jeeps). I discussed the memo and outlined my open-door policy, standards of behavior, etc. The sergeants nodded in agreement and left the meeting. Feeling a sense of accomplishment, I moved on to the next task. I needed to organize the equipment area filled with hoses, couplings, and other items used for refueling helicopters. I planned for the 100 percent equipment inventory within ninety days. I had to see and inspect each item before I signed the "hand receipt," or the document assuming responsibility for the property.

A few days after my sergeants meeting, a gangly, six-foot-tall Black E-5 (sergeant) spokesman, whom I'll refer to as "Sergeant P," came to my office. He wanted to talk to me about my memo. I wondered why Sergeant P came to the office instead of my White E-7 (sergeant first class) platoon sergeant. Cautiously, he approached me with a slight stutter: "Ma'am, we can't read this." Sergeant P explained that he and the other sergeants could not read what I considered a perfect memo outlining expectations. Even though I explained the memorandum to them, Sergeant P said that the other sergeants could neither read it nor explain it to their soldiers. Sergeant P suggested that I call everyone in the platoon together and talk to them myself. He shared that many of the soldiers had never worked for a woman and that they had never seen a Black female officer. My presence in the unit shocked them.

Sergeant P taught me a valuable communications lesson. Regardless of what a leader intends, what the recipient understands is more important. He said the sergeants wanted to support me and do a good job, but they couldn't understand me when I talked. Sergeant P advised me that I used too many college words and talked too fast. I understood that I had to step back, slow down, and be very deliberate and methodical about my communication.

I was unsure what he meant until a few of the soldiers asked me where I was from. One soldier approached me with a childlike curiosity, asking, "Ma'am, where you be from?" I replied, "Fayetteville." He looked surprised and said, "I didn't know the Army made y'all." He'd never seen a Black female officer. His comment gave me a visual of a Black female officer factory that produced clones.

To remedy my ineffective communication style, I led several "Preventive Maintenance Checks and Services," or motor stables (the Army term for conducting basic vehicle maintenance). By checking the troops' maintenance procedures with this step-by-step method, I could learn about the vehicles, work on my speech delivery, and obtain immediate feedback if I wasn't understood. After morning formation, I directed everyone to their vehicles, and I read the vehicle operator's manual for inspection aloud. Example: Step 1—Raise the hood of your vehicle. Step 2—Locate the oil dipstick and remove it, etc. After each step, I walked the vehicle line to check for compliance. After a few motor stable formations, I got to know the soldiers and observe them at work. I learned from them and gradually saw pride and communication within the ranks. They knew that I cared.

Restoring pride within the ranks did not extend to the soldier who was supposed to be my right arm, my E-7 platoon sergeant. My first platoon sergeant was a thin, gawky White man who had served in Vietnam. He barely spoke to me and was reluctant to take me to the helicopter refueling sites, to assist with inventory, and to perform basic foreman or supervisory tasks. I eventually asked for him to be replaced because he was insubordinate and not supportive. I called my father and asked him for recommendations on how to handle the disrespectful platoon sergeants. He basically said to fire them if they didn't do their jobs or disrespected me. And that's exactly what I did. I believe that within a year, I had about three or four platoon sergeants who were Black and White. Race didn't matter. I was a woman. None of them wanted to work for me or with me.

Although most of the soldiers in the unit respected and supported me, some of them did not. I received catcalls from the barracks windows, threats of turning off the lights in the warehouse, and allegations of inappropriate relationships whenever I went to check the refueling sites with a Black sergeant. In one conversation with the battalion commander (my third line supervisor), I expressed frustration about the lack of military courtesy and the rumors. He advised me that "boys will be boys." He also cautioned, "Don't put yourself in those situations," meaning that I should not allow myself to be in an area wherein I would receive these comments that could lead to allegations. He implied that it was basically my fault that I was a woman in the Army who was the object of disrespect and harassment.

Fortunately, the brigade commander, or my fourth line supervisor, Col. John C. "Doc" Bahnsen, was a prominent and visible advocate. Colonel Bahnsen graduated from West Point the same year that I was born. He was an imposing six-foot-tall Armor and Aviation officer (i.e., he worked in military tank units and flew helicopters) who resembled the World War II commander Gen. George S. Patton. Colonel Bahnsen told me to call his office if I had problems. My naiveté did not allow me to consider that second lieutenants did not call a colonel directly. I understood the chain of command, but I knew the chain of command below Colonel Bahnsen neither understood nor supported me. After a few months in the 108th, I felt that my chain of command regarded me as a problem or someone merely to tolerate. Colonel Bahnsen connected me to a fellow WAC on base whom I'll call Colonel D. She was a short-stature White WAC with dark ear-length hair and wore black-rimmed glasses. She called me regularly to check on me and offer support. These two officers wanted me to succeed and knew that I needed support.

Despite the harassment, in the back of my mind I knew that if I didn't fall out of formation during PT runs with the brigade and Colonel Bahnsen, I had a chance to survive this assignment. I believe that completing the periodic five-mile morning runs and PT with Colonel Bahnsen and the brigade helped me earn his respect.

In any military assignment requiring responsibility for property and equipment, an initial 100 percent property inventory is mandatory. When I was assigned to the 108th, despite many requests, no one assisted me with the inventory. After several attempts, I focused my energies on learning the job and motivating the troops. I no longer worried about conducting an inventory and signing for the property on the "hand receipt." I held fast to the golden rule of a quartermaster officer, "if you don't see it, don't sign for it." And I didn't sign the hand receipt. When the new company commander arrived, he conducted a change of command inventory. My unsigned hand receipt resulted in a Report of Survey investigation for missing equipment.

The Report of Survey was a farce. The total inventory value was $11,259. Approximately $500 of equipment was not accounted for, and the incoming commander could have considered missing items as an acceptable loss due to mission operations. However, he chose to find me pecuniarily liable for $448.32, meaning that I had to pay for missing equipment. My before-tax monthly salary was $773.00. Paying for missing equipment would have been a financial hardship and could have ended my military career before it started. Fortunately, Colonel Bahnsen reviewed the report and found me not liable for the loss. I'm forever grateful to Colonel Bahnsen and Colonel D, who provided me with top cover or morale and professional support.

After a year as platoon leader, I received orders to transfer to the Air Traffic Control (ATC) School to train as a company-level executive officer (XO) or second-in-command to the captain. My responsibilities to supervise administrative tasks and serve as commander in the commander's absence gave me the feeling of finally beginning to have a career. The dark cloud of imminent failure no longer hung over my head. Students attending this school had some of the highest GT scores in the Army. The leadership team was accustomed to working with military women and showed me more respect than I experienced in the 108th. These ATC soldiers were proud to be in the Army and excited about their future.

The ATC company participated in parades, wherein I had to walk with the other staff officers behind the captain company commander. Following Dad's advice, I broke starch and spit-shined my boots to ensure I presented a professional appearance for the generals and parade guests. After one parade, the commander directed me to report to Fort Rucker's headquarters. Apparently, I was being transferred to work in the Protocol Office. But I heard "Port Call." My first thought was that I was being shipped out somewhere overseas, and I panicked for a moment. My commander was upset because I had been in the XO position with the ATC company for less than a year. Another staff member in the unit suggested that I was being transferred because I was Black.

I called Colonel Bahnsen and shared my concerns about a perceived race-based transfer. He responded by advising me that I was a damn good officer, and if anyone said that I was getting the job because I was Black then tell them "*#^%$!" I also called Colonel D, who explained the new job. She advised me that the job was "Protocol" and not "Port Call." Furthermore, it was a good assignment, and I would enjoy the work. She was right. I accepted the assignment, and I did not repeat Colonel

Bahnsen's message. I felt stupid because I had never heard of a military Protocol Office.

Protocol Offices manage the reception and scheduling for dignitaries and visitors to military installations and work directly for the commanding general. Fort Rucker's visitors included generals speaking at the biweekly flight school graduation ceremonies, ambassadors, international officers, and other distinguished personnel curious about the latest aircraft or flight school operations. My job was to develop itineraries and ensure visitors had a positive experience while visiting Fort Rucker.

The assignment as a protocol officer expanded my knowledge about Army functions and structure. Once again, I was treated with respect and courtesy. The officers and staff at headquarters made no demeaning remarks about women and minorities. I was now working at a level that demanded the highest degree of military professionalism. My duties included escorting dignitaries from the airport and sometimes flying with them in the commanding general's aircraft.

I am proud to claim that I only lost track of one general in the year and a half of my assignment. The visiting general I lost saw military personnel at the airport and automatically followed them to their vehicle. Neither party verified themselves, but the general eventually realized that he was in the wrong car. Twenty years later, I met the general's son in the Pentagon and told him about losing his father at the airport. Then, the lost general scenario made for a great story, but it wasn't a light moment when it happened.

I also learned about menus and the foods that should never be served together, such as steak and peas. I was chastised because when a VIP cut his steak, peas fell into his lap as the steak slid across his plate. The food preparer should have been notified about the tough steak. However, my boss's best solution was to advise me not to have steak and peas on the VIP menu.

I also learned a valuable lesson about friendship while stationed at Fort Rucker. Everyone should have someone in their lives to encourage them and push them upward. I made friends with the two other Black female officers on the installation. One of them suggested that I use my

GI Bill benefits to obtain a master's degree at the local university, Troy State. I hadn't considered the option of attending graduate school. She advised me that obtaining a graduate degree would give me something constructive to focus on outside of work and give me a competitive edge when I left the Army. As it happened, I was already planning my escape from the Army. I knew that I would leave; I just didn't know when. The GI Bill paid 75 percent of the tuition. My work schedule as an XO and protocol officer provided a work-life balance I hadn't experienced in my earlier positions and allowed me time to complete the coursework.

In 1979, I enrolled at Troy State University in Dothan, Alabama, intending to pursue a master's degree in counseling. Troy became my refuge from the military, but that respite was short-lived. A professor in a group dynamics class implied that I thought I was better than everyone in the class. Since I did not share enough of my personal feelings and hardship, he did not believe that I showed empathy during group exercises. He was upset with me because I never cried or consoled those who cried. One older Black female enlisted service member in the class had more life experiences; she was raising children and had gone through a divorce. Perhaps he measured me by her standard. Other classmates experienced family death, alcoholism, and an array of life's misfortunes. But I had nothing to share in this room of strangers. I was twenty-two years old, fulfilling a career goal, unmarried, with a good job, and I loved my parents. I also had a cute car with a sunroof. I guess my life experiences did not meet his emotional barometer.

The class didn't have a final exam, just group work, but somehow, I managed to get a C in the course. In grad school, a C is equivalent to a failing grade. I may have received the C because I gave the instructor my "cold prickly" during a group exercise where we had two items to give away to symbolize our feelings about people in the room. I believe we had cotton balls and a round item resembling dried sweetgum sticky balls. He wanted me to be honest, and I was. I gave him my cold prickly and explained why. I don't remember what I said, but I guess he didn't like it. When I received my grade, I went to his office. I exchanged words with him and stormed out. I'm sure I slammed the door and immediately contacted my academic advisor and asked what other master's degree I could obtain with my current courses. I changed my major to "Foundations of Education." My course correction worked. I graduated in March 1981.

With a lifted spirit, renewed confidence, and a master's degree, I prepared to travel to my next assignment, South Korea. The commanding general of Fort Rucker and the Army's Aviation School, Maj. Gen. Carl H. McNair Jr., presented me with my first military award, an Army Commendation Medal. The award cited an outstanding period of performance from October 1978 to March 1981.

I left Fort Rucker with a real sense of pride in my own accomplishments and pride in the first and second Black women to graduate flight school during my assignment. In 1979, 2LT Marcella Hayes (Ng) was the first Black woman to become a military pilot when she graduated flight school at Fort Rucker.[14] In 1980, 2LT Christine Knighton became the second Black woman to graduate.[15] I was excited to witness the achievements of these women.

Leaving Fort Rucker for my first overseas tour, I knew South Korea would be a wonderful assignment. I was going to live in another country known for its good shopping! About four months prior to my departure, I connected with a childhood acquaintance who was completing his Infantry Advanced Course at Fort Benning, Georgia. He was no longer the geeky nerd I remembered but now a tall, sculpted, six-foot-two Airborne Infantry Ranger who had achieved a perfect score on the five-event physical fitness test. He was going to an assignment in South Korea at Panmunjom, or the Demilitarized Zone. My new friend, Walter, was from my hometown and neighborhood in Fayetteville. His last name was also Cummings (no relation, though). He was three years older than me and had a hard time remembering who I was when we connected during our first phone conversation. Our families already knew each other, and we became immediate friends. Enticed by the shopping, travel, and a new friend, I was excited to make the journey.

In late March 1981, I arrived in Seoul, Korea, and went to my new home in Uijongbu, about an hour north of Seoul. This place wasn't a military base but a compound, or a large open space surrounded by concertina wire. A horizontal wooden gray sign at the entrance of the compound that listed the top five clubs with venereal disease greeted me when the jeep entered the gates. For ease of removal, each club's name was on a wooden plank. Apparently warehousing and maintenance operations were not the unit's only focus or priority.

The compound had a variation of Quonset huts and one-level buildings dating back to the Korean War. This place would be my home for a year. I checked in with the clerk on duty and went to my new residence, a Quonset hut. I reached out my arms and touched both walls. My new residence was the width of my arm span. I sat down on the dingy white-and-black striped mattress on the twin bed with unfolded linen and a green wool blanket. I cried. "What am I doing here?"

4

THE LAND OF THE MORNING CALM

VENEREAL OR SEXUALLY TRANSMITTED DISEASE (STD) warnings took precedence over other messages to soldiers in South Korea. The STD sign at the entrance of my new unit, hereafter referred to as "the Compound," seemed to embody an attitude about women that prevailed in the Army: "Women are here for your enjoyment—but be careful. If you visit these clubs and hire a prostitute, you will contract an STD." During the 1980s, prostitution was illegal in Korea, but military and local authorities only acted when an allegation arose.[1] The clubs, massage parlors, and other establishments sometimes served as fronts for houses of prostitution.[2] The Army probably thought that the sign was helpful to the troops. I regarded it as just another reminder that the Army was where I did not belong.

Along with the public STD notices, a couple of senior noncommissioned officers (NCOs) warned me that if a Korean looked at my rear end at midnight, it was because they wanted to see if I grew a tail. I wasn't worried too much about anyone checking out my rear end at midnight—a curfew was in effect that required everyone to be off the streets before midnight.[3] But the international racist supposition that I might grow a tail was as devastating as the public display of sexism. Almost four decades later, I learned that the Black soldiers and WACs stationed in Europe during World War II experienced those same comments.[4]

This was my home for the next year. Uijongbu was best known as the setting for the hit television series *M*A*S*H**, which told the story of a field hospital unit during the Korean War, or the Forgotten War.[5] Sandwiched between the thriving metropolis of Seoul and the Demilitarized Zone (DMZ), Uijongbu was a city within an hour's access to two worlds. One city boasted a progressive lifestyle while the other maintained an active wartime stance.

After the Korean War, the peninsula was divided into two countries, North Korea and South Korea. The war never formally ended; the countries signed an armistice, or truce, to end hostilities. The 38th northern parallel separates North and South Korea.[6] My assignment was to manage the warehouse and provide supplies and equipment to the units in the area whose mission it was to protect the DMZ.

The Compound was protected by military guards and concertina wire. The main unit was a company of approximately two hundred soldiers. The company had two other female officers, one of whom was also Black. My job title was technical supply and accountable officer. I supervised a warehouse to issue vehicles and vehicle repair parts to the twenty-seven units in the region. After three years in the Army, I was finally working in warehouse operations, the job I'd trained for at Fort Lee. Under my supervision were thirty-six US Army soldiers, ten Korean Augmentation to the United States Army (KATUSA) soldiers, and fifteen Korean National civilians. With this robust staff, I felt that I could have a successful assignment in this austere environment.

My Korean National civilian counterpart was a male chain smoker who supervised the Korean National workers. He often spoke about how much Korean wealth had been lost during the Korean War. The Korean Nationals provided operational continuity of the warehouse despite the yearly rotations of the American soldiers. About half of the Koreans were fluent in English, and the others may not have had the language fluency but were a hardworking and dedicated workforce.

An exhaustive list of rationed items and prohibited activities accompanied my orientation to the Compound and Korea. Military personnel could not exceed monthly rations. I'd heard about rations from the World War II era, but I never thought I would be in an environment where purchases of cigarettes, alcohol, hair products, and other personal items were rationed or had monthly purchase limits. Rations prevented items from turning up on the black market or being sold to Korean civilians for an inflated value for high-demand items, such as Johnnie Walker bourbon. Some of these items are still rationed.[7] Military personnel were also prohibited from purchasing over-the-counter (OTC) medication from Korean drugstores. The ingredients in some OTC medications contained illegal drugs and other military-banned substances.

After a month, I moved from the narrow Quonset hut to an individual room in a one-level building on the Compound. My room measured approximately 16 by 20 feet and faced the "ammo dump" where the unit stored ammunition. Since I managed Class IX repair parts and not Class V ammunition, I didn't know what type of ammunition was stored there. But I did not find comfort facing that fence each time I opened the door to my room. I always felt that one lightning strike or errant cigarette butt would be catastrophic—but no explosion or incident ever occurred. Despite the proximity to the ammo dump, the amenities were comfortable. I had a telephone, a private bathroom, television reception, a hotplate for cooking, and a refrigerator.

For a nominal monthly fee, a "house boy," or young Korean male, shined my boots whenever I sat them on the front stoop of my room. My housekeeper, or "Ajumma," cleaned my room and ensured that my uniform was laundered and starched. Seoul, Dongducheon, and Osan provided a robust shopping network. My personal tailor customized outfits that I saw in fashion magazines. I bought eel skin purses, sent home packages filled with tennis shoes, sweat suits, one-inch-thick mink blankets, and brass novelties. I had a Korean cobbler to make boots, shoes, and anything else that I wanted. All I had to do was to show a tailor or "sew lady" a picture, choose fabric, and any outfit I could imagine became a reality.

Silk dresses with American labels hung in the streetside shops of Yongsan outside of the Eighth Army Headquarters. Polished to entice, the glistening brass lamps, candleholders, and figurines became part of my weekly shopping tour. Much of my current home décor consists of Korean furniture, brass figurines, and other items now considered vintage. Along with mink blankets, furniture, brass candleholders, and figurines, I still have several eel-skin clutch purses and a few unused ornate hairpins.

Shopping in Korea allowed both physical and mental escapes from the daily drudgery of my job as a warehouse and motor officer. I was either checking shelves and supply requests or in the vehicle repair area ensuring that the equipment was operational. I was basically maintaining a vehicle parts and repair facility for close to thirty military units.

Teaching provided another break from my job. With a master's degree, I was eligible to teach at Los Angeles Community College (LACC). LACC was located on a military base in Seoul and offered military personnel the opportunity to work toward a college degree while on active duty. Although I was embarrassed by my C grade in group dynamics while in graduate school, LACC's director didn't care. He believed my educational background and experience qualified me to teach "Introduction to Psychology." The classes were held in a room at the Compound or at a classroom at the Army base in Seoul after duty hours. I taught two academic quarters to soldiers pursuing degrees. My biggest challenge was finding the time to type out the tests and make copies on the blue paper the school provided. Teaching and talking to soldiers as students offered mutual calm and a safe space for both of us. The students and I, in my role as a teacher, felt a sense of accomplishment outside of the Army. While the work provided a break from the job, the extra money funded my shopping excursions.

Korean repurposing and recycling reminded me of life on my grandparents' farm. Nothing was wasted. The command issued guidance not to discard any military paper in a garbage can. I understood that classified information required special handling when discarded. But I didn't comprehend why unclassified paper could not be placed in garbage cans. I understood this guidance better when I ordered Yaki

Mandu (fried dumplings) from a local vendor, and they were served wrapped in pages of a discarded military phone book. During an Army Training and Evaluation Exercise, the "cease-fire" (a pause in the weapons firing) allowed Korean Nationals to pick up the brass casings from our blank and live ammunition cartridges. Now I knew why there was an abundance of brass items for sale.

In 2012, when I visited my daughter, who was teaching English in Busan, we took the train to Seoul. I felt as if I was in any US metropolitan city. I was not tempted to shop but instead chose to sightsee and reminisce about my time there in the 1980s. Shopping malls and department stores had replaced the individual shops that had decorated the sidewalk with their alluring merchandise. The Korean vendors had relocated to the subway retail areas or to a special area marked "Traditional Korean Market." Cafés, restaurants, and bright boutiques now line the streets of Seoul and Yongsan.

During the 1980s, the military was paid monthly, and an automatic payroll deposit to banks was optional. Some soldiers wanted to be paid in cash. At least twice during my assignment, I performed duties as a "Class A Agent" (payroll officer) to pay soldiers. Cash payment required me to report to Eighth Army Headquarters Finance Section in Seoul and travel with a loaded .45 caliber pistol. My driver was armed with an M16, and he drove me to pick up thousands of dollars in cash. The finance clerk provided a roster of names and the amount of each soldier's pay. I set up a pay table, or a mobile bank, to disperse funds at the Compound. My driver stood guard, and twenty to thirty soldiers waited in line for their turn to approach the pay table with a salute. "Ma'am, Private/Sergeant 'Smith' reporting for pay." I returned their salute, counted their money to them; they saluted again, I returned that salute, they signed for their money and left. To allow for soldiers in the area to receive pay, the duties lasted until approximately 1600–1700 hours (4:00–5:00 p.m.). Forty-sixty salutes later, my driver, the KATUSA soldier, and I returned to Seoul with an empty payroll—unless a soldier didn't show up to receive pay.

Although I was initially terrified by the Class A Agent assignment, my experience as a cashier at Hardee's and at the Fort Bragg Smoke Bomb Hill Post Exchange gave me some confidence to perform payroll duties.

The ultimate objective was to count the money correctly. If any funds were missing when I returned to Seoul, it came out of my personal funds. To prevent a miscalculation, I developed my own three-count system that I learned from being a cashier. When a soldier reported for pay, I counted the money to myself before I paid the soldier, I counted the money to the soldier when I dispersed the funds, and then I requested the soldier count the money again before signing for the funds. Fortunately, my payroll sheet was always accurate, and I never had to use my weapon to protect the payroll.

Once again, misogyny permeated the ranks. Sometimes it was on public display during morning runs with the unit through the streets of Uijongbu. The cadence caller sang disgusting Jody calls or cadences about what men would do to women as motivation for running. I approached my company commander and requested that he neither use nor allow female anatomy descriptions in cadences during morning runs. His response: "I talk about men too. I call them d*cks." His boss, a White male battalion commander was equally misogynistic. He openly stated that he intended to have an all-female staff. He wanted the other battalion commanders to be jealous of him when he walked across the parade field. His wish came true. He had an all-White female staff, with some 2LTs. One of the White female 2LT battalion staff officers shared her discomfort with me. She felt unqualified and did not understand why she had been placed on the battalion staff. Usually, staff officers' positions are assigned to officers who have been in the Army at least three years, and not recently commissioned 2LTs who had been in the Army less than a year. She knew her primary job was to be a trophy.

In addition to shopping and teaching, I found relief from the unwelcoming environment at the Compound with my new friend Walter. He was the first African American commander to be on assignment at Camp Kittyhawk located on the DMZ. Most of the soldiers stationed at Camp Kittyhawk were at least six feet tall, including the KATUSA soldiers. This height requirement was meant to provide an imposing presence before the Korean People's Army (KPA), or North Korean, soldiers.

My first trip to visit Walter on the DMZ was nothing short of terrifying. I traveled by taxi to Camp Casey, located approximately thirty-five minutes, or twenty kilometers, from my compound, to catch another bus, the DMZ Express. The trip to the DMZ took another thirty to forty-five minutes. The closer the bus got to the DMZ, the lower the inside and outside noises became, as if some external force controlled the atmospheric volume. The quiet was unnerving and reminded me of stepping into a funeral parlor to view a corpse.

Approximately five kilometers from the DMZ, a KATUSA military policeman (MP) boarded the bus, trailed by a US Army policeman. It was as if the KATUSA MP owned the territory, and the Army policeman followed his lead. The KATUSA MP checked the Korean driver's ID and vehicle credentials. He then checked Korean passengers' IDs and questioned them about their destination. The US Army MP checked the identification cards for the Americans. Unlike the KATUSA, he didn't question them about their destination.

I breathed a sigh of relief when I finally arrived at Camp Kittyhawk. Without a doubt, these soldiers were ready for war. The Army did not assign women to this type of unit since it was designated as combat arms. This designation meant that there was a high likelihood that personnel in this unit could have physical or tactical contact with an enemy. In 1976, the KPA killed two Army officers in this Joint Security Force Company (JSF) with axes, one of whom was the JSF company commander, Capt. Arthur Bonifas. The incident resulted in White House–level decisions and a military operation entitled "Paul Bunyan."[8] In January 1981, my new friend, Capt. Walter C. Cummings Jr., assumed command of the JSF Company.

This was a type of assignment wherein conflicts could erupt at any time. One evening while watching *Armed Forces Korean Network News* (*AFNK*) on television, I heard Walter's name. The North Korean soldiers on the DMZ were taunting him and calling him "nigg*r." He issued a strong public statement about not tolerating racial insults by them. Another incident involved the KPA soldiers throwing rocks at the US troops. The incidents seemed to be part of a constant stream of antagonism aimed at disrupting the fragile peace. Weekends and holidays did not exist for Walter's unit unless the soldiers requested time off. The operations were around-the-clock because a conflict could erupt when the United States least expected it. Walter shared that each Christmas the North Korean president, Kim Il Sung, promised to celebrate the holiday in South Korea.

Walter met with his KPA counterpart either in a wooded area on the DMZ or in the robin-egg blue building where the United Nations Command Military Armistice Commission (UNCMAC) held meetings. His UNCMAC flag that sat on the table during his meetings now sits on a small table in my dining room alongside a picture of him at one of the UNCMAC meetings. Whenever the North Koreas wanted a meeting to discuss an incident or just wanted to meet outside of the routine UNC-MAC meetings, Walter had to meet with them.

The UNCMAC meeting site was also a tourist attraction. The one time I visited the UNCMAC building, I witnessed a US soldier engaged in a stare down with a KPA soldier. The only time I'd seen precision movements mimicked as mirror reflection exercises was in a comedy mime routine on television. The US and KPA soldiers walked a white narrow line approximately three inches wide inside the UNCMAC building. They sometimes faced each other nose to nose, neither touching each other nor flinching. The behavior seemed childish and petty, but the intimidation tactics were real, and so was the threat of violence.

After witnessing these North Korean intimidation tactics and antics, I knew that Walter and the rest of his soldiers were on the brink of a conflict daily. My job didn't seem so bad after all, but I still wanted out of the military. I didn't like the constant grunge, misogyny, and marginalization. I would never be good enough for the Army.

I visited Walter whenever I could, and on occasion, we spent time together in Seoul or traveled to Osan for much-needed rest and relaxation. About halfway through my assignment, I shared my plans with him to leave the military. I told him that I was going to get out of the Army and buy furniture and items for my life in the United States. He offered to buy the furniture and didn't want me to plan a future without him. Of course, I said "Yes"—he could buy the furniture, and I would include him in my future. We spent the remainder of the tour planning our future and shopping for unique household items. Since I didn't want to leave anything to chance or misinterpretation, I verified that he was asking me to marry him. That was his proposal, a confirmation that he wanted to get married. With that affirmation, I also started a collection of cute hairpins for our future daughter.

In February 1982, I was promoted to captain. This is a promotion career milestone, and officers who outranked me welcomed me to the Army. I'd made it through the gauntlet of lieutenant-hood. A promotion signals positions of increased responsibility and a requirement for advanced education. My next military course requirement was the Quartermaster Officer Advanced Course at Fort Lee when I returned to the United States, but I declined to attend. Instead, I requested an assignment at Fort Bragg, to transition from the military and begin my new life as a military wife. My coworkers supported my decision to leave the military. They probably realized that as a Black woman I could have a better life out of uniform. My leadership's response was unremarkable. Besides, I had a master's degree, and I was confident that I could find a job if I had to. Walter and I discussed our career options and lifestyle. Working for me would be optional since he was confident that he would get promoted to the next rank of major. I looked forward to the transition to civilian life. I was ready to take off the uniform.

I returned to the United States in May 1982, rented an apartment in Fayetteville, and began my final military assignment at Fort Bragg at the Materiel Management Center for the XVIII Airborne Corps Support Command (COSCOM).[9] I planned mobilization training exercises for reservists and reviewed and developed supply policies. I enjoyed the job and the people, and I felt a sense of purpose. After I'd served in Korea, COSCOM's mission made sense. I'd seen how an adversary threatens stability in a region and understood that the Army had to be ready to meet these challenges.

After leaving the JSF Command in Korea in July 1982, Walter was due for an Army assignment with one of the three *R*'s—recruiting, reserves, or ROTC. He was assigned to ROTC at the Virginia Military Institute (VMI) as an assistant professor of military science.[10] He was disappointed with the assignment, because he was the first Black officer to be assigned to VMI and did not want to be scrutinized in a predominately White academic community where he would be a novelty. As a graduate of

North Carolina State University in Raleigh, he couldn't understand why one of the VMI alums did not receive the assignment. Despite his pleas for another location, his assignments officer at the Personnel Center in Washington, DC, would not acquiesce. To make matters worse, while looking for housing, he was told where we should live for his safety—in a Black neighborhood. He was frustrated that the Army had put us in this situation. He preferred being with the "real Army" with the troops and not in Lexington, Virginia.

My last day in the Army was March 1, 1983, and we were married on March 12, 1983, in our home church in Fayetteville, First Baptist on Moore Street. After our honeymoon in Jamaica, I joined Walter in a home that had formerly been a church parsonage. He found this gem of a house to rent in one of the Black neighborhoods of Lexington, located about three blocks away on a hill behind VMI. It was a three-level, 2,300-square-foot home built in 1932, with four bedrooms, one bathroom, and a front porch.

Other than my involvement as a military spouse, I was done with the Army and donated my Army uniforms to a thrift store. I was free from bombastic rhetoric, black boots that left horizontal black marks on the dorsal side of my foot, and olive-drab uniforms. I requested cookbooks for wedding gifts so I could assume the "push out logistics mission" just as my mom had done for my father. I'd be a housewife and support Walter's military career. After I saw the stress and intensity of his life as an infantryman in Korea, I knew that I had to support him.

Other than becoming a supportive wife and mother, I didn't have any career plans or a specific goal. I knew that I could find a job if I wanted one, and Walter didn't care whether I worked. We agreed to manage our finances with one salary and save additional income if I decided to get a job. This was the beginning of my own fairytale with my personal Prince Charming. As an extra bonus to my fairytale, I didn't have to fill out paperwork to change my last name.

PART II

LESS THAN A 5 PERCENT CHANCE

You may not control all the events that happen to you, but you can decide not to be reduced by them.

—Maya Angelou

5

MELTED BANANA POPSICLE

LOCATED ALONG THE BLUE RIDGE PARKWAY, Lexington, Virginia's rolling terrain, so similar to that of Boone and Uijongbu, soothed me with its familiarity. Mountains seemed to be a constant in my life. I knew to expect harsh winters with icy roads and snowdrifts. Lexington's winters did not disappoint.

Leaving the Army, planning a wedding, getting married, and moving to Lexington kept me busy. I spent most of my days unpacking boxes, putting away belongings, and learning my way around Lexington and the neighboring towns of Staunton and Buena Vista. During the 1980s, the phone book provided the best city guide. MapQuest and navigation systems had not been developed yet. I located places of interest in the Yellow Pages, called the location, and got directions.

Although I said that I was done with the Army, the constant mail from the Army Reserve was enticing. The Army Reserve lured me into its ranks with the opportunity of being a part-time soldier. With a softened attitude about the Army, I wrote to Army Reserve units hoping to find a position, but I never received a response. Being a military spouse, I knew that I would never have a steady job. If I joined a reserve unit, the extra money from reserve duty would be a means to stash extra cash. Since I never received a response to my letters, I joined the Army Reserve as an Individual Mobilization Augmentee (IMA). An IMA assignment was the perfect fit for my lifestyle. IMAs replace active-duty Army personnel in the United States when they deploy or go overseas. All I had to do was attend two weeks of training at an IMA unit, pass a PT test, and take Army correspondence courses to maintain the requisite military education.

To help me adjust to my role as an Army wife, the other Army wives quickly indoctrinated me to the VMI community. At social events, I felt comfortable talking to the men about military topics, but I worked hard to connect to the wives about recipes, shopping, and family matters. Even so, I didn't enjoy cooking, we didn't have children, and I felt like an outsider. I experimented with new dishes from the cookbooks I'd gotten as wedding gifts and obtained new recipes from the wives from the luncheons and dinners we attended. Thanks to my cooking experiments, Walter gained about twenty pounds in six months.

After I unpacked and learned my way around the community and the kitchen, I craved something else to do with my time. We became friends with a couple who lived across the street. He was a schoolteacher, and his wife spent many days tending to the lawn, cutting grass and trimming the hedges. While growing up in Fayetteville, I had only raked pine straw and leaves. I'd never seen a woman cut grass. "How do you use a lawn mower and trim hedges?" I asked her. "Easy," she responded, "just push the lawn mower back and forth and cut the tops of the hedges." She was right. I enjoyed this new outdoor routine and added the occasional lawn care to my fitness routine of jogging through the community, on the VMI track, and working out on our home exercise equipment. Although I surprised Walter with trimmed hedges and a cut lawn, I assured him that lawn care was not my primary responsibility.

To break the routine of household chores, shopping, and sporadic lawn care, in the fall of 1983, I began substitute teaching in Rockbridge County, where Lexington was the county seat. The flexible teaching schedule provided another outlet and helped me learn more about the community. One of my high school girlfriends, Lorraine, later connected me with a local school official who knew of an opening at an alternative education school in downtown Lexington. With my military background, the school official felt that I would be a good fit for the job.

Alternative education was an initiative to provide disruptive middle and high school students an opportunity to attend this school rather than be suspended. Most of these students were economically disadvantaged and at high risk of not graduating from high school. Most of them were close to going to a juvenile detention center. During the summer months, the county paid them to attend the program. The cost and benefits of them attending the program was a better investment than the students continuing along an unproductive path. The goal was for these students to return to a traditional school.

Teaching alternative education was unlike anything I'd ever done before. I'd been a cashier, a substitute teacher, and an Army officer with four different jobs. None of these jobs had required me to teach and motivate students considered juvenile delinquents. Like the military assignments for which I had not been specifically trained, I figured out how to do this job through trial and error. I was glad that I had listened to my mother's advice to get a teaching degree to have something to fall back on. At the time, I didn't understand why she rendered that advice. The Army was my only goal in college. Perhaps my mom knew that I might need a plan B in case the Army didn't work out. While at ASU, I majored in social studies and selected the teaching track or curriculum. My last college semester required me to be a student teacher. I student-taught at my high school, Reid Ross in Fayetteville, and lived with my parents. One of my students, Wayne Cummings, became my brother-in-law.

When school started in the fall, approximately ten students were in my alternative education class. The students' schools provided their schoolwork. My method to teach each of these students based on their individual needs required an Individual Education Plan (IEP). I expected to see an ethnically diverse group; instead, I saw young White students ranging in ages from thirteen to seventeen who lived in poverty. Other than gender, the only thing diverse about these kids was their life experiences. Their unifying theme was that they had been kicked out of school. A female student talked openly about her abortion at age thirteen; a male student discussed his family's home in the "hollar" (that is, the hollow, a community located in a valley). His home did not have indoor plumbing.

Using beige manila folders, I developed IEPs and allowed the students to complete schoolwork at their own pace. I tutored each student, checked assignments, administered tests, and held group discussion events. For history field trips, we walked to places of interest in downtown Lexington, such as the Oak Grove Cemetery, the burial place of Stonewall Jackson.[1] Reading grave markers in the cemetery seemed to give the students insights into the lives of local historical figures and their families. One of my proudest moments was when a female student returned to high school. I don't know if she graduated, but the alternative education program had given her a second chance.

Fort Bragg, North Carolina, was my first two-week IMA assignment. In May 1984, I was pregnant, and I reported to the Fort Bragg in-processing section wearing civilian clothes. The male military clerk gave me a weird look. "You don't have a uniform?" he barked. "No. I am pregnant and don't have any uniforms that fit," I retorted. My response was partially true. I'd gotten rid of my Army uniforms and did not live close to an Army base where I could purchase new ones. Deep down inside, I felt a sense of rebellion and defiance by not reporting in a uniform. My excuse for defying Army protocol was plausible since the Army didn't issue maternity uniforms until the early 1980s, and they were difficult to find.[2] After I signed in, I took the picture for my red-and-white reserve identification card in civilian clothes, and I purchased a couple of maternity uniforms. I was now officially an Army Reservist. For the next two weeks, I lived with my parents and worked where I had when I left the military and vowed not to return, COSCOM.

The return to teaching following my IMA assignment was short-lived. I taught the alternative education class until six weeks before our son, Walter IV, was born in November 1984 at Stonewall Jackson Hospital. After giving birth, I resigned from the teaching position but remained in the Army Reserve. I spent days comparing newborn notes with another new mother whose husband taught at VMI and taking the Quartermaster Officer Advanced Course by correspondence. I received a stack of course materials and books, filled in the answer boxes, and mailed them back to the graders at Fort Lee.

After three years at VMI, in the spring of 1985, Walter received an assignment to Fort Monroe, Virginia. We were relieved to finally leave Lexington and looked forward to a vibrant and diverse community in the Hampton Roads area. We purchased our first home in Newport News. In Newport News, I experienced a segment of the military that I'd never known about, "Active Duty for Special Work." These are Army Reserve assignments for less than 180 days where reservists work alongside active-duty personnel on Army Reserve issues. Army Reservists can have multiple assignments if they do not exceed 180 consecutive active-duty days, which counts against the Army's end-strength. Reservists who performed multiple short tours were referred to as "tour babies." As a new "tour baby," I accepted a three-month assignment at Fort Eustis, Virginia. I later found another civilian job teaching military logistics courses through one of the military consortium colleges. In the summer of 1986, I attended the Quartermaster Officer Advanced Course at Fort Lee for two weeks and worked in a two-week IMA assignment at Fort Meade. In the fall of 1986, I started a full-time teaching job at a magnet school in Newport News, and I taught seventh-grade reading and eighth-grade civics. Compared to the Army, the hours didn't seem full-time; my classes were from 8:00 a.m. to 3:00 p.m.

In December 1986, Walter was selected for early—or Below the Zone—promotion to major. Early selection meant that he was chosen ahead of his peers for promotion and had a higher-than-average chance of achieving general officer rank. We were proud and humbled by his achievement. He loved the Army and worked hard to excel.

Angst and anxiety prevailed the following year. In March 1987, while I was four months pregnant, my obstetrician advised me, "You will not carry this child full term." I had three large fibroids in my uterus with the fetus. One fibroid was covering the placenta, the organ providing oxygen and nutrients to the fetus. The obstetrician offered me the option to terminate the pregnancy and handed me a brochure to make arrangements. I chose not to terminate. In August 1987, we welcomed our daughter, Nisa. She was placed in the neonatal Intensive Care Unit

(ICU) because of blisters covering the lower half of her body. The pediatricians thought she might have a rare disease, Incontinentia pigmenti of the central nervous system, affecting skin, eyes, teeth, and the skeletal system. After a month of her being poked and tested without any confirmed diagnosis, I stopped taking her to specialists. Instead, I heeded the advice of the doctors and watched for signs of impairment. She continued to develop as a normal child, and the blisters faded. Nisa is now a brilliant thirty-five-year-old international English teacher who graduated from college with honors.

In late 1987, Walter received an assignment to attend the nine-month residence course at Command and General Staff College (CGSC) at Fort Leavenworth, Kansas. The class began in August 1988 and ended in May 1989. CGSC is the gateway class for promotion to colonel and making general officer. Without completing this class, officers would not be selected for battalion command or promotion. After CGSC, the Army would relocate to us another assignment, hopefully somewhere in the United States.

An application to attend CGSC in person as an Army Reservist arrived in the mail, which I discarded. A voice in my head repeated, "Forget about it. Don't do it." The other voices told me that it would be impossible to balance a demanding courseload and two small children. Yet at the urging of a friend, Deloris Dillard, who'd served with me in Korea, I changed my mind and sorted through the garbage for the CGSC application. She reminded me of our time in Korea, saying something to the effect of, "You'll be there anyway, and you can handle anything for four months." Since the Army Reserve residence requirement for CGSC was only four months, I wiped the garbage stain off the CGSC application and mailed it in. Included in the application was my official Department of the Army photo in a maternity uniform.

Along with welcoming a new daughter, Walter was attending graduate school. For some unknown reason, by early 1988, he was no longer a hearty eater, had lost about fifteen pounds, and was sleeping more than usual. He complained about his eyesight failing and tingling in his hands. We felt that he was tired from trying to balance work, graduate school, and new fatherhood. The doctors diagnosed him with carpal tunnel syndrome, put one of his arms in a cast to limit mobility, and gave him a new eyeglass prescription. Other than the carpal tunnel syndrome, the medical tests came back negative for abnormalities. After the biannual PT test, he came home and sat on the end of the bed. Clearly, he was frustrated. "I almost failed the 2-mile run," he said. As an infantryman, failing a PT test would end his career.

In late July 1988, we packed up a U-Haul trailer and, with two toddlers, began a two-car convoy from Newport News, Virginia, to Fort Leavenworth, Kansas. Walter led the way in his manual un-air-conditioned two-seater beige Toyota truck. I drove our navy-blue manual transmission Volvo 740 station wagon. We arrived, located our house on the military installation, and unpacked as we awaited the arrival of our furniture and other household items. I visited the employment office in the city of Leavenworth to inquire about a babysitter. I met someone there who said she knew a lady at her church who could provide in-home childcare. After interviewing the lady who was referred by her church member, I was set with a nanny for four months and looked forward to completing CGSC and preparing for our next assignment.

CGSC is a graduate-level curriculum.[3] The most difficult academic portion of CGSC is the first four months, or the common core subjects. The core subjects consist of Leadership, History, Resource Management Operational Strategy and Planning, Joint Doctrine, Army Doctrine and Tactics, Logistics, Resource Management, and Force Management. After completing the core course, officers enroll in elective courses about the military, the Advance Operations Course, or get selected for Senior Advanced Military Studies. As an Army Reservist, I had to complete the first four months.

Each CGSC class has approximately one thousand officers primarily from the Army, international officers, and members from the Reserve Components. The class is broken down into sections, and then further divided into four staff groups of about sixteen officers. During the 1988–89 academic year, I was advised that the goal was for each staff group to have at least one reservist (Army Reserve or National Guardsman), one African American, and one female. I fulfilled three of the diversity goals.

Military doctors at Fort Monroe advised Walter to have carpal tunnel surgery to alleviate the tingling in his hands. Walter decided to have surgery on both hands at the same time. Since the surgery was considered minor, Walter believed that the recovery time would not impact his studies, and the academic environment of CGSC would allow for recovery. Munson Hospital at Fort Leavenworth would not perform the surgery, and Walter opted for a civilian surgeon. After attending class for about a month, we paid for the surgery ourselves, and Walter began his recovery. He had casts on both arms and complained about his eyesight. About two weeks after the surgery, he felt weak, and I took him to Munson. He was admitted for observation, but doctors could not provide answers about his condition. From his hospital bed he whispered, "Go home and change clothes. I don't want anyone to lock your heels while in uniform." Obviously, he felt that I was getting annoyed with the military doctors, and he didn't want me to get into any trouble by confronting them about his treatment as an Army officer. To be heard, I needed to revert to the role of an Army wife.

Following Walter's advice, I went home, changed clothes, and returned to the hospital. A doctor reviewed his test results with me and advised that his white cell count was high, but they didn't know why. I sat with him for a while and returned home to relieve the babysitter. The next day when I visited him, the doctors advised me that they were relocating him to Fitzsimmons Military Hospital in Aurora, Colorado, for further tests. I called our families to advise them of his medical condition. His mother came to Leavenworth and accompanied him to Colorado as the physicians and specialists sought a diagnosis for his deteriorating health. I planned to terminate my enrollment in CGSC to focus on Walter and the kids. He encouraged me to remain in CGSS to create options for myself if something happened to him. Within a few days, he was transferred to Fitzsimmons. With mixed emotions of guilt and grief, I remained in CGSC.

His departure to Fitzsimmons and my return to class started a journey that I equate to a ring of Dante's inferno.[4] One CGSC instructor, whom I'll refer to as Lieutenant Colonel M, subtly reminded me that as the triple diversity student, I was the weakest link of the class. My overall grades were above average, but that didn't matter. Apparently, I was a prime example of someone likely to be exploited by the Soviets. I would be the one whom the Soviets perceived as weak. Unlike my White male classmates, some from West Point, I was a Black woman reservist. Since reservists are only part-time military, they are not the main line of defense. Clearly, I was the weakest link.

Using the Socratic method, Lieutenant Colonel M called on me more than other students. Walking into his class, I waited to hear my name called: "Captain Cummings, what do you think of XYZ?" or something similar. He often made cynical remarks such as, "I guess you didn't read the assignment" when he felt my answer was not as complete as it should have been. Occasionally Lieutenant Colonel M taunted other students with his cynicism. In one instance, Lieutenant Colonel D threw a gummy bear candy at a male Hispanic student for answering a question correctly. When the student caught the gummy bear and ate it with an affirming smile, Lieutenant Colonel D reminded him that Pavlov was Russian. Lieutenant Colonel M continued the lecture, noting that the student's response to the tossed gummy bear illustrated what the Russians hoped to achieve with their exploitative tactics: "They lure you in with psychological manipulation then attack." One of the other instructors advised me of Lieutenant Colonel M's teaching style and apologized on his behalf. Lieutenant Colonel M. never apologized to me for the academic harassment, but he confessed that he had been unaware of Walter's illness.

After weeks of tests and biopsies, the doctors at Fitzsimmons could not diagnose Walter's condition. I visited him for two to three days and accompanied him to his doctor's appointments. He continued to lose weight, and the doctors could only treat the symptoms. Ruptured blood vessels in his eyes caused neovascularization, and his blood oxygen levels were decreasing.

Walter tried to use humor as he described losing his sight: "The floaters in my eyes look like small black animals with tails scurrying. There goes another one." He'd point to the wall as he watched the floaters move in his field of vision. As his vision worsened, he mentioned black-and-gray hazes with white spots appearing without any color images. Afterward, lines or sketches replaced the haze. Then darkness.

Finally, in early November, the doctors identified his condition as light chain deposition disease (LCCD).[5] It was and still is a rare disease.

In 1988, fewer than ten cases had been reported nationwide. The disease was terminal. Fitzsimmons did not have treatment protocols, so they referred him to a specialist at the Mayo Clinic in Arizona. We waited for Munson to finalize the arrangements for Walter's departure.

LCCD caused his system to produce excessive amounts of protein and increased the viscosity of his blood. Blood with high viscosity levels becomes dense and thick. It can no longer flow through the body normally and nourish the organs, thereby starving them and causing them to shut down. Walter's shutdown began with neuropathy symptoms in his hands, causing the carpal tunnel syndrome. His lungs and eyes were next, explaining the floaters and breathing difficulty. The doctors advised us that if the treatment was unsuccessful, it was only a matter of time before his kidneys failed. Renal failure would most likely be the cause of his death.

Like an officer leaving command, Walter and I met with his staff advisors and CGSC leadership to bid farewell. While he shared his diagnosis and prognosis, everyone seemed to have the blank, thousand-meter stare. With glazed eyes and heavy hearts, people could not believe that Walter would succumb to this disease. I probably didn't believe it, either. Walter told me that a few people had asked him if I understood that he was terminally ill, because I didn't cry or seem emotional. I sat in the meetings and responded with polite and optimistic comments like, "I believe that he can beat this" and "We'll be okay." I now know that deep shock and grief do not always produce tears. Sometimes they produce extreme optimism or silence.

Word about Walter's illness traveled fast throughout the school. Several CGSC classmates asked me, "Is there anything I/we can do?" I usually responded, "Thank you, I appreciate it, but we are OK." Realistically, there was not anything anyone could do. However, I did sell my daughter's crib and a few other infant items to a fellow pregnant classmate.

After the end of one class, fellow classmate Maj. Ronald Johnson, a Black male West Point graduate who had heard about Walter's illness, approached me and asked, "What are you going to do?" I responded, "I'm going back to my home in Fayetteville." Johnson pleaded with me,

"Don't do that." I explained to him my childcare dilemma. I would need help raising the kids, and my parents would be there to assist me. He suggested that I return to active duty. He and I went back and forth about why I should not return to Fayetteville. I could not envision returning to the Army's grunge. Johnson, however, offered assurances about my maturity and ability to have a successful career. Furthermore, if I returned to active duty, I could build a better life for myself and the children. I disagreed. I could not foresee my life on active duty as a single parent. He finally told me to stop thinking about it and just sign my name. He told me about his decision to attend West Point and how he had been hesitant about committing. He just signed his name.

At Johnson's continued urging, I contacted the Reserve advisor and applied to return to active duty. With Walter's illness, I would now be the primary breadwinner and needed a career jump start. I devised a plan to regroup in the Army for a couple of years. Later I could become an IMA or join a reserve unit if I was unable to manage raising a family and serving. Walter and I discussed my return to active-duty full-time. He agreed that it would be a good idea. I signed my name on the dotted line to return to active duty full-time in the Active Guard and Reserve (AGR) program. Ronald Johnson later became a two-star general and chief of the Army Engineers. I've often shared with him that I attribute much of my military career to our conversation.

In early December 1988, Walter and his mother departed on military medical evacuation aircraft (MEDEVAC) to the Mayo Clinic to begin his chemotherapy treatment. After the initial treatment, he returned to Fitzsimmons to continue the treatment with hopes of chemotherapy stopping the excessive protein production.

On December 15, 1988, I graduated from CGSC. I bought a live Christmas tree and began to decorate it. Since Walter was partially blind, I wanted him to smell the scent of the pine tree when he returned home. But he never did. On December 18, his mother called with an update and a question: "He's in ICU and not expected to live. What do you want to do?" I'm sure I responded with, "Keep him alive until I get there" or some similar statement. She explained that his death was imminent within seventy-two hours. I felt as if I were a character in an awful movie or a television show wherein someone packs a suitcase, grabs the kids, leaves home, and never returns. I called my neighbor and friend Charlene "Charlie" Briscoe in hysterics. Her husband, Bill, had been stationed at Fort Monroe with Walter. She came over and made flight arrangements for me as I packed. One or two suitcases and the kids and I were out the door. I'm unsure who drove us to the airport. When I arrived at Fitzsimmons ICU, Walter was on a metal gurney with a sheet covering his lower body awaiting a toe tag and a body bag. The kids and I went into the room to say goodbye. With his eyes wider than usual, his cornea glistened with a snow-like whiteness, and he turned his head slightly and stared at us. I picked up both kids and told them, "Say hi to Daddy, and tell him that you love him." We returned to the lobby area, where we waited to receive word of his passing.

I don't know how long we stayed in the lobby. In a daze, I probably took the kids to get some food and checked into the lodging on post. My parents and Walter's family had been notified, and over the next two or three days we waited and prayed. Everyone came to the hospital. Our prayers worked. Walter stabilized and came back to us from the brink of death. With his condition stable, he moved into a hospital bed on the oncology ward.

When Walter arrived on the oncology ward, the nurses were surprised to see him. A Black male nurse assured Walter of his resilience and applauded his miraculous recovery: "We didn't expect to see you again! You had a big ole knot on your head when we found you on the floor." Walter had had an episode known as a thrombotic thrombocytopenic purpura that caused a seizure, renal failure, and high blood pressure. He regained consciousness, but he was now weak and totally blind.

When Walter condition's stabilized, my mother took the kids with her to Fayetteville. Within three days, the physical and medical evaluation boards determined that he was not fit for duty. His prognosis was a 50 percent chance of death within two to three years. After two weeks of sleeping in hospital rooms and in temporary lodging at Fitzsimmons, I wasn't feeling well and made an appointment for myself. My diagnosis: bronchitis. I had difficulty breathing in Colorado's dry air and high altitude. The doctors checked my weight; I had lost about fifteen pounds since August 1988.

With Walter's condition stable, he was medically retired, or an Army retiree for medical reasons. The Army offered him anyplace in the United States to live. Walter chose the Washington, DC, area to be close to his brother Wayne, my former student who had relocated there with his wife. Washington, DC, was also the location of the military's premier medical facility, Walter Reed. We felt that DC was a win-win situation, close to quality medical care and close to family. Within three weeks, Walter and I were on a MEDEVAC flight on our way to Walter Reed.

In January 1989, we arrived at Walter Reed. The doctors assessed Walter's condition and said that he had about six months to live. They also asked me if he worked around chemicals and weapons. I reminded them that he was an infantry officer, so of course he worked around weapons, but I was not aware of chemical exposure. After an extensive dialogue with one of the doctors, he advised me not to spend any money trying to find out how Walter contracted this rare disease. The doctor basically told me, "Get on with your life. He'll be dead, and you will go broke trying to figure out how he got this disease." There was no cure; he was dying. Although miracles could happen, this was not a case where a miracle could save him. Initially I did not accept the prognosis. I knew he would and could beat the odds of dying. During one of his many blood draws, I finally came to accept Walter's fate. Instead of blood, a yellow liquid filled the tubes. The liquid reminded me of a melted banana popsicle. The miracle I needed was to get me through Walter's transition to death. His new prognosis: six months to live.

For about two weeks, I lived in Walter's hospital room and occasionally slept at his brother's apartment. His mother, brother, and I took shifts staying with him. He was blind and afraid but lucid enough to push me to find stable housing. "Have you found a house yet?" he kept asking. I rented an apartment in Greenbelt, Maryland, and rented bedroom, living room, and kitchen furniture. Walter stabilized enough to get released from Walter Reed and come to the apartment, and I took him to dialysis three times a week. My parents and a few of his friends visited. It appeared that after each chemotherapy treatment, he had an episode wherein he would have to be hospitalized due to low blood levels, seizures, and an array of other symptoms. The doctors explained that chemotherapy kills the good cells right along with the bad cells. The side effects from the cure were as bad as the disease.

While in vigil mode at his hospital bedside, I sought solace and comfort in books. Two books in particular helped me to make sense of my chaotic life. Sidney Sheldon's protagonist in *Windmills of the Gods* was a woman who lost her husband suddenly.[6] The character's dialogue and thoughts prompted me to write Sheldon and share with him how much I connected to his character and why. He wrote back to me and shared that he wrote about his late wife, Jorga, who had passed away three years prior. Harold Kushner's *When Bad Things Happen to Good People* asked the ultimate question, "Why?"[7] The premise made sense to me: life is chaotic, and God helps us to restore order into chaos. That's exactly what I needed, order. I needed to reduce the chaos in my life. But how?

With my all my possessions at Fort Leavenworth, Bill and Charlie told me that they had everything under control. I assigned them power of attorney to manage our affairs at Fort Leavenworth, and I never returned. They packed household goods and sold Walter's Toyota truck. One of my classmates drove our Volvo station wagon to Greenbelt in March 1989. After experiencing how my Army friends and community supported me through this tragedy, I knew with certainty that I was making the right decision to return to active duty. The bond of military families is powerful. Military families know how to get things done and support each other through life's darkest moments.

In April 1989, I was offered an opportunity to return to active duty as a full-time reservist in the capacity of an AGR. The AGR program is full-time active duty working alongside the active-duty force as the subject-matter expert for reserve issues. AGRs ensure that the Army Reserve is included in Active Army and Department of Defense (DoD) policies. With absolute resolve, I expressed my assignment request: "I have to be stationed in Washington, DC." The assignments officer emphatically stated that was *not* going to happen because this was my first assignment in the AGR program. I initially refused to return to active duty and requested my name be removed from the list. But a female major reminded me, "Continue with your life; your husband's fate is sealed."

Fortunately, in May, I received an assignment at the Office of the Chief Army Reserve (OCAR) in Washington, DC. OCAR's headquarters is located at the Pentagon. At the time, the satellite officers were in Rosslyn, Virginia. OCAR establishes policy for the entire Army Reserve. I panicked. Although I had requested a DC assignment, my uncertainties about the area emerged. The traffic was a nightmare, and I was worried about childcare. I didn't want to leave the kids with my parents for an extended period.

Full of guilt and uncertainty, I went to Fort McCoy, Wisconsin, for two weeks for AGR orientation training. Walter's mother was living with us and stayed with him while I was away. When I returned, Walter said that he no longer wanted to be on dialysis and was ready to die. He was still very physically strong and required sedation for dialysis and other treatments. He signed a Do Not Resuscitate (DNR) document. Finally, in mid-June, I asked his doctors, "How long will he live without dialysis?" "About a week," one of them responded. I told Walter that he would die within a week without dialysis, and I needed the time to allow everyone to say goodbye. We negotiated his death date. We reviewed his burial plans; he wanted to be buried near his father in the cemetery across from the Veterans Administration hospital in Fayetteville. He kept asking if I had located a home to purchase. I assured him that I had. One of the dialysis nurses knew a real estate agent who helped me find a house in Laurel, Maryland. Coincidentally, I assumed a VA home loan from a veteran who was dying from Lou Gehrig's disease.

Since Walter's death was certain, one of my supervisors suggested that I sign out on thirty days leave at OCAR. I now had a thirty-day leave deficit. I could not take any time off for vacation until I accrued leave, which would take about a year. While working on this manuscript, an April 2023 headline caught my attention, "Troops can now take two weeks of leave after death of spouse or child."[8] I wish that I could have had at least two weeks to grieve my husband's death in 1989.

On Father's Day, June 18, 1989, our families visited Walter; he said goodbye and drank a strawberry milkshake. Nisa fed him ice. He told the kids to "behave for Mommy." Around noon on June 19, I walked out of his hospital room with our son to get lunch. My father and mother-in-law were in the room with him. When we returned, the nurses met me in the hall, one of them grabbed both of my hands: "I'm sorry."

I looked at Walter. He seemed to be asleep. I touched the inside of his forearm. The dialysis line was no longer active with the quiet churn of the central venous catheter. From a spiritual perspective I believed that Walter had lived long enough for me to find a house and a job before he died.

In Walter Reed's parking lot, I explained to our five-year-old son that Daddy had died and was now with the angels. His response, "You didn't tell me that people died. Now what I'm supposed to do without a daddy?"

I had no answers.

6

BRINGING DOWN
THE GAVEL

CHILDREN EXPRESS LIFE'S EVENTS TO make sense of the chaos and disruption they experience. My five-year-old son's reenactments of his father's funeral were interesting to observe. He drew pictures of his father ascending to heaven. His GI Joe dolls died, had a funeral, and soared into heaven with the angels. I reminded him daily, "Daddy is no longer with us, but we have to keep on going." And that's what we did—we kept on going. The kids and I acknowledged our pain but kept on going. Oftentimes, I felt as if I were an amputee reaching for a missing limb, realizing that it was just a phantom pain of losing my husband, my activity partner, and my best friend.

After Walter's funeral at First Baptist Church on Moore Street, the same church where we were married and dedicated (that is, requested public prayer for) our children. I returned to the apartment in Greenbelt and prepared to move into our new home. I contacted Bill and Charlie Briscoe, who arranged for my household goods to be delivered. My father decided to live with me to help me unpack and settle into a new home. With hopes of Walter returning from the hospital, I had purchased a four-bedroom brick rancher home with a one-car garage and a full basement, built in 1970.

While I was still in Fayetteville preparing to return to Maryland, my girlfriend Lorraine, who referred me for the job in Lexington, Virginia, told me about her niece Paula. Paula had graduated from college and was job hunting. I offered her a four-month stint as a live-in babysitter. I proposed that living with me, she could save money to job hunt and return to Fayetteville. I could locate a permanent babysitter during her stay. The plan worked. I was set for four months with a babysitter. My dad returned home, and I began my new life as a single parent.

My morning routine consisted of driving to the New Carrollton metro station in Maryland and boarding the Orange line to my Pentagon satellite office in Rosslyn, Virginia. During lunch, two to three times a week, I walked to the Key Bridge Marriott for a workout in the gym and a run over the Key Bridge to Georgetown. I learned about the Washington, DC, metro area by running throughout the city. Those lunchtime runs provided a soothing that I didn't know that I needed. Running over the Potomac River, through the trails, and around the monuments made me feel a sense of accomplishment. I began to believe in my ability to make it as a single parent.

My first position at OCAR was reviewing the policy for Army schools in various career management fields and assessing the impact on Army Reservists. I reviewed documents and gathered data from Army schools about how changes to Military Occupational Codes and skills would impact training and qualification. My job was to ensure that the correct information about Army Reserve policy made it to the regulations or was addressed by the appropriate Army school.

Learning how to navigate the Pentagon was both intriguing and frustrating. The Pentagon is constructed in concentric rings from A to E, with A being the inner ring. Addresses contain the floor level number, the ring alpha character, corridor number, and the room number. An office or paperwork with an E address such as "1-E-200" referred to an office on the outer ring. Since the majority of the civilian presidential appointees and generals' offices are located on E Ring, the "E-Ringers" symbolize power and authority. More importantly, those offices have windows with outside views of the Pentagon. Everyone else is in a cubicle or in an office without a window.

One fact that I didn't comprehend during my first four years in the military was the authority of senior civilians.[1] They run the military. Every major office in the Pentagon has a civilian in charge at the Senior Executive Service (SES) level who reports to the secretary of the service (that is, Army, Navy, etc.) who reports to the secretary of defense, then to the president, the commander in chief. Hundreds of "SESers" oversee and establish DoD policy. The generals and soldiers in the field execute or perform the policy as directed by their chief of staff (four-star general or flag officer), who works for a service secretary (for example, secretary of the Army). As a lieutenant or captain, I never worked with civilians who oversaw the military personnel. Now I watched many officers reporting to the Pentagon with a hard-core military style get humbled by SESers during presentations and office visits.

The warrant officer computer technician taught me some computer basics, including how to use email and format the five-inch floppy disks to save work in the event of a power failure. He reminded me to print a paper record of actions and not to trust the computer or the disk, because they were easy to corrupt. Whenever I asked him for assistance, his favorite acronym and response was "RTFS [Read the F**ing Screen]," meaning that the blinking prompt on the screen provided the solution. I also attended classes and learned the groundbreaking Enable software package for Word Perfect and Harvard Graphics (the precursor to PowerPoint). I learned to synthesize pages of information to a few talking points and how to create colorful graphics or a cartoon to convey concepts. We developed horse blanket briefings with data on 14″ × 17″ sheets of paper. A picture is worth a thousand words held a new significance. One of my bosses would tell me, "Edna, let me see the cartoon. I can understand it if I can see it." I was sure these new computer and cartoon skills would come in handy when I left the Army.

My confidence about single parenthood continued to increase. I managed the workload, navigated the metro, and developed a childcare network. I met other single parents, and we all shared our childcare challenges. We rushed to catch the train to pick up our children from daycare or relieve a babysitter to avoid paying hefty late fees. Some co-workers were not as understanding about single parents. One female officer advised me that she did not submit my name for a project because I had kids, and she knew that childcare would be an issue. I later received feedback from colleagues who overheard my conversation with her. Apparently, I chewed her out. I should have taken her out of earshot of others to advise her, "Do not *ever* speak on my behalf about my children or whether I could meet a requirement." But I did not. I unloaded in the office because I was angry that she had a sexist attitude about me as a single parent.

A White male superior taunted me with rude comments when I arrived at work in the morning or when he invaded my personal space in the tight little copy room. Often, he stood behind me close enough to whisper in my ear, but not close enough for his body to touch mine: "It must be hard being a single parent." I'd turn around and see him smirk. I never responded and tried to keep a distance from him. Avoiding him was like playing office dodgeball. He was the ball. I was trying not to get hit or, in this case, "hit upon." I requested a transfer from that office due to childcare issues. I didn't report his harassment, because I would have created a problem for the office. I'm sure that my allegation against him would have been viewed as noncredible and unsubstantiated. When I advised him of my transfer, he responded as if he were issuing an office edict: "No more single parents!"

Another female officer—I'll refer to her as Colonel Z—dealt with sexist attitudes with an extreme and dramatic method. Colonel Z entered the Army as a WAC and trained at Fort McClellan. She never sugarcoated words or worried about being polite. One day, I noticed an approximately six-inch pink fake male "private part" on her desk. Colonel Z explained, "I wasn't born with one, and I have to take this with me to meetings." Her explanation included how men listened when she held the fake male anatomy. She was tired of the male officers holding meetings in the men's restroom and making decisions about her program. Colonel Z demonstrated how she slammed the anatomy on the table like a judge with a courtroom gavel to get their attention. I don't know if she got her fellow male officers' attention, but she sure got mine. I knew not to cross Colonel Z.

My home life was becoming a routine. The hardest part was going through Walter's personal items and deciding what to donate or keep. As I met new friends and coworkers, a few shared similar experiences of love and loss. Occasionally I received calls from people who had learned of Walter's death. I felt that I had to console them instead of them consoling me. The Pentagon was also a military crossroads for previous coworkers. I ran into a few pilots who had undergone flight school training at Fort Rucker, classmates from Fort Lee, and Walter's friends who knew of his passing. Many offered their condolences and supported my return to active duty.

I am unsure when I received notice of my promotion eligibility, but my name appeared on the promotion list for major. In May 1990, almost one year after I became a widow, I was promoted. The Army and other branches have three categories of officer (O) ranks, company grade lieutenant through captain (O1–O3) field grade, major through colonel (O4–O6), and general officer (O7–O10). I hadn't thought about the possibility of promotion, nor had I expected to become a field grade officer. With each promotion, the Army reminds us of increased positions of responsibility. The Army was correct. In August 1990, the Gulf War began.[2] I had more responsibility.

On August 2, 1990, nearly one hundred thousand Iraqi troops invaded Kuwait and overran the country. The Kuwait invasion led to a United Nations Security Council embargo and sanctions on Iraq and a US-led coalition air and ground war, Operation Desert Shield (ODS).[3] The 1990 Iraqi invasion of Kuwait led to the largest call-up, or mobilization, of reserve forces since the Korean War. More than thirty-five thousand Army Reserve soldiers from 626 units helped liberate Kuwait by providing combat support and combat service support. The Army Reserve was among the first to fight and the last to leave. I couldn't help but think about my decision to return to active duty. If I had remained as an IMA or joined a reserve unit, I would have been mobilized for this war, been ordered to deploy, and disrupted my family. I was blessed to be in the active ranks and not called up for the war.

With the ground war came a new workplace for me, a classified area in the basement of the Pentagon, the Army Operations Center (AOC), and new responsibilities, Army Reserve family programs. I spent twelve to fourteen hours a day in the AOC ensuring Army Reserve soldiers had the resources to perform their duties. I also worked with programs to ensure families had the needed support. Computers and internet access were not tools available to connect communities. I organized the shipment of thousands of manuals, guides, resource aids, newsletters, and whatever the Army thought would help support reserve families during this war.

When the Army Reservists returned home after the war, another battle ensued—the fight for benefits. My focus then shifted from family programs to a benefits program known as incapacitation pay. The vivid medical descriptions of soldiers' injuries demonstrated their sacrifices—a soldier caught in a tank turret, chronic obstructive pulmonary disorder, post- traumatic stress disorder resulting from sexual assault (now referred to as military sexual trauma), and many more.[4]

The ground war, or ODS, ended in January 1991, and Operation Desert Storm, the air campaign, began.[5] I still spent time in the AOC, supporting Army Reserve actions, but another internal culture war began—the fight against sexual harassment. In September 1991, upward of sixty-five women alleged sexual harassment and misconduct by male officer attendees at the Navy's Tailhook Association in Las Vegas, Nevada. The subsequent investigations resulted in a revamp of the military's sexual harassment policies.

The revamp of these policies escalated the focus on the Army Reserve's sexual harassment policies. Along with my incapacitation pay duties, I was assigned equal opportunity (now diversity, equity, and inclusion) and women's issues. I now had three programs to manage, which increased my travel to conferences, workshops, and to the Defense Equal Opportunity Management School in Cocoa Beach, Florida, to obtain certification.

Each of these jobs was educational, challenging, and demanding. I attended meetings and events with the military's top generals and civilians. The Tailhook investigation generated the Navy's stoplight approach to sexual harassment.[6] The "Red Light, Green Light" traffic-light colors defined acceptable and unacceptable forms of behavior. Critics then and now maintain that the colors oversimplify the complexities of behavior.[7] But I felt empowered when I told a male senior officer that he was engaging in "Red Light," or inappropriate, behavior by commenting on how nice my legs looked in a skirt. He got the message without me wasting words.

Prior to my departure to my next assignment in 1995, several White male officers apologized to me, with one saying, "You are a damn good officer." He expressed remorse because he'd thought I was part of an affirmative action plan. He mentioned that when more Black women came to the organization, he felt that they (White men) were being overrun and forced to work with us. Everything made sense now. The microaggressions, extra assignments, and additional questions about my tasks were deliberate. I'd had to prove my qualifications and worthiness above and beyond what was required—over and over again.

In 1995, I received an assignment as an assistant professor of military science in the ROTC department at Georgetown. I could not believe I landed the assignment. I was working at the university that defined college basketball and the epitome of a quality education. Most of the students in Army ROTC had scholarships and required little motivation. I admired these students carrying the extra academic load and commuting from colleges in Washington, DC, and Maryland to attend classes. Unlike ASU, Georgetown did not offer academic credit for Army ROTC.

The Army ROTC office was and still is in the Car Barn. Crossing the Key Bridge from Rosslyn provides a view of a brick building with a clock affixed to the rooftop. Constructed in the late 1800s, the Car Barn was originally a consolidated streetcar station and storage garage. Our office location was most known for the stone steps adjacent to the building—or the "Exorcist steps," nicknamed for their appearance in a famous movie scene.[8] These Exorcist steps became a training regimen for the ROTC cadets. The active-duty ROTC sergeants conducted cadet PT on these steps. We also performed PT on the racetrack, and I prided myself on my ability to run faster backward than some of the first-year cadets could run forward. I met the track coach, who was a former Marine, and I could see the glow in his face as he watched the cadets get into shape. I also have fond memories of a homeless man on M Street who stood up and saluted one day while I took a walk during lunchtime. He said that he was proud of me. I thought that it was sad that a homeless person rendered me more respect than some uniformed personnel in the Pentagon.

Along with teaching leadership classes, I was the recruiting operations officer (ROO) in charge of increasing enrollment in ROTC. One of my best recruiting successes was convincing a young man to attend Georgetown instead of West Point, the Army's military academy. I basically told him, "DC is the center of the world, and West Point will not match the experiences and freedoms that you have at Georgetown." I reminded him of three things: (1) he would only be eighteen once; (2) he was in a win-win situation, and he would become an Army officer whether he attended West Point or Georgetown; and (3) not all Army generals attend West Point. He attended Georgetown and later became the cadet battalion commander. When I convinced him to attend Georgetown, his father's eyes rendered approval.

While dressing for work one morning in late 1995, my stomach cramped and quivered. I staggered into Fort Meade's Kimbrough Army Hospital's emergency room. After examining me, the doctor delivered disturbing news. The fibroids that I'd developed during my second pregnancy had grown. One was the size of a grapefruit and was pressing on my kidneys. They were too large for surgery, and my blood levels showed that I was anemic. The doctor recommended a treatment of Lupron injections to reduce the fibroids and prepare for surgery. My mind flashed back to my husband's illness and the impacts on our children, and tears flowed as the doctor explained my medical condition. Regrets flowed through my mind about inattention to my health: "I wished I'd gone to the doctor earlier instead of suffering through the monthly pain caused by fibroids." The doctor assured me that I would be okay. I hoped he was correct.

After my diagnosis and surgery four months later, I knew Georgetown was going to be my last active-duty assignment. My body was breaking down, and I was no longer going to allow the Army to control my life.

This was now the time for me to focus first on my health and family. The kids were doing well in school. By working at Georgetown, I was able to place them in Holy Trinity School across the street from my office. The private school tuition for two children was cheaper than childcare. I now had a deliberate plan for my life. The children were thriving, seemed happy, and loved their school. After I recovered from surgery, I began a passive job hunt in the Washington, DC, area.

In the fall of 1996, the Army notified me of my upcoming promotion board to the next rank of lieutenant colonel (LTC). It didn't matter. I planned to leave the Army and become a "tour baby," or IMA, but the Army enticed me with another fascinating opportunity. My assignments officer advised me my new job would be at Fort Gillem, in Atlanta, Georgia, as a Military Support to Civilian Authorities (MSCA)[9] officer to work with the Federal Emergency Management Agency Regions IV. Of course, I complained about uprooting my family. He reminded me that I had not moved since 1989, almost eight years. I reminded him that other officers (all White) had been in the area for as long as I had been if not longer. I asked, "Why do I have to move?" After several back-and-forth conversations, I consented to move—with prejudice. The kids had meltdowns. But I told them it was a new adventure, a new city. They didn't care.

When I left Army ROTC in Georgetown in 1997, one of the NCOs wrote a two-page farewell speech and read it aloud, "Nightmare on Prospect Street," wherein he refers to me as Major Hyde (of Dr. Jekyll and Mr. Hyde fame). I held onto this 1997 farewell speech to remind myself of the bond and respect that we had as a team preparing these cadets for the Army. My guidance to NCOs was not to let me do something stupid. We took care of each other. Until I read his farewell speech, I never knew I displayed such a broad personality range.

In June 1997, I was promoted to lieutenant colonel and received orders for First US Army Headquarters, Fort Gillem, Georgia. First Army's mission is to prepare the Army Reserve and Guard and Reserve for a range of tasks including disaster response. My new job fell into the disaster response or all hazards area and was part of the staff who worked in the Operations Center and tracked hurricanes and trained for disasters. These disasters included acts of violence or threats against the United States. World events required civilian and military assets to address terrorism threats within the United States. In February 1993, the World Trade Center was bombed, killing six people and wounding one thousand; in April 1995, a truck bomb exploded at Alfred P. Murrah Federal Building in Oklahoma City, killing 168 and wounding hundreds; in August 1996, Usama (Osama) Bin Laden issued his first declaration of war against the United States and the West, calling for the death of Americans; and in July 1996, there was a pipe bombing at Centennial Olympic Park during the Olympics in Atlanta, Georgia.[10]

I reported to Fort Gillem in July 1997 and began duties as one of five MSCA officers. We trained and coached first responders in the five Federal Emergency Management Agency (FEMA) regions east of the Mississippi about how to work with the military. Our basic mission was to help first responders understand that the military supports and does not lead disaster response effort and improve civil-military interoperability. The only exception was immediate response wherein "DoD officials may provide an immediate response by temporarily employing the resources under their control, subject to any supplemental direction provided by higher headquarters, to save lives, prevent human suffering, or mitigate great property damage within the United States. Immediate response authority does not permit actions that would subject civilians to the use of military power that is regulatory."

To further understand this assignment, I attended classes and learned about the Robert T. Stafford Disaster Relief and Emergency Assistance Act, domestic law, posse comitatus, and emergency response.[11] I had an additional duty as the Response Task Force (RTF) personnel officer, or J-1, in another aspect of disaster response, Weapons of Mass Destruction (WMD).[12] WMD included a range of nuclear, radiological, chemical, biological, or other devices intended to harm many people.

Overall, Fort Gillem was an enriching assignment. In my role as the personnel officer for the WMDRTF, we supported real-world events, trained with the Department of Justice, and deployed to sites within the United States. The leadership was professional, but one of my White male peers, a lieutenant colonel, seemed to have an issue with my authority.

Prior to departing for one location, I sensed that the lieutenant colonel was annoyed because I was his supervisor. Once we arrived, I, along with rest of the staff, was exhausted. We took a brief rest from traveling and setting up operations to prepare for the following day's events. I sat down in a chair and propped my feet upon another chair. The lieutenant colonel walked by my makeshift rest area at a rapid pace. While staring straight ahead, and swinging his arms, he knocked over the chair with his left hand that I was using to rest my feet. He kept walking as my feet fell to the floor and almost caused me to fall out of my chair. Without thinking, I kicked the fallen chair in his direction. The lieutenant colonel kept walking as if he was oblivious to his deliberate hostility and aggressive behavior toward me. I don't know if the chair I kicked hit him.

Unbeknownst to me, the one-star general in charge of our team had witnessed the entire event. He responded, "Now, now, children," and righted the chair that I had kicked. Afterward, the general seemed to talk to me more than usual. I believed that after he witnessed the officer's aggression toward me and my response, I either earned his respect, or he became aware of the hostile environment. I was embarrassed by my behavior, but the other options to address the behavior would not have been as impactful. If I had confronted the lieutenant colonel or chastised him, I would have escalated the situation. He could have alleged that I was being hostile and concocted a scenario wherein he was walking fast, swinging his arms, and "accidentally" knocked over the chair. After the chair incident, the lieutenant colonel did not exhibit any additional hostile behavior toward me. Perhaps he didn't dare.

While at Fort Gillem, the Army selected me to attend the Army War College's distance learning correspondence course. The course was two years long with in-person classes in the summer. Being selected for this course indicated that I had a chance for promotion to the next rank, colonel. This course required writing papers on assigned military topics and attending a two-week residence phase in the summer.

My assignments officer called me about a Pentagon assignment and a follow-on to my current MSCA duties. At the time, the Army oversaw disaster response for the military as the executive agent. The Consequence Management Program Office (COMPIO) had a mission to organize WMD response capabilities in the National Guard and Army Reserve forces.[13] COMPIO's primary focus was to stand up the initial ten WMD–Civil Support Teams (WMD-CST). The ultimate plan was to have one WMDCST in each state.

A 1998 Tiger Team report or Army study group about disaster relief and its function as a state mission established COMPIO's mission. Given the unique nature of a WMD attack, requests for federal assets would be required much earlier than during typical disasters. Managed by the National Guard (a state asset), the WMD-CSTs served as the initial military response, or the tip of the military spear with the civilian communities' first responders.

In 1999, I moved back to the Washington, DC, area to the Pentagon. Fortunately, I had kept my house and didn't have to house-hunt. My son was glad to leave Georgia; my daughter was not. I felt bad uprooting them again, but this time we were going to a familiar place. I was COMPIO's deputy director. Twice a month, we briefed the Office of the Secretary of Defense about the status of the program and funding expenditures.

One of the biggest challenges we encountered was convincing the rest of the military that these assets were vital at the state level and that threats against the homeland were imminent. We ended each briefing with the phrase, "It's not a matter of if, but when." A domestic lawyer advised our team not to use the term "homeland defense" because we'd instill fear into the American public. At the time, homeland defense was not a primary mission area for the military and was referred to as an operation other than war (OOTW).[14] OOTW programs included humanitarian assistance and MSCA. COMPIO's mission aligned with OOTW and although important, it was not a warfighting mission or aligned with the functional or warfighting combatant commands such as Central Command, European Command, and so on.

FEMA managed the cleanup, or aftermath (consequences), for all disasters, and the FBI managed investigation, or the criminal aspect, of violent acts. DoD did not oversee either disaster response or criminal investigations within the United States, providing support only when requested. The WMD-CSTs belonged to the National Guard and not the military, and the states are under the command of the governor, who manages the response. We spent a lot of time defending our actions and approach. In the fall of 2001, COMPIO was disbanded, accused of mismanagement, having too much civilian equipment, poor acquisition strategy, and a range of other accusations outlined in a Defense Department Inspector General's report.[15] Reading the report, we surmised that the investigators did not understand civil-military interoperability. We knew the challenges of working with civilian communities, rapid fielding requirements, etc. Our team did everything we could to ensure seamless integration—and with the leadership's approval.

We disputed several of the items that were later removed from the final report. In May 2001, I attended a congressional hearing about our office with my two-star general. My father called and asked me if he had seen me on television. I replied, "Yes, I was in the hearing." He wanted to know if I was in trouble and if I needed his help. I assured him that I was okay. None of us in the office received any punitive action, but we all felt the same way—defeated and unappreciated. After two years of hard and thankless work, in August 2001, our office was disbanded. The functions transferred to other DoD agencies. We were proud of our accomplishments and the ten WMD-CSTs that resulted from our efforts. We may not have done everything right, but we didn't do it all wrong.

On July 20, 2001, I graduated from the Army War College with a master of strategic studies degree. A new assignment usually follows the completion of a military course, but I didn't know what mine would be. With COMPIO disbanded, I worked in OCAR's office in Rosslyn, Virginia, on various training and readiness programs. In September 2001, my neighbor's father died. My daughter begged me to go to his funeral. She was close friends with his grandson, but I was on the fence about missing work. When COMPIO disbanded, I had to complete several evaluation reports for the staff. I was late with my former secretary's report, who had been reassigned to the three-star general in charge of personnel, or the Army's G-1. The funeral was on September 11, in Davidsonville, Maryland, about thirty miles from the Pentagon. I decided to attend the funeral but not the graveside ceremony. My focus that day was delivering the late evaluation to my former secretary. I planned to drop my daughter off at school and go to the Pentagon with hopes of obtaining my secretary's signature on her evaluation. The service began at 10:00 a.m.

Approximately ten minutes away from the funeral home, I received a frantic call from a close friend. He wanted to know where I was because a plane had hit the Pentagon. When I arrived at the funeral home, several people were on their cell phones. I tried to use my cell phone, but the call would not go through. The funeral director allowed me to use her office landline to call my sister Jackie to let her know that I was not at the Pentagon. I asked her to call our family and friends to let them know that I was okay.

My son's school closed early. He arrived home without knowing if I was alive. He later shared that he had collapsed in the classroom. My mom and other family members had similar responses. Everyone mentally buried me on 9/11. My former secretary's office was in the impact area, and everyone in the office was killed. But my former secretary was still alive. She was in Florida attending her mother's funeral. In the days immediately following 9/11, my parents and I received countless phone calls checking to see if I was alive and uninjured.

In August I had been reassigned to an office in Crystal City, Virginia. I don't remember if I went to work September 12 or 13, but I do remember the smoke from the smoldering Pentagon as I drove across the 14th Street Bridge to my office. The Pentagon was still burning. Once I got to work, I prepared to assume duties in the AOC one door down from my old COMPIO office. Our task: to prepare the military for war.

Yellow police tape held the Pentagon's doorways open to allow fresh air to circulate. Everything smelled like burnt charcoal. One of the security guards who controlled access to the Pentagon smiled when he saw me come through the turnstiles. He hadn't seen me in a few days and was wondering if I'd survived the attack. I heard several stories like mine about people who were scheduled to be in the Pentagon on 9/11 but were not. An officer I worked with received second-degree burns from leading others to safety. I'll always remember how he later sat in a chair discussing the rescue with his face scorched from the Pentagon's flames.

In March 2002, I held a ceremony for my promotion to colonel (COL), or O6. My three-star general sent me a note with a phrase that made this promotion seem special: *Historically speaking, less than five percent of a year group makes it to colonel.* This meant that regardless of race or gender, less than 5 percent of officers who join the Army get promoted to the rank of colonel. I'm sure he sent a similar note to everyone who made colonel, but I kept it as a reminder. I beat the odds of making colonel.

I wanted this promotion to be different from the others, and I honored my father with a ceremony. A two-star general read a Certificate of Appreciation for his service. I asked my father to wear his 503rd/80th Airborne Anti-Aircraft Artillery Association burgundy blazer. It was a way to honor him and the Black soldiers who served in segregated units.[16] My father spoke and shared that he was proud to see the progress that the Army had made. After the ceremony, I knew that I would undoubtedly move on to another assignment, hopefully in the Washington, DC, area. I did not want to move again.

Prior to 9/11, the April 2002 Unified Command Plan created a new combatant command, US Northern Command (NORTHCOM), and assigned it the mission of defending the United States and supporting the full range of military assistance to civil authorities.[17] NORTHCOM was located at Peterson Air Force Base, Colorado Springs, Colorado, and it was also the headquarters of US North American Aerospace Defense Command (NORAD) with a scheduled activation date of October 1, 2002. I was offered a job at Fort Belvoir, Virginia, or USNORTHCOM.

I could not tolerate a three-hour round-trip daily commute to Fort Belvoir, and I didn't want to move to Virginia. On the other hand, if I moved to Colorado, it would be my third move since 1999. I was unsure if I wanted to move again. The kids were not excited about the move either. But I would be standing up a new command with a mission that I knew inside and out was enticing. Besides, this was probably the first time in my military career that I felt selected for a job wherein I knew that I already had the deep knowledge and experience to make a lasting impact. I was confident that I was the best person for this job in a new command.

The activation of NORTHCOM marked the first time since Gen. George Washington that a single military commander was charged with protecting the US homeland. NORTHCOM's area of responsibility (AOR) includes all air, land, and sea approaches to North America, encompassing the continental United States, Alaska, Canada, Mexico, and the surrounding water areas out to approximately five hundred nautical miles.[18]

In my innermost being, I knew that wherever I landed, this would be my final military assignment. Instead of another round of the Washington, DC, traffic and congestion, I chose Colorado.

Me at about age four, ca. 1960

My father, Staff Sgt. (E6) Willie R. Cummings, in the mid-1960s

First dream fulfilled—becoming a
cheerleader at age fourteen

Second dream fulfilled—receiving my commission as a second lieutenant at Appalachian
State University in May 1978

My first Army assignment as a second lieutenant at Fort Rucker, Alabama. (Courtesy of the Department of Defense)

My late husband, Capt. Walter C. Cummings Jr., meeting North Korean soldiers at the United Nations Military Armistice Command Building in Panmunjom, South Korea, in 1981. (Courtesy of the Department of Defense)

Serving as an Army first lieutenant in Uijongbu, South Korea, in 1981

Our last family portrait, taken at Fort Leavenworth, Kansas, in 1988, for the Command and General Staff College yearbook

Beating the odds—my promotion to colonel in Arlington, Virginia, in 2001, with my parents pinning my eagle wings

Wearing the eagle wings as a U.S. Army colonel in March 2001

The last photo of me in uniform, shaking hands with Maj. Gen. Raymond Rees, Colorado Springs, in August 2003

My first 6888th moment, beside the 6888th Central Postal Directory Battalion Monument at Fort Leavenworth, Kansas, in November 2018

Maj. Charity Adams inspects the 6888th Central Postal Directory Battalion, before the King Edwards School for Boys in Birmingham, England, in February 1945. (Courtesy of the National Archives, 111-SC-200791)

Members of the 6888th Central Postal Directory Battalion: Sylvia Benton (*rear of Jeep*); Romay Davis (*seated in front*); Alyce Dixon (*standing in front*); the woman standing in the rear remains unidentified. (Courtesy of the Department of Defense)

Speaker Pelosi, Janice Martin, whose family member served in the Six Triple Eight, and myself on March 3, 2022

The Six Triple Eight Congressional Gold Medal signing ceremony on March 3, 2022, with former Speaker of the House, Nancy Pelosi, and four family members and three members of Congress in attendance

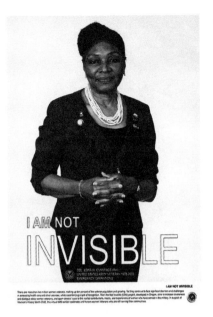

My portrait for the I Am Not Invisible campaign to highlight women veterans, in June 2022. (Courtesy of the Department of Veterans Affairs)

Portrait of Air Force Retired Maj. Fannie McClendon (age one hundred and two) for the I Am Not Invisible campaign to highlight women veterans, in June 2022. (Courtesy of the Department of Veterans Affairs)

In May 2019 the documentary team traveled to the United Kingdom as guests of the U.S. ambassador, who presented a blue plaque to the King Edwards School for Boys commemorating the Six Triple Eight. *Left to right:* James Theres, the author, Ambassador Robert W. Johnson, Acting Chief Master Keith Phillips, Retired Brig. Gen. Clara Adams-Ender, Retired Master Sgt. Elizabeth Helm-Frazier, and Director Garry Stewart

The rededication of Fort Lee, Virginia, to Fort Gregg-Adams, in April 2023

Veterans Day breakfast at the White House in November 2022 with Second Gentleman Douglas Emoff, Vice President Kamala Harris, and First Lady Dr. Jill Biden. (Courtesy of the White House)

Designs for obverse and reverse sides of the Six Triple
Eight Congressional Gold Medal, with Lt. Col. Charity
Adams to the right. (Courtesy of the U.S. Mint)

7

A BLACK BEAN AND
THE PARKWAY PATRIOT

IN THE SUMMER OF 2002, I arrived in Colorado Springs following wild-fire season. The remnants of burning timbers created an odor and haze from the forest fires with occasional gray-ash winds. The black-and-gray burned trees laced the evergreen mountainside. The "Springs" is the home of Pike's Peak, one of the most famous mountains in the country.[1] The mountains created a picturesque rolling landscape of hills and valleys, but the trees only had two colors, green and brown. I prefer the greater biodiversity of Boone's Blue Ridge Parkway mountains with the varying trees and colors. I felt the pangs of East Coast homesickness creeping in, and I hoped work responsibilities would soon replace my discomfort.

My new assignment was chief readiness and integration and re-serve forces advisor. NORTHCOM required manpower to assume its new mission but was still without an increase in force structure. Other commands had to decrease their personnel allocations and give them to NORTHCOM. Reserve Components would fill personnel shortfalls. My main responsibility was to find qualified reservists for this new mission.

An additional responsibility required duty at Cheyenne Mountain to monitor activity in the Operations Center. I'd seen movies wherein NORAD and Cheyenne Mountain thwarted alien attacks and tracked Santa Claus, but I never expected to work here. It was better than anything I'd seen on television or could have imagined. I was extremely lucky to work with the Air Force. Hollywood replicated the myriad of monitors tracking activities but not the office comforts. Unlike the Pentagon and Fort Gillem's OPS centers with basic swivel office chairs, NORAD's OPS Center had high-back leather chairs *and* midnight meals. During one midnight meal, I jokingly asked one of the cooks, "You got any chocolate cake back there?" After I sat down to eat, he appeared with a humongous slice of dark chocolate cake and icing. I'd heard that the Air Force lifestyle was softer than the Army's, and everything I'd heard was true. The chocolate cake was just the beginning.

Softening my Army writing style was the next sign of a different and less intense military culture. I had been taught the authoritative Army writing style with guidelines to state the "bottom line up front," or BLUF. My first guidance memorandum was returned. My Air Force supervisor advised me to change my sentences containing "will" to "shall." He told me that my Army writing style was too harsh.

Whenever I visited the Army post Fort Carson, located about twenty-two miles south of Peterson Air Force Base, I knew just how lucky I was to be assigned to Peterson. Fort Carson is home of the 4th Infantry Division and other warfighting units. A deep silence always seemed to envelop Fort Carson's tan camouflage-pattern landscape. Few people smiled; they all seemed preoccupied. I once stopped a group of soldiers in the middle of a walkway who were talking and had ignored me while I was in uniform. I asked, "Did you forget to salute?" I'm pretty sure I held up traffic. It took them longer than expected to acknowledge my rank as an Army colonel. Their focus was somewhere else, perhaps their next deployment.

USNORTHCOM/NORAD's commander was a four-star Air Force fighter pilot, Gen. Ralph "Ed" Eberhart. His leadership style was unlike any other that I'd ever experienced. During our morning staff meetings, he sat at the head of the rectangular wooden espresso-colored conference table with his key staff officers. I may have been one of only two or three African American officers in the meetings of about thirty people and the only Black woman. The most vocal in the meetings were the Army and Marine generals. The Navy rear admiral seemed to speak after everyone else spoke, but not as loudly. General Eberhart only spoke to ask a question or to give guidance. He did not engage in idle chitchat. When he spoke, he silenced the room with a steady and emphatic tone, only slightly above a whisper. Everyone had to stop talking and almost lean in to hear him. Brilliant! I thought. He did not need to yell or scream to make his point. It was clear that he was in charge.

I only saw him annoyed twice. The first time he squirmed in his chair before he spoke to an SESer visiting from Washington, DC. The second time was when he approached me. He advised me of a reserve officer who kept calling his office for a job, complaining that I wouldn't give her the assignment. He wasn't mad at me; he was annoyed at the officer. I called the officer's superior to ensure that she never called General Eberhart's office again. During my time at NORTHCOM, I'm sure that I stood out like a black bean on top of white rice, but he made me feel welcome and appreciated. Once during a social event, he actually smiled and told me to "Get a life." He'd seen me at multiple events that week. I was easy to remember.

The landscape in Colorado Springs during summer and fall is deceiving. Unlike on the East Coast, summer in the Springs was not humid. The dry air seeped into my system. Running at the high altitude seemed to cause everything from my nose to my toes to hurt. One day, I limped into sick call because of excruciating pain in my right foot. When the doctor reviewed my X-ray, she asked, "When did you break your foot?" My response: "I don't know." Scar tissue had formed around the injured area. My mind flashed back to my surgery in 1996, how I'd ignored the pain until it was unbearable. "Never again," I thought and rendered personal kudos to myself for seeking treatment. The treatment? Physical therapy to break up the scar tissue that cracked while the therapist twisted my foot a couple of times a week.

Achieving the rank of colonel did not make me immune to protocol and escort duties. While awaiting the arrival of a general at the Colorado

Springs airport, a captain approached me and asked, "Colonel Cummings, do you remember me?" I did not. He introduced himself as one of my former Georgetown ROTC cadets, now assigned to the president's bomb squad. I was proud to know that one of my former students was now working at the highest levels in our nation. I was impressed that he took the time to say hello and seemed excited to see me. Seeing him and many others of my former soldiers achieve success gave me a sense of accomplishment.

In the spring of 2003, my daughter pointed out that no one would come to her graduation in Colorado Springs, Colorado. As a tenth grader, I suppose she was contemplating her junior and senior years of high school. She said that she didn't have friends and was miserable. The "Springs" was also the coldest I'd been since I was on a nighttime exercise in Korea. The powdery snowdrifts were sometimes six feet high. After snowplows moved snow, I drove in brown slush to work or rode with one of my neighbors who had a pickup truck.

I realized then just how exhausted I was. I was tired of being sick and achy, tired of being cold, and tired of moving. I was tired of being tired. In April 2002, I stopped unpacking boxes and contemplated retirement. As I pondered my next steps, someone reminded me, "You are working for 50 percent of your paycheck." Bemused, I questioned the math. The individual reminded me that when I retired, I would receive 50 percent of my paycheck. He then asked me to evaluate if the constant moving and disruption was worth it. I decided that it was not. It was time for me to retire and gain some control of my life.

For the fourth time in six years, I packed my household goods for another relocation. This time would be the last time for sure. Once again, I moved back to my home in Maryland. After twenty-five and a half years of military service, I would leave the Army and become a military retiree. This time, I would not return.

As an Army officer, I could have held my retirement ceremony at Fort Carson with other Army personnel who were retiring, but I decided, "No ceremonies or early wake-ups for me." I didn't want to go to parade practice at 0800, or 8:00 a.m. Instead, I had a pizza party with my coworkers and staff in the USNORTHCOM conference room. My twenty-five-year military career ended with a pizza, a cake, and a fond farewell.

Wise counsel from the Army transition counselors remained with me as I began the next phase of my life as a retiree. The counselors emphasized that personnel leaving the Army should find something meaningful to occupy their time. The divorce, death, and suicide rates escalate among veterans for several reasons: loss of military camaraderie, depression, and broken relationships. They shared stories of how Army personnel of all ranks often broke down in tears as they packed their offices. I was sure that with my children, parents, and employment prospects, I had more than enough to keep me busy. I felt immune to becoming a transition tragedy.

Finally! Arriving back at my home in Maryland was a dream come true. I looked forward to sleeping in, taking my time to unpack and arrange furniture and discard the boxes. I could now ignore military movers' advice, who told me to keep packing boxes for the next move. I was especially excited to greet Nisa when she returned home from school and looked forward to active participation in her last two years of high school.

At last, I was a stay-at-home mom. I began my ritual of preparing breakfast and greeting her after school. After less than a week of my domestic bliss, while picking at the fluffy omelet that I'd crafted for her, she politely asked, "What are you doing, and what is this?" Nisa then requested that I not make her breakfast and begged me not to feel the need to be at home when she returned from school. The transition had officially begun. I had never been home in the mornings when she went to school, nor had I ever been there when she returned. The transition counselors had been on the mark. Military families are not accustomed to the service member being around, and they, like my daughter, develop their own routines. It was not my place to change her routine overnight but instead to develop new ones—gradually. She had to get accustomed to me as a civilian.

Along with adjusting to my new family routine, working as a nonmilitary or civilian required a new mindset. I was lucky to have worked with the Air Force prior to my transition. The softer writing and communication style proved helpful to me as a civilian. Both my tone and writing styles were much softer and not as authoritative—or so I thought.

Sometime in the fall of 2003, I accepted a position from a defense contractor who supported the federal government. The military and other federal agencies do not manufacture machinery or equipment. Instead, the federal government procures goods and services (including manpower) from commercial companies. Each of the ten classes of supply that I learned about in Quartermaster OBC is manufactured by a civilian company. Some of the items, such as uniforms, become standard military issue, and others are strictly commercial off the shelf (e.g., some types of software). When the military needs people to perform noncombat tasks and short-term tasks, or needs a certain expertise, they hire contractors. I was one of those contractors, or a "Beltway Bandit." Instead of a "Beltway Bandit," though, I referred to myself as a "Parkway Patriot," a term I heard from one of my former military supervisors.

The Beltway and Parkway are the major highways and routes in the thirty- to forty-mile radius of the Washington, DC, metropolitan area. Calling contractors "bandits" evolved from the multiples or price variant required to sell or offer a good or service to the federal government. As an example, if a contract employee makes fifteen dollars an hour to perform an administrative task for a federal agency, the company may charge the government thirty to forty-five dollars per hour to cover overhead expenses, benefits, fees, and more. Although the government approves the pricing and awards the contract to the defense-contracting companies, the contractors are often the brunt of jokes and jabs about their prices.

Other than managing the tasks performed for the government, federal contractors have no authority on jobsites. They work for the government and are given a statement of work based on the bid that they submitted. I was not prepared for the disdain that some federal workers had for defense contractors. Facing rank discrimination or hostility as a veteran was not something that I had considered. I had experienced the officer-enlisted division of labor in the ranks, but it had been a relationship of mutual respect and usually not one of total disdain toward officers. Some federal workers and contractors had been in the military and just didn't like officers, especially colonels.

"We don't hire colonels." That was how one of my military friends who was working for a defense contractor shared his company's policy. His managers felt that colonels were too difficult to work with. My absolute worst managers were former junior enlisted personnel who hated officers and worked to prove their own authority. On one jobsite, I learned that a coworker was a retired Army colonel. He sat in the back of the cubicle maze of contractors and seldom spoke. I approached him with an inviting conversational gambit: "I didn't know that you were a colonel, how are you doing?" He replied with a hint of jovial sarcasm indicating that he was "in the closet."

Rank and racial discrimination was prevalent in some of the corporate offices as well as on the jobsites. Oftentimes, I was "the only." I was the only female manager or the only African American. A White male coworker mentioned that I was not treated like the other retired colonels. I wasn't sure what he meant until a senior Black female manager at another company explained how we were an oddity and should not expect too much respect or authority. She was a former Pentagon SESer also frustrated with the lack of respect shown to her. Assuring me that I was not doing anything wrong or carrying myself unprofessionally, she expressed frustration about not receiving professional courtesy in the workplace. The former SESer felt that her authority was undermined, and she provided examples of how junior White men with less experience received instant credibility during meetings. She advised me to cash my check and not to worry about marginalization, assuring me I could always find another job or just work for myself. Her advice validated my perceptions.

While working for one of the defense contractors as a program manager, I won a multiyear, million-dollar contract and thought I had a promising career with the company. When the win was announced, everyone high-fived me and gave their congratulations. However, after working there for almost three years, I gave the manager my resignation, saying that the two-and-a- half to three-hour round-trip commute in the Washington, DC, Beltway traffic was too much. That was partially true, but I was also tired. The other truth was that when I had asked a question about a contract, one of the managers (White male) without flinching asked, "Do you think this is beneath you?" In my mind, he'd called me "uppity." When he made the comment, several responses ran through my mind, but none would have seemed either professional or appropriate at the time. He was probably unaware of the impact of his comment. Being a manager, he may have spoken to other employees the same way. But it didn't matter to me. I felt that if I surfaced the comment with him, I would have been labeled a "complainer"—or one of those "sensitive types." I mentally checked out of the company. I refused to deal with overt racism and misogyny again. I had no fight left in me for his attitude and comments. I'm sure I thought, "If he said something like that once, he'll say it again, or his behavior will show how he feels."

I was confident that I would find another job. In fact, I found another job *before* I left the company. When I announced that I was leaving, several male coworkers applauded my decision and assured me that I was doing the right thing. They either wanted me gone or empathized with my pain at being disrespected. I expressed my ambivalence about leaving to a White male coworker. He advised me to never look back and never go back. This company taught me a lot about defense contracting and the art of the "graceful exit." More importantly, I learned not to burn a bridge that I might have to cross again. Years later, while working for another defense contractor, I worked with that same manager who had implied that I was uppity. We exchanged pleasantries, and all was well with the world. We were both working on an eight-figure contract bid.

As I job hunted, I became familiar with the term "suitability," wherein an applicant may be qualified but not suitable for a job. Suitability for corporate culture is another discriminatory tactic. One employer was uncertain if I could fit in the organization. She believed that since I had been in the military, I would be too heavy-handed. She offered an opinion about how the "carrot" approach was better than the "stick" while dealing with the workforce. I reminded her I was a mother, and as a military officer, I'd had to motivate soldiers from all backgrounds to perform and to do their best. I was hired for the position, but the interview frustrated me to the extent that I had second thoughts about accepting the offer. I also received feedback from another position where I applied; the manager wanted to know whether I had ever served in combat. He was concerned about whether I was calm and stable enough to work with the executives. I'd never met the manager; he only read my résumé.

Unfortunately, education, experience, and a track record of stellar performance are not enough to combat the negative stereotypes about veterans. These attitudes frustrated me and many other veterans entering the workforce. I empathize with the thousands of veterans who are rejected by employers based on preconceived notions about their suitability for the workforce. A 2018 *Psychology Today* article states, "Regardless of whether the veteran agrees with the stereotype brought forth by such a question, it can *still* generate anxiety or stress."[2]

After five years of working for other companies, in 2008 I started my own consulting company, Cummings & Cummings, LLC, specializing in management and proposal consulting. I saw many startups and small businesses struggle with understanding the federal government's bid and proposal process. Sorting through proposals and compliance documents was cumbersome. Many small businesses and startups had neither the manpower, talent, nor time to pursue federal contracts.[3]

Modeling my approach after other consultants, I developed a hybrid model of employment. I worked with small businesses part-time while I worked for larger companies as an employee. To avoid conflicts of interest, I did not accept clients who pursued work similar to my full-time employment. If my workload was too heavy, I hired independent consultants to assist me.

Working with smaller companies also taught me about their business. Pursuing contracting opportunities enhanced my abilities to develop and maintain client relationships and promote and market products and services. Responding to the federal government's Request for Proposals (RFP) requires companies to understand the government's acquisition strategy and evaluation criteria. A proposal is a legal document stating that companies intend to perform tasks outlined in a Statement of Work within the cost and parameters in their bid. I've seen companies default on multimillion-dollar contracts because they could not perform within the submitted price.

I encouraged companies and individuals to find a glowing quotation from their evaluation reports and awards to use in a biography or in a statement about themselves as a new business owner. I reminded them that those hidden gems are unique to them, and no other business owner can claim those specific phrases. Oftentimes, I was as excited about their services as they were. I enjoyed watching the expression on a CEO's face after revising a proposal's executive summary and the "Why Us?" statement. By isolating value proposition and attributes, the "Why Us?" statement sets the tone for the proposal to convince a buyer that a company's products or services are better than those of the competition.

Being a retiree also allowed me more opportunity to join civic organizations and boards. Three and a half decades after graduating from ASU, I joined their Foundation Board of Directors. As a board member I established the Warrior Fund Scholarship for veterans and their children attending ASU. When I visited ASU in 2008 for homecoming, I was impressed by the energy on the campus. I became active in their African American Alumni chapter and established a network of new friends. In the Washington, DC, area, I attended more events with military organizations such as the Association of the United States Army (AUSA) and the Military Officers Association of America (MOAA). Then, in January 2018, I read an online donation request from a professional development and mentoring organization, the ROCKS, Inc., for a 6888th Central Postal Directory Battalion Monument project at Fort Leavenworth, Kansas. I'd read online about the 6888th a few years prior, and the project excited me. I wanted to help honor these World War II–era Black women.[4]

Consisting of 855 members, the 6888th was the only Black WAC unit to serve overseas during World War II. A few years prior, I had read their history and about how they navigated gender and racial discrimination to reduce the mail backlog in the European Theater of Operations (ETO). I donated to the 6888th Monument and called the project director, Retired US Navy Cmdr. Carlton Philpot. As mentioned in this book's introduction, I'd met Commander Philpot in the early 1990s when I bought

Scout's Out, a Buffalo Solider print, to raise funds for the Buffalo Soldier Monument, also located at Fort Leavenworth.[5] I asked how I could assist him with the 6888th Monument. We spoke for around an hour about the project. He needed help fundraising. That hour-long phone call began my journey to bring international recognition to this group of unsung World War II heroes.

Reading about the importance of mail to troops reminded me of the joy my mom and I felt when we received letters from my dad when he was Vietnam. After I returned from Korea and waited for Walter, reading his cards and letters provided me comfort and love. I still have some of the letters and cards from my dad and Walter. These personal examples of how mail calmed my spirit during separations strengthened my resolve to heighten awareness about the 6888th and honor their accomplishments. The 6888th awakened a new passion and purpose in me. I wanted to share their story with whomever would listen.

A 3 PERCENT CHANCE

Nothing has ever been achieved by the person who says,
"It can't be done."

—First Lady Eleanor Roosevelt

8

COLONEL "EDNA" MEETS MAJOR CHARITY "EDNA" ADAMS AND THE 6888TH

JANUARY 2018 BEGAN MY 6888TH MONUMENT fundraising quest laced with excitement and doubt. I was excited to join the 6888th Monument Committee but uncertain how to raise the additional forty to fifty thousand dollars needed to complete the project. Tapping into my experience with the ASU Foundation Board, I knew fundraising needed a public relations approach to engage donors. Through social media along with my personal and professional networks, I began a campaign to educate the public about the 6888th and drive donors to the 6888th Monument website's donation page. Commander Philpot introduced me to another veteran, Retired US Army Master Sgt. Elizabeth "Lizz" Helm-Frazier, who also lived in Laurel, Maryland. He designated us as the "East Coast 6888th Monument Committee." Lizz and I met for lunch, devised a plan to contact potential donors, and prayed for guidance. We didn't know how long it would take for us to raise the funds, but we knew that we would get it done.

Along with fundraising, I attempted to learn as much as possible about the unit. I read books and articles about the 6888th and other Black WACs from that era.[1] Based on my own career, I was curious about how Black women fared in a military segregated by gender and race. Speaking with some of the living 6888th veterans, I was surprised to learn that just like me, many of the women joined the Army because of a newspaper article. I also read Charity Adams Earley's autobiography, *One Woman's Army*. I related to her story in ways that I did not anticipate.[2]

While reading about Adams's military career, I also gasped several times and experienced a range of emotions, including anger, empathy, and sorrow. Although she was in the Army seventy years earlier than I was, we shared similar experiences. In a 1992 interview, she responded to her many accolades by saying, "You don't know you're making history when it's happening." Truer words have never been spoken. My career goals were to graduate college and become a 2LT. By pursuing my career aspirations, and without knowing it, I became the first Black woman to graduate from ASU's ROTC program.[3]

Charity Edna Adams and I both have North Carolina roots. She was born in Kittrell on December 5, 1918, and spent most of her childhood in Columbia, South Carolina. She attended Wilberforce University in Ohio and graduated with a bachelor of science degree in math, Latin, and physics. While a graduate student studying vocational psychology at Ohio State, she joined the first class of 440 WAACs to attend Officers Candidate School at the first WAAC Training Center, Fort Des Moines, Iowa. Due to a 10 percent racial quota, the Army allowed forty slots for Black women. Adams described herself as one of the thirty-nine "ambitious, adventurous, and patriotic" [Negro women] in the class.[4]

After receiving her commission in August 1942, she commanded a segregated Basic Training Company at Fort Des Moines and traveled throughout the United States to other installations where more than 6,500 Black WACs were assigned. She was the first Black woman to be commissioned as an officer.[5] At twenty-six years old, Adams commanded a segregated unit that, on March 4, 1945, became the 6888th Central Postal Directory Battalion. Formed from the WAC, the Army Service Forces, and the Army Air Forces, the newly formed Black WAC unit, with the provisional name of RT-1051c, deployed to the ETO.[6] The ETO stretched across the entire continent, from the Atlantic Ocean to the Ural Mountains (bordering Europe and Asia) and encompassed campaigns in the Middle East and North Africa.[7]

Upon learning about her assignment, I believed Adams also knew that the 6888th's mission was greater than clearing the mail backlog in the ETO. Similarly, as a Black female officer, I always felt that since I was either the first or the only, I had an additional responsibility. My professional actions reflected on other Black military women. Adams's service in Europe represented hope for millions of Black women in the fight for freedom in the United States. She was fighting to prove that her unit deserved the opportunity to serve. She also recognized that the 6888th's success would resonate within the ranks and prove that if given the opportunity, Black women could meet or exceed standards alongside their White peers. When the unit then known as RT10–51c departed from Camp Shanks, New York, for England, Dr. Mary McLeod Bethune sent them a telegraph. Her telegraph highlighted the significance of them serving overseas: "You represent 15 million of us. Your success in this courageous service is ours. Think well. Realize your individual responsibility. Carve a niche for those who follow you." Clearly, their mission was larger than mail.

A relentless civil rights activist, Dr. Mary McLeod Bethune was vested in Black women joining the military and served as an advisor to the secretary of war, Henry L. Stimson. Prior to the first group of Black women joining the WAACS, in a 1941 note to Stimson, she wrote, "We are anxious for you to know that we want to be and insist upon being considered a part of our American democracy, not something apart from it. We know from experience that our interests are too often neglected, ignored, or scuttled unless we have effective representation in the formative stages of these projects and proposals. . . . We are incensed." Stimson invited the National Council of Negro Women (NCNW) to become a member of the Women's Interest Section, paving the way for the NCNW to become nationally recognized as a representative of African American women.[8] When World War II began, Dr. Bethune was named an honorary general of the Women's Army for National Defense.[9]

The mail mission was one of the most vital lines of communication between Americans in the ETO and loved ones at home in the United States.

Due to the June 6, 1944 (D-Day) preparations and afterward, warehouses in Birmingham, England, were filled with millions of pieces of mail and packages intended for the seven million US military, government, and Red Cross workers as well as American politicians and civilians in the ETO. Prior to D-Day, and most likely for security reasons, the military censors ended outgoing mail delivery. Adding to the backlog was the Battle of the Bulge (December 16, 1944–January 18, 1945), due to which approximately six airplane hangars of Christmas packages sat undelivered.[10] In total, airplane hangars and warehouses held almost two years of undelivered packages and mail. The constant influx of mail added to the backlog, and not receiving mail from loved ones at home was hurting morale. One general estimated that the backlog in Birmingham would take six months to clear. Other military units had tried but failed to restore reliable mail service. With a final personnel strength of 824 enlisted personnel and 31 officers, the 6888th's unit structure was modeled after the "Invasion Force Post Office," or the 17th Base Post Office (BPO). Since April 1944, the 17th BPO had worked alongside the 1st BPO in Sutton, Coldfield Warwickshire, England, until the 17th BPO could relocate.

To further complicate routing the mail and clearing the backlog, many personnel in the European Theater shared the same names (for example, 7,500 Robert Smiths). Ideally, the service member's locator cards and serial numbers aided in the routing of the mail to the correct person. But due to low literacy levels in the United States, many envelopes and packages contained incomplete addresses and were addressed to service members' nicknames (for example, Buster or Junior). Under Adams's leadership, the 6888th established a twenty-four-hour shift system and processed upward of 65,000 pieces of mail and packages per day for ninety days, or approximately seventeen million pieces. She implemented efficiencies in the mail sorting system and reduced the massive mail backlog in England, after which the unit relocated to Rouen and Paris, France, to clear additional backlogs. The Army gave them six months to clear the backlog in Birmingham; they did it in three. In her book, Adams notes, "Each piece of mail was 'worked' for thirty days, and if undeliverable, was returned to sender." Prior to returning to sender, the 6888th also physically examined personal items to determine the recipient. In a 2019 interview, 6888th veteran Elizabeth Johnson describes how she handled a crumbling package containing a watch, read the inscription with the serial number, and located the service member. She recalled, "It made me feel so good that I could forward it to him."[11]

Throughout her time in the ETO, Adams displayed confidence in her leadership abilities. On February 15, 1945, two days after the 6888th disembarked from the eleven-day Atlantic journey to Europe, General Lee requested the opportunity to inspect her troops. With a unit she'd never met or supervised, she readied her troops for inspection and led them in a historic parade in Birmingham, England. Within months of assuming command, she stood up to a White male general who wanted to replace her with a White lieutenant, two ranks below her rank as a major. She responded, "Over my dead body." The general initially planned to file court-martial charges but later apologized and said that she had earned his respect. In her book, Adams does not disclose the identity of the general but cites the date of his visit as March 30, 1945.

The general who threatened to replace Adams could have been the inspector general, or IG, who visited the post offices within the ETO's postal network. Upon the 6888th's arrival in Birmingham, they were assigned to the 1st BPO Headquarters unit. According to *Letters for Victory*, by Martin Collins and Frances Collins, in mid-1945, an unnamed IG visited the 1st BPO located in Sutton Coldfield, the primary American forces ETO post office, Army Post Office number 640.[12] The IG checked to ensure salvageable items were not being disposed of to reduce the mail backlog. However, the IG found a letter bearing his name in a bag of mail to be discarded instead of delivered. This infraction resulted in the dismissal of Maj. D. C. Jernigan, commanding officer of the 1st Base Post Office. The *Sutton News* in 1945 wrote, "Major D. C. Jernigan has been relieved by Brigadier-General E. F. Koenig, Commander UK Base Communications Zone second in Command of the European Theater of Operations for neglect of duty" and that "Major Jernigan had failed to follow every detail of [A]rmy regulations governing the disposal of parcels that have lost their identifying wrapper or are badly damaged in transit." It's plausible that the same IG attempted to inspect the 6888th, and when Adams refused, he had the authority to impose the same type of punishment rendered to Major Jernigan. Neither the *Sutton News* nor Adams revealed the name of the IG or general who visited the 6888th, but the Collinses' book emphasized strict penalties for violating the Army's mail handling policies. Army officers lost their jobs.

While in the ETO, Adams also had a twofold mission to improve morale. Her primary mission was to improve the morale of the frontline troops by restoring reliable mail service throughout the ETO. The 6888th's motto, "No Mail, Low Morale," embodied this mission.[13] Although not stated, but as a basic leadership premise, her second mission required her to maintain the morale of her own 855-member unit. The 6888th was a self-sustaining unit. Adams and her staff organized responsibilities within the unit and assigned the 6888th members according to their skills.[14] They cooked their own food, maintained their vehicles, and set up hair salons to ensure that women had some of the comforts of home. Red Cross workers and nurses in the ETO also visited the 6888th's hair salon. As a leader, Adams shielded them from gender and racial indignities by refusing the Red Cross's offer for a segregated recreational facility in Birmingham and an off-duty hotel in London.

Adams mentions in her book the diverse talent in the unit, consisting of a band, sports teams, an entertainment troupe, and recreational activities.[15] Unfortunately, their talent did not stop racism from interfering with their livelihood. The Army rescinded an invitation to a basketball tournament when they discovered the 6888th was a Black unit. In another instance, the 6888th was unable to board a train to attend a basketball tournament in Stuttgart, Germany. They contacted Lieutenant General Lee, who intervened and added a separate car for them to continue the trip. The ten-member basketball team, coached by 1st Lt. Mercedes Jordan 6888th from New York City, won the tournament and received self-winding wristwatches along with a trophy.[16]

With the war ending in Europe on May 8, 1945, and the workload decreasing, three 6888th members received discharges and held jobs in Paris.[17] A December 1945 *Afro American* article notes that Rosalie Hassell, Beatrice Morris, and Carolyn Poole worked in the Graves Registration Bureau. Other members attended schools in France and

Italy. Cpl. Dorothy Baily, from Boston studied motion picture and stage production at the Biarritz American University Theater in France. According to the article, "A highlight of her career was managing the 6888th variety show 'Wacacts.'" In May 1945, Pfc. Mary Bankston and Pfc. Mary Barlow were two of the thirty-six 6888th members who appeared in a USA-Anglo show attended by three thousand British and US personnel held in Birmingham, England.[18] In July 1945, two of the Wacacts, Private First Class Bankston and Private First Class Barlow, and Sgt. Delores Browne lost their lives in a vehicle accident in Rouen while returning from a social event. Like most troops who died abroad, the Army did not send the bodies back to the United States for burial.

According to Bill Brands, a historian with the American Battlefield Monuments Commissions, the paperwork in the women's Individual Deceased Personnel Files shows that Pfc. Mary Barlow and Pfc. Mary Bankston died in the accident on July 8, 1945, and were buried at St. Andre Military Cemetery, Normandy, France on July 11. Sergeant Browne succumbed to wounds sustained in the accident on July 13, 1945, and was buried at St. Andre Military Cemetery on July 14.

Brands provided me with crucial context for these wartime burials: "During World War II over 400,000 Americans were killed. The collection, identification, and burial of these dead was the responsibility of the Graves Registration Service. The main concern of the GRS was to properly identify, mark, and bury these dead as quickly as possible in temporary cemeteries close to where they fell. Such peacetime practices as embalming and casketing were not possible due to the scale of the task and the austere conditions."[19] At the time, the proper way to conduct a wartime burial was to envelop the remains in a white cotton mattress cover, used as a shroud or burial garment. The Army also used other materials such as bedsheets, tablecloths, curtains, blankets, parachute canopies, discarded canvas, or tarpaulins. If these materials were not available, the dead were simply buried in their clothes.

Due to the wartime burial policy, Adams collected funds to pay for coffins built by the German prisoners and tapped into the unit's expertise to give the women a respectful service. Among the many skills of the soldiers in the 6888th, some had experience working in funeral parlors and prepared the women's bodies for burial, including such tasks as applying makeup, styling hair, and dressing them in a military uniform. Brands indicates that for most soldiers, this preparation was designated on official forms as "shroud."

After the war, the three women's families completed the request for permanent disposition of their remains. In 1948, the women were permanently interred at Normandy American Cemetery, Colleville-sur-Mer, France. Customary military funeral services were conducted over the grave at the time of the burial. Only four women are among the more than nine thousand troops who were laid to rest at Normandy, and three are from the 6888th. The other woman was Elizabeth Richardson, a Red Cross club mobile worker who died in a military plane crash near Rouen.

Between December 1945 and March 1946, the 6888th returned to the United States, to Jim Crow segregation laws and locales with limited job opportunities. They also returned from the ETO unheralded and unrecognized for their accomplishments overseas. Many of the women left the military and pursued civilian careers. Some got married, raised families, and used the GI Bill to continue their education and buy homes. At war's end, then Lieutenant Colonel Adams had achieved the highest rank possible for a woman in the WACs besides the WAC director. She was the highest-ranking Black woman in the Armed Forces. Charity Adams Earley died on January 13, 2002.

Adams's career also caused me to reflect on other parallels between our careers. When Adams traveled to Europe, she did not have postal operations training. She didn't know where she was going until she boarded the plane from the United States and opened her orders mid-air. When I arrived at Fort Rucker, I didn't have specialized training in petroleum operations. But Adams and I both had leadership training that taught us to problem-solve and lead troops. I felt overwhelmed and misled by the Army at Fort Rucker, but Adams had confidence in her abilities to optimize the postal operations and increase mail throughput. I had had doubts.

But as I matured and developed professionally, the Army repeatedly placed me in positions where I did not have formal skills training. I'd like to think that the Army believed in my aptitude to develop a solution and complete the task. The Army codes some assignments as branch immaterial, or a basic branch without a specialty, and expects leaders to solve problems and enhance operations regardless of their training or experience.

In our most challenging assignments, Adams and I both had White male officers with power and influence who were our mentors. They provided guidance and support to assist us to navigate our military assignments. Adams's advocate in Europe was Lieutenant General Lee, the Communications Zone commander, and my advocate at Rucker was Brig. Gen. John C. "Doc" Bahnsen. Both White male senior officers realized that we Black women were in situations where we were not wanted but where we were needed to get the job done. They made it possible for us to succeed.

Like Adams, I also received apologies from White male officers and a few noncommissioned officers when they realized that I was capable of exceeding mission requirements. Adams and I both knew that meeting the standards was never enough; we had to do more. I also related to the lack of military courtesy and flagrant disrespect Major Adams received in World War II from White male superiors and subordinates. Many times, regardless of race or gender, military personnel in the Army or other services didn't salute me either or acknowledge my rank. While in uniform I've been called sergeant although I was a colonel.

I also related to her experiences when she discusses not being assaulted. I thought about how she must have felt going to work every day, hoping that no one would assault her physically but accepting verbal harassment as the alternative. On several occasions I mentioned the crass language and received nonchalant responses from male superiors. I soon learned not to expect any supervisor to address sexual harassment or inappropriate language. As I developed professionally, I developed my own methods to put people on notice about their inappropriate behavior. Unfortunately, sexual harassment and assault are still at the forefront of the military's challenges. Finally, in 2022, the White House made sexual harassment a military crime.[20]

On Adams's return trip to the United States, the White WACs on the ship did not want to serve under her command. She reminded them that she was in charge and told them to leave the ship. Adams heard a voice behind her supporting her statement to the White WACs and repeated the order, telling them to leave the ship. The WACs remained under Adams's command. The scene reminded me of the White officer who kicked my chair to undermine my authority, and I also heard a reassuring statement, and not a reprimand, from a general who witnessed the event.

Post war, Adams returned to Ohio State to complete her master's degree and exchanged words with her professor. He kept her after class and chastised her for not participating and reminded her, "We kept education just as it was." Another professor objected to her receiving a master's degree after only three academic quarters. Reading about her graduate school encounters reminded me of my confrontation with the professor at Troy State. Perhaps our shared educational experiences highlight the challenges veterans experience in academic environments. We may be perceived as not participating or contributing when we remain quiet in class. Many of us observe more than we speak.

Adams and the 6888th's story and fight for respect further fueled my quest to erect the 6888th Monument. To assist with marketing and public relations, I contacted military friends with strong public relations backgrounds. Retired US Army Ranger and Maj. Frank Phillips was a public relations professional who had assisted me with branding and marketing when I formed my company. Frank's methods were direct and candid—"Make people remember you; and they will want to talk to you." He added, "They may not know what you are selling, but at least they will want to talk."

Frank connected me to Retired US Army Maj. Edgar Brookins (now deceased), who was a distribution manager for the nation's oldest Black-owned family newspaper, the *Afro American*. Edgar's nickname was "Mr. DC" due to his vast media network in the Washington, DC, metropolitan area. Edgar connected Lizz and me to Dr. Renee Allen, a highly decorated twenty-two-year Navy and Navy Reserve veteran, also known as the People's Emcee. Dr. Allen hosted a Washington,

DC–based weekly internet television show, *Renee Allen and Friends.* Lizz and I appeared on her show, shared the 6888th story, and asked for donations. I used a basic marketing technique of product placement and asked Edgar if Ben's Chili Bowl, a well-known DC landmark, would hang a 6888th Monument poster inside the restaurant. Not only did Ben's Chili Bowl hang a sign in the restaurant, the owner and founder, Ms. Virginia Ali, posed for a picture with the 6888th poster alongside Edgar and Renee Allen. When I attended events, I asked people, "Can you hold this 6888th poster for a picture?" I then posted their picture on social media.

To increase awareness and raise funds for the monument, I consulted my then twenty-seven-year-old cousin Candice. I knew the basics of how to share, retweet, and like posts but not how to create content. She schooled me on tagging (@) and hashtagging (#) and provided other techniques on how to increase followers. I was familiar with the hashtag symbol but was curious about its function. A search of a particular word or phrase yielded results, and I couldn't understand why a hashtag was necessary.

One of my clients who specialized in cybersecurity and blockchain explained the hashtag function.[21] The hashtag represents a mathematical function from blockchain computations. The # ahead of alphanumeric characters assigned a unique contract to the character throughout the blockchain's distributed ledger. In social media, the # indexes alphanumerics, which then become a unique character, and easier to find. I used #sixtripleeight, #6888th, #blackwacs, #6888WW2, hoping these hashtags would trend or at least draw people to the posts. To increase interactions, Candice advised, "Use trending hash tags; you gotta know what's trending." Daily, I scanned the web and social media for 6888th information, posted 6888th Monument updates, and posted 6888th veterans or Black World War II WACs stories and pictures. The social media posts increased our donations and raised public awareness about the 6888th. When I'd meet people at events and share information about the 6888th, they knew me by my social media names, Twitter @CCLLC2008 and Instagram 6888WW2. Frank's methods were working. People wanted to talk to the person behind the social media posts.

Each year, the Congressional Black Caucus Foundation (CBCF) presents an "Avoice" award to recognize outstanding individuals and organizations who make humanitarian contributions to society. In January 2018, I contacted them about one of the living 6888th members, Ms. Millie Dunn Veasey, who was the first female president of the Wake County National Association for the Advancement of Colored People (NAACP). Ms. Veasey also hosted Dr. Martin Luther King when he traveled to Raleigh. Based on my recommendation, in February 2018, Ms. Veasey received the Avoice award alongside Gen. Colin Powell and Navy veteran Ginger Miller, the president of the Women's Veteran Interactive Foundation.[22] Ms. Veasey's nephew received the award in her honor. She died the following month, in March 2018. In September 2023, when I became an Honorary Member of Zeta Phi Beta Sorority, Incorporated, I was humbled when her family gifted me some of her sorority items.

In January 2018, we knew of eleven living 6888th members. One of the veterans, Elizabeth Barker Johnson, lived an hour from Boone, in Hickory. I contacted her daughter Cynthia and arranged to meet them in Lenoir, North Carolina, in May, when I attended an ASU Foundation Board quarterly meeting. I met Ms. Barker and Cynthia at a restaurant. At ninety-eight years old, Ms. Barker's wit and recollection of her time with the 6888th was beyond impressive. I gave her a 6888th World War II veteran hat, flowers, and placed a 6888th poster on the table. A lady walked by Ms. Johnson and thanked her for her service and asked her age. When Ms. Johnson responded, "I'm ninety-eight," the lady complimented Ms. Johnson about her lack of facial wrinkles. Without flinching, Ms. Johnson replied, "I have wrinkles in places where you can't see them."

Originally from Elkin, North Carolina, after the war, Ms. Johnson used her GI Bill benefits to attend Winston-Salem State University (WSSU) in 1945 and earned her diploma in 1949. She was the first veteran to enroll in WSSU using the GI Bill. After completing her degree requirements, she accepted a teaching position, but her principal would not allow her to attend her graduation ceremony. Ms. Johnson regretted not having the opportunity to don her cap and gown and walk across the stage.[23] A former advancement officer at ASU who encouraged me to join ASU's board, Dr. LaTanya Afolayan, was now the vice chancellor at WSSU. I shared Ms. Johnson's story with LaTanya, and LaTanya visited Ms. Johnson at her home in Hickory. In May 2019, Ms. Johnson's story received national media coverage when she graduated and received her diploma. Ms. Johnson died on August 23, 2020.

My mother asked me to check the 6888th list for the name of one of her friends, Ms. Davetta Butler Sheppard, a native of Sampson County, North Carolina. Ms. Sheppard's name was indeed on the 6888th list of women from North Carolina. I located a January 1945 article in the *Afro American.* archives detailing Davetta Butler's confinement at Camp Breckenridge, Kentucky, for refusing to repair bedsprings in a damp and cold barracks. We did not know that our family's friend had taken a hard stance against unfair treatment. After the war, Ms. Sheppard attended Fayetteville State University and became a civil servant. My mother donated $688.88 to the monument in honor of her friend Ms. Sheppard.

The 6888th story led me to other stories about Black WACs who served in World War II. Black WACs were court-martialed, beaten, and imprisoned for violating Jim Crow segregation laws in the United States and for refusing to perform menial tasks. In April 1944, the *Afro-American* reported that two WACs received labor sentences at Fort Jackson, South Carolina, for breaches of military discipline, and in December 1945, a police officer slapped a WAC for drinking from a water fountain at the police headquarters.[23]

I spoke with Sandra Bolzenius, the author of *Glory in Their Spirit,* about the court-martial of four Black WACs at Fort Devens, Massachusetts, who went on strike rather than perform menial tasks at Lovell Hospital.[24] Within the span of eight days between February and March 1945, four other members of the Black WAC detachment at Fort Devens attempted suicide. The Army's surgeon general also blocked three of the women from overseas duty with the 6888th Postal Battalion based on "a domestic urgency for persons with their training." In August 1945, three Black WACs were beaten for sitting in the waiting room designated for Whites at the Greyhound bus station in Elizabethtown, Kentucky. Pfc. Helen Smith of Syracuse, New York, was taken to jail while bleeding from her injuries and spent a week in the hospital recovering. Pfc. Georgia Boston and Pvt. Tommie Smith were also beaten. They were later court-martialed and found innocent of the charges. Without a doubt, these WACs were at the forefront of the civil rights movement.

By midsummer, Lizz and I had helped raise the balance of the funds needed for the monument. While we awaited a date for the dedication ceremony, we continued to share the 6888th story whenever the opportunity arose. James "Jim" Theres, a documentary producer, contacted the Monument Committee. He asked for our help making a documentary about the 6888th. In 2018, Jim had produced a documentary, *The Hello Girls*, about 233 World War I women from AT&T who served as telephone operators in France.[25] By the end of World War I, the Hello Girls had connected more than twenty-six million calls, and Gen. John J. Pershing recognized them for their service. Due to gender discrimination, the Army denied them veterans' benefits when they returned from World War I. Further research reveals that one of the Hello Girls, Renee Messelin, was a Black woman from Chicago who passed for White.[26] The Hello Girls did not receive benefits as veterans until 1977, under the GI Improvement Bill. Jim saw the similarities in the 6888th story and the Hello Girls and wanted to interview some of the living 6888th veterans.

Jim and Lizz both worked at the Department of Veterans Affairs in Washington, DC, and met to discuss the documentary. At first, Liz's close residential proximity to me had seemed coincidental, but Jim and Lizz's occupational proximity appeared as more than a coincidence. The three of us began to believe that our prayers to honor the 6888th were working. Luck, coincidence, or divine connections were working in tandem for us to share the 6888th story.

The 6888th Monument dedication was scheduled for November 30, 2018. Five living veterans had agreed to attend. Jim and his film crew planned to film the ceremony, the living veterans, and their families. To create a media buzz, I shared the dedication ceremony on social media and sent emails and thank-you notes to everyone who donated.

However, I was apprehensive about returning to Fort Leavenworth for the dedication. It was the place where I had experienced one of the worst tragedies in my life, learning that my husband was terminally ill. Leavenworth was where I had packed a suitcase and left with two kids to a new life filled with uncertainty and fear. Returning to a reminder of the horror and heartbreak was not something that I wanted to do.

However, I had to let go of my fears, ignore the phantoms, and honor these women—in person.

I'd worked diligently to raise funds for the 6888th Monument. Now was the time for me to face my Leavenworth ghosts.

9

FROM A MOMENT TO
A MOVEMENT

KNOTS FORMED IN MY STOMACH and my spirit stilled on November 28, 2018, when I drove a rental car from the Kansas City airport to the Holiday Inn at Fort Leavenworth. Remnants of snow alongside the roads and white mounds in the parking lots hinted at the uncertainty of the weather and the onset of the Christmas holidays. Tarnished 1988 visions of a live pine Christmas tree and holiday cheer during my late husband's terminal illness replaced the anticipation of seeing the 6888th Monument. Yet the horrors of returning to Fort Leavenworth vanished when I stopped at the security gates and showed my military identification card. Nothing in the city or on the military base looked familiar from my 1988 assignment. Nothing. Entering reality was much better than replaying the thirty-year-old images in my mind. I still wanted to visit the home that I'd left with a couple of suitcases, never to return. I checked into the hotel and attended the evening meal with the 6888th veterans and families. Ms. Barker Johnson's wit and dry humor did not disappoint. Ms. Barker questioned my wearing of a 6888th hat: "You weren't in the 6888th!" I advised her that I was a 6888th supporter, and she responded with a deep questioning stare, sans smile.

Each monument and statue at Fort Leavenworth's Buffalo Soldier Park glistened in the beaming sunlight of November 29. The sparse cotton clouds lacing the electric-blue sky provided an ideal backdrop for an outdoor gathering. The melting snow mounds lined the sidewalk but did not disrupt the gathering of 6888th veterans, families, and supporters. The five 6888th veterans surrounded the new monument for a photo session. Lizz slipped away from the crowd and rested her hand on the new 6888th Monument with Charity's bust and 844 names. Lizz mentioned that she needed a moment to give thanks and say a prayer. We had accomplished our fundraising mission. An Army photographer captured Lizz touching Lt. Col. Charity Adams Earley's monument bust in a solemn moment. Through that monument, Lizz appeared to touch the spirit of the 6888th and perhaps released energy for us to meet the next day and continue the 6888th recognitions.

November 30, 2018, began with a 6888th parade from the hotel at Fort Leavenworth to the dedication ceremony held at Frontier Chapel.[1] Full of emotion for the unsung 6888th women, the ceremony's attendees were left in emotional awe of the 6888th Monument. Senator Jerry Moran's (R-Kansas) voice cracked with earnest sentiment when he spoke about his gratitude for the 6888th, who'd kept his father, a World War II veteran, and his mother together during his father's service abroad. Senator Moran's remarks reflected the 6888th's mission and impact during World War II. I, along with members of the audience, fought back tears while he spoke. He then unveiled an enlarged copy of Senate Resolution (SR) 412, passed in October 2018.[2] SR 412 expressed support for the monument, recognizing the service of the 6888th Central Postal Directory Battalion and the mission of the Buffalo Soldier Educational and Historical Committee. The resolution encouraged celebration of the accomplishments and contributions of African Americans during Black History Month and throughout 2018.

I made a mental note to contact Senator Moran's office and ask if he would be interested in introducing a bill to award the Congressional Gold Medal to the 6888th. Prior to arriving at Fort Leavenworth, Jim Theres had mentioned his work with a staffer of Sen. Jon Tester (D-Missouri), on a Congressional Gold Medal project for the Hello Girls.[3] Jim thought it would be great if the 6888th received a Congressional Gold Medal as well. Jim provided me with the Hello Girls Congressional Gold Medal draft. I prepared the 6888th draft prior to my departure for Fort Leavenworth. Yet after speaking with several members of the House of Representatives to introduce the legislation, my optimism about pursuing the Gold Medal had waned. If I could not motivate the House to sponsor the legislation, then the Gold Medal was merely a dream that would never become a reality.

At the reception following the dedication ceremony, a man introduced himself as Kevin Hymel. I recognized his name and thanked him for writing the 6888th article, because I used it as a reference for the Congressional Gold Medal draft.[4] He was surprised that I knew who he was.

Jim and I then turned our focus to the documentary. We discussed the best approach for interviewing the 6888th veterans and their families. After a day filled with activities, we didn't want to tire the veterans with the interviews. Jim filmed the dedication ceremony and interviewed a few veterans in the evening and on the following day. Listening to the 6888th veterans' stories, I gained incredible knowledge and insight about these Black women who never thought much of their military service. The common theme among the interviews was that the veterans didn't think their military service was a big deal. None of them dwelled on the racism or sexism they had experienced; they were soldiers doing their jobs, and they loved America, their home.

The documentary interviews uncovered some remarkable stories. The 6888th family members' recollections were as enlightening and educational as those of the veterans themselves. Although the 6888th was designated as a Black or Negro unit, not all the women assigned to it were African American.[5] The daughter of a 6888th veteran, Lydia Thornton, revealed that Lydia was Mexican American. When she was given a choice to join either the White or the Black WAC unit, she chose the Black unit. I reviewed her enlistment records; Thornton's race is listed as "Negro Citizen."[6]

Retired US Army Lt. Col. Rodger Matthews and his sister Betty Murphy, daughter of 6888th veteran Vashti Murphy, also provided incredible insight into their family. Vashti's father, Carl H. Murphy Jr., copublished the *Afro American* and sent war correspondents to Europe. While in Europe, Vashti wrote articles for her family's newspaper.[7]

Along with filming the documentary with Jim, the Congressional Gold Medal draft was looming without a sponsor from a member in the House of Representatives. Although Senator Moran spoke in earnest about the 6888th, I also needed a House sponsor. The 2018 political environment seemed toxic and harsh, and I did not want to enter the fray. I called a friend and mentor, Retired US Army Maj. Gen. Dorian Anderson, whom I'd met while working with one of the contractor companies. Coincidentally, my late husband, Walter, often spoke about Anderson and how he respected him as an infantry officer. I ranted about the possibilities and downfalls of engaging in politics. He paused and responded, "How are you going to feel if you don't pursue this, or at least try?" I regarded the question as rhetorical, and I'm sure he did not expect me to provide an answer but rather just to consider the response. I replied with angst, "Okay, I'm going in." Like a soldier heading into a field of fire, I decided to advance in the direction of the perceived political hostility. I asked him to provide me with "top cover," meaning prayer. He closed with the statement, "Edna, sometimes your calling calls you."

With my "calling and covering" ahead of the December 2019 congressional recess, I reached out to Senator Moran's office and asked his Defense Fellow if Senator Moran would sponsor the Six Triple Eight Congressional Gold Medal. Leveraging the Pentagon staff officer technique, I provided the draft document with references, and ended the conversation with, "Please let me know what I can do to assist." On February 28, 2019, Senator Moran introduced S. 633, the "Six Triple Eight" Congressional Gold Medal Act of 2020. The Defense Fellow contacted me and advised me to contact other Senate staffers and ask them to cosponsor S. 633 to achieve a two-thirds majority (sixty-six cosponsors). He also reminded me that the bill needed a House companion bill. I was on the fringes of panicking about the lack of support. I had already contacted at least three House offices, and no one had agreed to sponsor the bill. I could not understand why no one from the House saw value in introducing the companion bill about these incredible veterans.

Jim and I scheduled other interviews and storylines to include in the documentary. Jim requested that I tell the 6888th's story as one of the documentary's talking heads. During my research, I located a 1925 Army War College Study that concluded that Black Americans who served in the military were only suited for menial tasks.[8] The study set the tone for the military and public attitude about Black service members and their ability and overall lack of mental capacity to perform duties aside from menial tasks. Once again, I felt unsettled, misled, and betrayed by the Army.

In July 2001, I had graduated from the esteemed US Army War College with a master of strategic studies degree, having never heard of the 1925 study. Jim opened the documentary with a segment of me discussing the impact of the study and the military's attitudes toward Black soldiers.[9] As he edited the documentary, I requested that he not show "angry Black women." I wanted the documentary to reflect the patriotism, challenges, and perseverance of the 6888th women—not scowls and victimization. He listened.

Jim established the documentary's timeline with the goal of completion by mid- to late March. Lizz and I marketed the documentary ahead of its completion. I posted the documentary trailer and the Congressional Gold Medal request for cosponsors on social media. On March 23, 2019, we hosted a sneak peek preview at the Sandy Springs Slave Museum in Olney, Maryland. We wanted the sneak peek to double as a focus group. The feedback was positive. We were on the right track. Just five days later, we premiered the *Six Triple Eight* documentary at the Military Women's Memorial at the gates to Arlington National Cemetery. Both venues held standing-only crowds. Since Senator Moran had introduced the Congressional Gold Medal, we talked about the Gold Medal and documentary to anyone who would listen. Tapping into my business branding resources, I ordered *Six Triple Eight* documentary postcards with screening schedule labels on the reverse. I brought copies of letters for film attendees to send to their senators, asking them to cosponsor the legislation.

I realized the impact of our documentary would be significant when, a few weeks earlier, I received a message from the US embassy in London via Twitter. The embassy wanted me to follow them and sent a direct message (DM) to establish communication. Thanks to my cousin, I knew how to "follow" and DM the US embassy. The US embassy wanted our production team to travel to the United Kingdom in May 2019 to screen the *Six Triple Eight* documentary throughout the United Kingdom in celebration of the seventy-fifth anniversary of D-Day. In mid-May, James Theres, Lizz, Brig. Gen. Clara Adams-Ender, and I traveled to the United Kingdom to meet with Ambassador Robert W. Johnson and the Lord Mayor of Birmingham, Yvonne Mosquito.

In May 1981, some of the 6888th veterans had visited Birmingham and met with the lord mayor.[10] We were repeating history. Ambassador Johnson dedicated a blue plaque at the King Edwards School in Birmingham, England, to mark where the 6888th lived during World War II.[11] In the United Kingdom, a blue plaque is a historical marker that celebrates the links between past notable figures and the buildings where they lived and worked.[12] The UK trip vaulted our moment at Fort Leavenworth to a movement, one that would change history.

Along with traveling throughout England, Brigadier General Adams-Ender and I traveled to Scotland and screened the documentary at the University of Glasgow and met the US consul and American interns. Jim and I remained after the tour and visited Rouen, Paris, and the beaches of Normandy and Normandy American Cemetery. Hosted by Stephen Ambrose Tours, in June 2023, I returned to Europe with a group of 6888th descendants and supporters on a historical tour. Following the 6888th's assignments, we began in Scotland and ended the tour in Paris.[13]

Through social media, I established an ongoing relationship with the American Veterans Center (AVC) in Arlington, Virginia. The AVC hosted information on their website about the 6888th and interviewed some of the veterans for their oral history collection.[14] After we returned from the United Kingdom, Lizz and I accompanied three 6888th veterans who served as grand marshals for the May 2019 National Memorial Day Parade.[15] In October 2019, the AVC also presented the six 6888th members with the Audie Murphy Award during the televised American Valor Awards. Our UK trip and connection with the AVC taught me two invaluable lessons about social media: quality content matters, and having a large quantity of followers does not always yield quality results. At the time, my Twitter account had fewer than one hundred followers, and yet I went to the United Kingdom and was working with a premier veterans' organization.

I continued my marketing efforts with email blasts to family members and supporters and asked if anyone knew a member of the House of Representatives who would introduce the companion bill. In mid-March, Sheree Robertson, daughter of 6888th veteran Anna Robertson, who lived in Milwaukee, Wisconsin, contacted me. She had attended Marquette University with Rep. Gwendolyn Moore (D-WI) and asked, "Do you still need a sponsor?" I most certainly did.

In April I met with Chris Goldson, Representative Moore's legislative director (LD), who showed me a list of more than four thousand bills and pending legislative actions. The Gold Medal bill needed 290 bipartisan cosponsors to pass the House. The LD commented, "The Gold Medal is important, but your team's grassroots efforts have to get it done." He gave me the what (get it done), but I had to figure out the how (rallying supporters around the legislation). He drafted the bill for Representative Moore's review. I had a flashback. The meeting with the LD reminded me of being in the military and analyzing a mission. Although thousands of bills fail to pass Congress each year, I did not want this bill to fail.[16]

On June 5, 2019, Jim and I hosted a documentary screening at the War Memorial in Milwaukee to honor Ms. Anna Robertson. More than three hundred people attended, and Representative Moore announced the House companion bill, H.R. 3138, the "Six Triple Eight" Congressional Gold Medal.[17] While I celebrated the legislation, Representative Moore's LD's comment to me about the thousands of bills under consideration overrode the joyous occasion. Between 2017 and 2022, more than thirty-four thousand bills were introduced in Congress, and only 2 percent were enacted into legislation. My advocacy for this legislation had a 98 percent chance of failure. According to GovTrak, of the 16,601 bills introduced in the 116th Congress (January 2019–January 2021), only 344 (3 percent) were enacted or signed by the president.[18]

On June 30, 2019, the Reginald F. Lewis Museum, Baltimore, hosted a *Six Triple Eight* documentary screening.[19] Among the approximately one hundred attendees were six captivating and stoic middle-aged Black men wearing ebony blazers and matching military flat service caps embroidered with the National Montford Point Marines Association (NMPMA) logo. I recognized one of them from the National Memorial Day Parade. A three-inch Congressional Gold Medal brass replica hung around his neck.[20] I marveled at his medal and shared my quest for the 6888th's Gold Medal. He urged me to call Retired US Marine Corps Master Gunnery Sgt. Joseph "Joe" Geeter. Joe had led the drive for the Montford Point Marine Gold Medal in Congress for the NMPMA.

In 2012, the Montford Point Marines received the Congressional Gold Medal. They were the first African Americans to enlist in the US Marine Corps after President Franklin Roosevelt issued an executive order establishing the Fair Employment Practices Commission in June 1941. The recruits trained at Camp Montford Point in Jacksonville, North Carolina, from August 26, 1942, until the camp was decommissioned on September 9, 1949. On February 19, 1945, Black Marines of the Eighth Ammunition Company and the Thirty-Sixth Depot Company landed on the island of Iwo Jima. They were the largest number of Black Marines to serve in combat during World War II. They took part in the seizure of Okinawa, with approximately two thousand seeing action. Some of the Montford Point Marines participated in amphibious landings on Peleliu and Saipan. More than nineteen thousand Blacks served in the Marine Corps during World War II, with approximately thirteen thousand of them serving in units overseas.

My phone call to Joe Geeter resulted in learning new tactics, tools, and techniques that I never would have considered while working with Congress. My 6888th signage needed to be engaging. Since World War II photos were black-and-white, he advised me to introduce more color on posters and signage. Following his advice, I contacted Dr. Afolayan and her husband, a brilliant Nigerian artist, Tunde.[21] I provided him with 6888th archival photos, and he produced a vibrant portrait of a

Black WAC with a patriotic background, entitled *Women of Courage-1*. He granted me permission to use the painting's image to promote the 6888th's Gold Medal. I used the image on postcards, note cards, bookmarks, and anything associated with the Gold Medal campaign.[22]

Joe also suggested that I contact military organizations and ask them to send letters of support and add the Gold Medal drive to their legislative agenda. Once added, the organizations' lobbyists and advocates could obtain congressional support. MOAA, AUSA, and the Women's Memorial lobbied Congress to pass the Gold Medal legislation. Letters of support from veterans' organizations (for example, the Foundation for Women Warriors, Women's Veterans Alliance, the Rocks, Inc., National Black Veterans Coalition, and the Service Women's Action Network) increased the 6888th's visibility on Capitol Hill. When Representative Moore sent "Dear Colleague" letters to House members requesting cosponsors, she cited the letters of support.

Joe reminded me to visit Senate and House offices and specifically request meetings with the LDs to discuss the Gold Medal. Since the LDs are the gatekeepers for all bills, they are the key staffers to engage. He told me to wear something with visible 6888th and military markings when I visited Capitol Hill. To carry the message with authenticity, he encouraged me to use my military rank and 6888th title. I had a military rank, but not a 6888th title.

I decided to call myself a "6888th citizen advocate." Although I was lobbying for the legislation, I was not a lobbyist. "Citizen advocate" indicated that I was functioning as a private citizen and not on behalf of an organization. In 2019, Senate and House offices were open to the public without an appointment. My title, organization, and clothing markings could hopefully diffuse any perceived uncertainty about my presence. For my walk-in visits to offices on Capitol Hill, I wore a baseball cap embroidered with the words "Woman Veteran" and *a Six Triple Eight* documentary T-shirt with the 6888th inspection photo on the front and the Gold Medal bill numbers on the reverse. Since the LDs were seldom available for a meeting, I obtained their business cards and left 6888th postcards with the bill numbers. Once I returned home, I followed up with an email, beginning with:

Dear—(LD),

I visited your office earlier this week to discuss (S.633 or H.R.3138). I sincerely hope that Representative or Senator—will co-sponsor this legislation to honor the 6888th Central Postal Directory Battalion. Attached is a list of 6888th veterans from—[state].

Respectfully,

Edna W. Cummings
Colonel, US Army (Retired)
6888th Citizen Advocate

The rest of the letter included information about the 6888th and links to recent media coverage.

Only one visit to a right-wing senator's office made me uncomfortable. Just as Joe instructed, I entered the senator's office with a big smile, wearing my "Woman Veteran" hat and 6888th T-shirt. The White female staffer's back stiffened and her eyes widened when she saw me. I believed she either pressed a panic button or cameras had tracked my entrance. Two White male staffers appeared from the back office and asked how they could be of assistance. Without flinching, I talked about the 6888th and the members from the senator's state and asked for their support. The staffers became less tense, we exchanged pleasantries, and I left with a knot in my stomach. I suspected the staffers expected a hostile attitude or complaints from me.

Joe provided other valuable insights about navigating Congress. LDs and staffers must respond to emails and inquiries. Most of the time they did respond. If they didn't, I followed up within thirty days. Many of these emails resulted in a response of either "Thanks for flagging" or "We'll take a look." Approximately 50 percent of the responses resulted in a cosponsor. After each response, I sent a note to the office of Senator Moran or Representative Moore to follow up.

I told Joe that he was my Gold Medal mentor and called him often. I teased him about the Marines claiming to pave the way for the Army.

In this instance, the claim was correct. He reminded me that if the Gold Medal legislation failed to pass the 116th Congress that ended January 3, 2021, it would have to be reintroduced all over again in the next session of Congress. With rare exceptions, Congressional Gold Medals seldom pass in the session they are introduced. The Montford Point Marines Congressional Gold Medal took two sessions. With warmth and encouragement, Joe told me not to give up.

Each year, AUSA holds an annual convention in mid-October at the Washington Convention Center. The Army Women's Foundation (AWFDN) holds a Women's Leadership Symposium featuring a guest speaker, panels, and other discussions about women in the military. In October 2019, the AWFDN featured the 6888th and invited one of the living members, Ms. Indiana Hunt-Martin. Ms. Hunt-Martin, now deceased (1922–2020), was born in Ulvada, Georgia, and grew up in Niagara Falls, New York. After graduating high school, she cleaned restrooms at an explosives factory later known to be connected to the Manhattan Project and the atom bomb. In 1942, she joined the WACs and played first base on the 6888th's softball team. A *Stars and Stripes* newspaper journalist published a story about Ms. Hunt-Martin.[23] Afterward, other media outlets contacted her for interviews. *CBS Evening News* aired a segment in November 2019, and CNN aired a segment in July 2020.[24]

A week after the October AUSA convention, I traveled to Phoenix for a documentary screening hosted by the Office of Military & Veteran Affairs at the University of Phoenix. Retired US Air Force Maj. Fannie McClendon, then ninety-nine years old, attended the screening.[25] Major McClendon was an Army first lieutenant in the 6888th and knew Charity Adams. She was also one of the officers who identified the 6888th women who died in a vehicle accident. After her return from the war, Major McClendon joined the Air Force when it became a branch in 1947. She retired in 1971 and became an antiques dealer in Mesa, Arizona. In 2020, the University of Phoenix and the National Society of Leadership and Success Foundation established a Major Fannie Griffin-McClendon scholarship to support military students in pursuit of higher education.

Through documentary screenings, visits with legislators, public appearances with the living 6888th veterans, presentations, and other events, the Congressional Gold Medal legislation continued to gain momentum. By the end of 2019, our volunteers were confident that the Congressional Gold Medal Bill would pass by January 3, 2021, the end of the 116th Congress.

One of my most educational 6888th experiences occurred in mid-February 2020, following a documentary screening at the University of Tennessee, Chattanooga.[26] The day after the screening, interpretative park ranger Brian Autry and Christine McKeever, executive director of the 6th Cavalry Museum, gave me a guided tour of a Civil War battlefield at Chickamauga and Chattanooga Military Park, Fort Oglethorpe, Georgia. More than one hundred thousand men fought during the Civil War there in the fall of 1863.[27] During World War II, Fort Oglethorpe was an overseas training site. In January 1945, the 6888th trained there for two weeks prior to their departure for Europe. The 6888th underwent gas mask drills, crawled under barbed wire, and readied themselves for a wartime and austere environment. With a map in hand, Brian and Christine drove me through the wooded battlefield and showed me where the 6888th had lived and trained. The 6th Cavalry Museum, located next to the battlefield, curated a 6888th exhibit and an interactive 6888th timeline of events.[28]

On March 11, 2020, Lizz and I were inducted into the Army Women's Foundation Hall of Fame for our contributions to Army women and work to recognize the 6888th. The ceremony was held at the Women's Memorial, Arlington National Cemetery, Virginia. Due to the outbreak of COVID-19 on the West Coast, individuals who traveled outside the United States within the past thirty days were asked not to attend. Instead of shaking hands, we bumped elbows.

On Friday March 13, 2020, due to the expanding COVID-19 pandemic, the president of the United States declared a national emergency.[29]

10

ADVOCACY DURING LOCKDOWN

WHEN THE PRESIDENT DECLARED A national emergency, I visualized one of the many pandemic Homeland Security Exercise scenarios from my military and consulting careers. Public panic, supply stockpiling, fuel rations, triggers for action, and a host of other preparatory actions ran through my mind. Without knowing the duration of the threat or the containment strategy, my parents were my main concern. During the last week of March 2020, I relocated to North Carolina for two months to help them during the early phases of the pandemic. At the time, they were in their late eighties and early nineties, and I did not want them grocery shopping or taking any unnecessary risks that might result in COVID exposure.

Since the nation was operating in a state of emergency, I stopped contacting Congress about the Congressional Gold Medal. Containing and mitigating COVID was the priority, and advocating for the Gold Medal could wait. By mid-March 2020, S. 633 had more than 50 percent of the needed 66 cosponsors, and H.R. 3138 had approximately 30 percent of the needed 290 cosponsors. Instead of emailing Congress, I researched the 6888th.

Edgar Brookins, the general manager of the Washington *Afro American* newspaper, connected me to the newspaper's online archives through Baltimore's Pratt Library. I researched the terms "6888th," "Negro WACs," "colored WACs," and any other search term that I thought would produce information about Black WACs. Those searches yielded results and uplifted the trajectory of the 6888th's narrative and my advocacy. I sent the articles to two 6888th researchers, Retired US Army Maj. Dominic Johnson and Margaret Cricket Holder. They cross-referenced the articles with the 844 names on the monument and confirmed six missing 6888th names.

One of the most valuable articles I located during my research contained the cities and the states of residence of 738 Six Triple Eight members who were the first contingent of the 6888th to arrive in Europe.[1] Prior to COVID, whenever I contacted Senate members, I sent a list of 6888th veterans by state. When I contacted the staffers in the House, I could not answer the question "Were any 6888th members from Representative XX's district?" From this new list, I could now identify the congressional district and include that specific information when I resumed emailing and calling the House to request cosponsors. I could now answer the LD's question and occasionally share pictures of 6888th women from specific congressional districts.

May 8, 2020, marked the seventy-fifth anniversary of the World War II victory in Europe. The *Afro-American* published an article that I coauthored, "The Silent Six Triple Eight," highlighting birthdays of four 6888th veterans.[2] The article served two purposes, highlighting the 6888th veterans and issuing a call to action for readers to contact Congress and request Congressional Gold Medal cosponsors. By late spring, other media outlets including the *New York Times* and CNN published stories about the 6888th, and organizations hosted virtual documentary screenings.[3]

In 2020, two 6888th veterans died from non-COVID-related illnesses. Ms. Elizabeth Barker Johnson died on my birthday, August 23, 2020, and Ms. Indiana Hunt-Martin died on September 21, 2020. Their deaths energized my resolve to continue to work on passing the Gold Medal legislation. Since I could no longer visit members of Congress, I increased the number of emails to their LDs. The 6888th story gained momentum, but the cosponsors in the House did not.

S. 633 reached 68 cosponsors on December 9 and passed the Senate on December 10.[4] H.R. 3138 had 106 cosponsors; 184 cosponsors short of the two-thirds majority. On a bold move after S. 633 passed the Senate, I sent the names of journalists and their email addresses to the House leadership's media points of contacts. My request? A statement about the passage of S. 633. None of the House leadership issued a statement. The "Six Triple Eight" Congressional Gold Medal Act of 2019–2020 did not go to vote in the House and failed to pass Congress. A January 2021 Pew Research Center article cites the 116th was overall one of the least legislatively productive Congresses of the past five decades.[5]

Failure either devastates or energizes a cause. In this case, the Congressional Gold Medal's failure in the 116th Congress energized the 117th Congress. Within weeks of the 117th congressional session convening, the Senate and House LDs and another staffer member from the House leadership held a virtual meeting with two 6888th volunteers (Retired US Navy Senior Chief Christine Martinez and Retired US Army Maj. Natasha Hinds) and me. They assured us that both bills would be reintroduced, advised us of their intent to monitor the legislation, and asked us to maintain our momentum. By February 12, 2021, the Senate and House reintroduced the "Six Triple Eight" Congressional Gold Medal Act. Both bills had new numbers, S. 321 and H.R. 1012, respectively.

With the new bill numbers, I revised my social media strategy. With each cosponsor, I captured a screenshot of the cosponsor's image and posted it on social media platforms. I added the number of cosponsors needed to pass each chamber, tagged the cosponsor and Congress, and thanked them. I posted Gold Medal cosponsor countdowns to the two-thirds majority needed in Congress.

Volunteers reported difficulty speaking with legislators outside of their district. Some legislators responded with an obligatory "Thank you for contacting us, we will consider the legislation when it goes to vote," or "Please contact your district's legislator." Since we were a grassroots decentralized community of advocates, I advised volunteers to use the title "6888th advocate" or "6888th family member" when they called offices.

Those titles carried more weight than citing their congressional district. I provided a script for volunteers to use for emails and telephone calls:

> Hello, I am (your name, or organization/ use retired military rank if applicable), a Citizen Advocate for H.R. 1012, the Six Triple Eight Congressional Gold Medal. I'd like for Rep. — to co-sponsor this bill to honor the 6888th Central Postal Directory Battalion, an 855-member unit of the Women's Army Corps who served in Europe during World War II. The bill has passed the Senate and only needs — co-sponsors to pass the House of Representatives.
>
> During World War II, the Six Triple Eight prevailed where others failed to improve troop morale in Europe by manually sorting more than 17 million pieces of mail for delivery in three months—well under the Army's 6-month goal. By restoring vital communications with loved ones, they helped our nation claim Allied Victory and end the war. As an all-female unit, they had to serve in a military segregated by gender. Similar to the Tuskegee Airman, the Harlem Hellfighters, and other World War II African American units who received the Congressional Gold Medal, the Six Triple Eight also rose above racial discrimination to serve.
>
> Attached is a list of 6888th women from (cities, state name).
>
> Thank you. I sincerely hope that Rep — supports this legislation. Representative Gwen Moore's office is the Point of Contact: —.

On March 27, 2021, Ms. Deloris Ruddock, a 6888th veteran living in Takoma Park, Maryland, died. Senator Moran and the Secretary of Veterans Affairs Denis L. McDonough attended her committal ceremony held at Baltimore National Cemetery on April 20. Senator Moran announced that S. 321 had achieved the two-thirds majority needed to go to vote. On April 29, S. 321 passed the Senate by unanimous consent with 75 cosponsors. S. 321's passage meant the Gold Medal was viable. The 6888th volunteers could now direct their focus on obtaining the necessary House cosponsors. Communications to cosponsors and organizations now touted bipartisan and unanimous Senate approval, a strong indicator of a bill's ultimate success.

In late April, Representative Moore's LD introduced me to a staff member, LaToya Bell, a Gold Star Fellow. A Gold Star family member is an immediate relative of a fallen service member who died while serving in a time of conflict.[6] Established during the 116th Congress, the Gold Star Fellows program provides Gold Star families an opportunity to work for Congress in a one-year paid fellowship. LaToya's husband, Sgt. 1st Class Russell Bell, died in Afghanistan on August 2, 2021.[7] His death occurred during an independent dismounted patrol, when an improvised explosive device (IED) detonated near Zharay, Kandahar Province. LaToya teleworked from Fayetteville, and like me, she was a young widow of an Airborne Ranger and a proud App State alum. We agreed that the universe had connected us and that "APP Nation and Mountaineers" would get the Gold Medal passed.

On my birthday, August 23, 2021, I received an extraordinary gift, or at least I thought it was just for me. H.R. 1012 reached 200 cosponsors, or the magic 200. Once a bill reaches 200 cosponsors in the House, other legislators notice. When the bill achieves 218 cosponsors, or the support of half of the 435 members of the House, the chance of passing the bill increases. My emails to senior House members who were not cosponsors highlighted these milestones. Their LDs responded either with a phone call or an email, "We will not cosponsor, but Rep. XYZ will vote for the bill when it reaches the floor." I could not understand why a House member would not cosponsor the bill but would vote for it. A cosponsorship indicates early support; a vote means the legislator approves the bill when it reaches the floor for a vote.

While continuing my research for 6888th articles in the *Afro-American* archives, I located a January 1945 article about an African American unit, the 255th Port Company.[8] Thus far, I'd read about the 65,000 pieces of mail the 6888th processed per shift and seen photos of the warehouses filled with undelivered mail and packages.[9] An average 65,000-per-shift processing volume equaled 195,000 pieces of mail per day, or 5.85 million pieces of mail per month, during the 6888th's time in Birmingham. This article provided specific details about the volume of mail backlog in the ETO.

The 255th Port Company landed in Normandy with the first wave of troops. In January 1945, one month prior to the 6888th's arrival in England. The 255th broke records in unloading an all-mail ship loaded with 130,000 bags, or 3,600 tons, of mail. The soldiers finished the job eight hours ahead of schedule and received a commendation. The mail was sorted and routed to Army Post Offices (APO)s. Some of the mail could have gone to Birmingham, England, or remained in France. Based on the article and simple "mail math," I calculated the 255th Port Company off-loaded approximately 40 million letters and packages—in France alone.

> 130,000 bags of mail—each bag weighed approximately 70 pounds.[10]
> 130,000 × 70 = 9,100,000 pounds.
> A standard letter weighs approximately 3.5 ounces.
> One pound = 16 ounces.
> 16/3.5 = 4.57 letters per pound.
> 9,100,000 × 4.57 = 41,587,000 letters approximately that could have been off-loaded by the 255th Port Company.[11]

Although 41.58 million letters represent an estimate of flat mail, with packages mixed with the mail, I surmised that 17 million pieces of mail and packages is a plausible and reasonable estimate for the 6888th's workload in Birmingham England.

The 255th Port Company article enriched 6888th presentations and discussions. The 255th received accolades and commendations for off-loading mail. However, I noted the disparity in highlighting 6888th contributions to improving morale. A June 1945 *Afro-American* article stated "the 6888th set new records in handling tremendous volume of mail" without mention of a commendation.

On Groundhog Day, February 2, 2022, H.R. 1012 reached 291 cosponsors. I exhaled, wiped away a few tears of joy, posted the results online, and notified supporters. Representative Moore's LD explained that since the House and Senate bills were identical, achieving two-thirds vote on H.R. 1012, sends S. 321 to vote. We now waited for the House to vote on S. 321. In mid-February, Representative Moore's office notified me to invite family members and a small group of supporters to her office to watch the vote scheduled for February 28. I had attended watch parties for sporting events but never a legislative watch party. Without any doubt, this event would be memorable. Approximately twelve 6888th family members and supporters gathered around the television in Representative Moore's office to watch the vote.

At 06:30:52 p.m., the House Chair announced as unfinished business (from earlier discussion) S. 321, To award a Congressional Gold Medal to the members of the Women's Army Corps who were assigned to the 6888th Central Postal Directory Battalion, known as the "Six Triple Eight." When the vote tallies appeared on television, we clapped at the yeas and shouted the nays (apparently accidental) into yeas. We cheered S. 321 to passage.

At 07:07:47 p.m., on motion to suspend the rules and pass the bill agreed to by the yeas and nays: (⅔ required): 422–0, S. 321, the "Six Triple Eight" Congressional Gold Medal Act of 2021 passed by unanimous consent.[12]

Earlier that day, another bill passed the House, H.R. 2142. This bill honored 6888th veteran Ms. Hunt-Martin. It read, "To designate the facility of the United States Postal Service located at 170 Manhattan Avenue in Buffalo, New York, as the 'Indiana Hunt-Martin Post Office Building.'" (On September 20, 2022, the Senate also passed H.R. 2142, and President Biden signed it into Public Law No. 117195 on October 11, 2022. On March 24, 2023, to further honor Ms. Hunt-Martin, the Buffalo County Erie Park Naval Museum held a grand opening of its *Two Wars* exhibit, featuring Ms. Hunt-Martin's uniform, her boots, discharge papers, and locater card.)[13]

As we awaited Representative Moore's return to her office from the vote, we slapped high-fives, hugged, and shed tears of joy. Representative Moore returned to the office and entered the door in a move resembling a religious holy dance. She and Lizz popped a bottle of champagne. We celebrated two victories for the 6888th, a Congressional Gold Medal and the renaming of a Post Office.

President Biden had ten days to sign S. 321 into public law. Representative Moore's LD felt that due to the February 24 Russian invasion of

Ukraine, the president would not hold a signing ceremony. Instead of a presidential signing ceremony, on March 3, the Speaker of the House, Rep. Nancy Pelosi, held a signing ceremony in her office.

As mentioned in the introduction to this book, the signing ceremony in Speaker Pelosi's office is one of my personal best historical moments. I took photos and selfies with the Speaker! She laid out eight pens and used each one to sign her name. Her meticulous signature strokes amazed me. I gave a congressional staffer my phone, and she took a picture of the Speaker handing me one of the ink pens.

On March 14, 2022, President Biden signed the "Six Triple Eight" Congressional Gold Medal Act into Public Law 11797. During the watch party in Representative Moore's office, I'd noticed the framed copies of signed legislation on her walls. Her office inspired me to request signed copies of the legislation to frame and present to the living 6888th veterans.

The Congressional Gold Medal takes approximately one year to eighteen months for the US Mint to design and make the medal available to the public for purchase. The US Mint designs and strikes one Gold Medal for display at venues cited in the legislation and offers 3-inch and 1.5-inch bronze replicas for public purchase.[14] About two weeks after the president signed the legislation, Representative Moore appointed me to serve as a citizen liaison to the US Mint to assist with the design of the 6888th Gold Medal. I asked Representative Moore's office to add Tracy Bradford, curator of the Army Women's Museum at Fort Lee, to the team. The citizens' design team consisted of Commander Philpot, appointed by Senator Moran; Tracy; and me. The US Mint considers our recommendations and refers the images for approval by the secretary of the Treasury. On April 18, 2023, the Citizens Coinage Advisory Committee met and voted on a design for Six Triple Eight Congressional Gold Medal for minting and recommended it to the US Commission of Fine Arts (CFA).[15] The CFA advises the secretary of the Treasury on the themes and designs of all US coins and medals.

Considering the advanced ages and declining health of the living 6888th veterans, I didn't want to delay their celebrations while we waited twelve to eighteen months for the actual medal to be produced. Senator Moran's office gave me seven copies of the signed legislation to frame for the living veterans and one for myself. The 6888th living veteran's families and caregivers determined the type of celebrations they wanted to have. I attended the celebrations of Retired US Air Force Major McClendon held on May 26, 2022 in Mesa, Arizona,[16] and Ms. Robertson's event on June 27, 2022, in Milwaukee.[17]

On June 15, 2022, the Women's Memorial at Arlington National Cemetery hosted a standing-room-only Congressional Gold Medal celebration.[18] Approximately three hundred guests attended, including 6888th family members, making it the largest gathering of 6888th descendants in recent years. Arlington National Cemetery also included the fourteen gravesites of 6888th members who are buried there on its website's list of notable African Americans.[19] Guest speakers at the Women's Memorial celebration included the Secretary of Veterans Affairs the Honorable Denis R. McDonough, WSSU president Dr. Elwood L. Robinson, award-winning actor Blair Underwood and his family, and the *Six Triple Eight* documentary production team. Underwood premiered the opening number from the upcoming 6888th musical and joined the 6888th family for a group photo.[20]

The Congressional Gold Medal celebrations did not end the 6888th recognitions and information requests.[21] In August 2022, I joined a panel hosted by former president George W. Bush's "Stand To Veteran Leadership Program" with Dennis Miller, a Bush Program Scholar and 6888th grandson, and *Sisters in Arms* author Kaia Alderson. We spoke about the 6888th and their impact on history and our personal lives.[22]

The 6888th's recognitions continue. Appendix 6 lists some of the honors and recognitions since 2018. The list includes an exceptional tribute by the historian John Monsky, *The Eyes of the World: From D-Day to VE Day*. Monsky tells the story of the final eleven months of World War II with music, video, photos, and letters. He includes a tribute to a 6888th veteran, Ms. Crescencia Garcia, one of the women from Puerto Rico who joined the WACs.[23] In 2019, another cousin, Monica Sanders, texted me an article about Ms. Garcia's COVID recovery. Ms. Garcia was in a World War II uniform. I located her name on the 6888th *Afro American*'s "first contingent" list and contacted her granddaughter Tara. Tara advised me that during World War II her grandmother worked in a hospital burn unit in Whitchurch, England, located about an hour north of Birmingham.[24] I asked Tara to check her grandmother's identification tags for the serial number. I also matched her serial number in the National Archives Access to Archival Databases. Ms. Garcia's serial number and timeline matched.

Ms. Garcia was one of an estimated two hundred Puerto Rican women who joined the Women's Army Corps. Due to Garcia's dark skin, she was assigned to the 6888th but worked in a hospital burn unit in Europe about an hour away from the 6888th's duty station in Birmingham, England. I verified 6888th reassignments with Major McClendon, who said that, depending on the skin tone of the 6888th women, some women were assigned to work elsewhere. Ms. Garcia was one of those women. I surmised that she was dark-skinned when she enlisted, but by February 1945, her tan had faded. Major McClendon mentioned that the staff would look at a very light-skinned 6888th member and say, "She won't be with us long." A light skin meant that if a 6888th WAC could pass for White, she probably would get assigned to White WAC unit.

Ms. Garcia received a standing ovation when she attended the 2021 Veterans Day performance at Carnegie Hall in New York. On June 6, 2022, six 6888th family members and I attended the performance at the Kennedy Center in Washington, DC. During the 6888th segment, the families got a standing ovation and a moment in the spotlight. I am grateful beyond words to Monsky's production team for including the 6888th in the World War II tribute.

Thanks to the efforts of many volunteers, we mobilized an international community who shared the overlooked 6888th story with the public and brought the story to the forefront. The 6888th community helped us to beat the odds and enact legislation to honor these unsung heroes. The 6888th's story is broader than being the first Black women to serve overseas. The larger story is about the unrecognized service of Black WACs during World War II who served at home and abroad.

PART IV

UNRECOGNIZED CIVIL RIGHTS PIONEERS

I'm no longer accepting the things I cannot change . . .
I'm changing the things I cannot accept.

—Angela Davis

11

WORLD WAR II BLACK WOMEN

Hidden Herstories of Intelligence, Patriotism, and Resilience

BEGINNING WITH THE REVOLUTIONARY WAR, hundreds of thousands of Black women have embraced the ideals of patriotism and democracy by either serving in uniform or supporting the war effort at home. Along with fighting for the nation, they also fought racial and gender battles with the tools and skills at their disposal. Their main weapons were education and resilience. Before women were allowed to wear the uniform, Phillis Wheatley used her voice and penned patriotic poetry during the Revolutionary War. The only documented woman to enlist in the Civil War, Cathay Williams, donned the uniform and served in the Black 38th US Infantry Regiment (Buffalo Soldier) as Cathay Williams.[1] Harriet Tubman demonstrated leadership during the Civil War and led enslaved persons to freedom and assisted the Union army in her many roles as a spy, soldier, and nurse. Tubman was posthumously named a one-star brigadier general in Maryland's National Guard in 2024.[2]

During World War I, a group known as the Golden 14 were the first Black women to serve as yeowomen and performed administrative duties.[3] Eighteen Black nurses served.[4] To release men for combat in World War II, more than six hundred thousand Black women worked in US factories as "Rosie the Riveters."[5]

World War II was the first war wherein a large number of Black women served as members of the US Armed Forces, and their educational levels surpassed those of most Americans. In 1944, the Army Nurse Corps allowed 56 Black nurses to join the Army Nurse Corps with approximately 479 finally accepted. [6] The Army required WAACs enlistees to be high school graduates between twenty-one and forty-five years old, between five and six feet tall, between 105 and 200 pounds, and "of good health and character." In 1940, 64 percent of twenty-five- to thirty-four-year-olds hadn't completed high school.[7] A report by Oregon's secretary of state cited evidence of the devastating impact of the Great Depression on public education. Hundreds of thousands of men signed their draft registration forms with a mark because they could not sign their own names. Before the end of the war, the Army established special schools to bring illiterate draftees up to a fourth-grade reading level. Of the approximately 20 million eligible young men for the draft, 50 percent were rejected the very first year, either for health reasons or illiteracy, and 20 percent of draft registrants were illiterate.

In 2022, the Defense Manpower and Data Center Casualty Analysis System reported that since 1980, 991 Black females have died worldwide in military operations, in the Persian Gulf and in contingency operations.[8] These numbers do not include deaths in the United States resulting from injuries sustained in combat or service-connected injuries.

Prior to reading about the 6888th, I was familiar with only two Black World War II military women. The first was Capt. Dovey Johnson Roundtree, who became a civil rights lawyer after the war. The second was 1st Lt. Martha S. Putney, who became a scholar and author after the war. Neither the works nor history of these WACs was part of my formal military education, nor were they mentioned as leadership examples in my military education or career.

The 6888th represents approximately 13 percent of the Black WAACs and WACs who served in the Army from 1942 to 1946, and theirs was the only Black WAC unit sent overseas. When the 6888th arrived in the ETO, an estimated 130,000 Black troops were in Britain along with 130 Black Army nurses and American Red Cross workers. Some of the Red Cross workers performed duties as "Donut Dollies" who operated a mobile service club, or "clubmobile," to give troops entertainment and food, alleviating homesickness.[9]

By solving the Army's mail crisis and restoring vital communications to and from the United States, the 6888th story is the most highlighted of the Black women who served during World War II. Due to the leadership of their twenty-six-year-old commander, then Maj. Charity Adams, the 6888th has elevated the historical narrative of these women who contributed to the nation's defense. One question arises when I speak to audiences about the 6888th's accomplishments and their receipt of the Six Triple Eight Congressional Gold Medal. How did they do it? My response: "Intelligence, Resilience, and Leadership."

A February 1945 *Afro American* article states that 85 percent of the 6888th were ex-schoolteachers or had college degrees.[10] Major Adams's education prior to joining the Army is evidence of her intelligence and aptitude for solving problems. If she had not joined the Army, she surely would have still made her mark in history. Her approach to solving the mail crisis is analogous to applying systems engineering principles to increase efficiency and throughout. The Defense Acquisition University defines systems engineering (SE) as a "methodical and disciplined approach for the specification, design, development, realization, technical management, operations, and retirement of a system. SE applies critical thinking to the acquisition of a capability."[11]

Adams was a solution architect and executed SE-type tasks for the mail with a methodical and disciplined approach. Before assuming command of the 6888th, she defined the mission and the mission needs and developed a system to optimize the mail operations. Due to segregation and lack of support from other units, Adams identified inherent capabilities in her unit to acquire and sustain their basic needs of food, shelter, security, and quality of life.[12] She applied critical thinking skills to ensure optimal performance and then replicated the model in Rouen and Paris. With the war winding down in August 1945, Adams outlined plans to retire or scale back mail operations and her role as commander.

Adams's leadership enhanced morale within the 6888th organization and for the millions of American troops and civilians in the ETO. Her

"Over my dead body!" response to a general's racist commentary is the most prominent example of her combating racial inequities. Where possible, Adams took a hard stance against the Army's segregation policies. While stationed at Fort Des Moines, Iowa, in the fall of 1943, Adams realized that Black WACs were not allowed in the White band. She encouraged the Black WACs to form their own band, later known as the 404th Armed Service Forces Band. In the summer of 1944, she faced accusations of "race-mixing" at the Officers' Club. While stationed in Birmingham, England, Adams refused Red Cross supplies for separate recreational facilities for the 6888th. She also refused separate recreational hotels in London. Her leadership approach was an example of her own systemic resilience to combat the harsh realities of racism in the United States and in the ETO.

In early March 1946, the Army deactivated the 6888th at Camp Kilmer, New Jersey, without recognition or praise for their service. Although each of the 6888th veterans I spoke with used educational or housing GI Bill benefits, racial disparities existed for many World War II veterans who could not access these services. In a lawsuit filed in December 2022, the Department of Veterans Affairs denied benefits for Black veterans at a higher rate than for White veterans. Some of the 6888th veterans used the VA hospital services much later in life. One veteran mentioned that a staff member advised her to "Go get your husband" when she went to a VA hospital in the 1970s. Thanks to the urging of 6888th advocates, she now uses some of the VA's medical services.

Nearly all of 6888th members returned to society as everyday citizens, raised families, and lived in obscurity for the rest of their lives, never discussing their military service. Empowered by living and working abroad, several of the women assumed leadership roles in their communities. Conversations with the surviving 6888th veterans revealed that they experienced freedoms in the British and French communities abroad that they did not have in the Army or in the United States. The 6888th veterans' stories reveal humility, pride, and patriotism, and a common theme of not seeking praise. A March 1946 *Afro American* article recalls a firsthand account from Pvt. Florence Collins's experience in England: "The English are quite aware of our color bar and go miles out of their way to make sure that we are happy and contented. We are treated like royalty."[13]

Approximately two decades after the war, in 1976, twenty-one former WAACs and WACs, including former members of the 6888th, gathered at a home in Hampton, Virginia, and discussed approaches to securing their history. They recognized that although Black women served in all of our nation's wars, no entity captured their history nor mentioned it in the media. During this meeting, these veterans formed the National Association of Black Military Women, whose mission is to "To seek out, record, maintain and tell the history and heritage of African-American Military Women who served and are serving in the United States Armed Forces."

The Black WACs serving during World War II blazed a trail for civil rights and social justice at home and abroad. The WACs serving in the United States were on the forefront of civil rights by demanding to do more than menial tasks. Through my advocacy for the 6888th, I met a World War II veteran, Ms. Millie Bailey, who died in April 2022 at the age of 104. Ms. Bailey was a WAC lieutenant (1942–45). When I asked about an event wherein a White lady spat at her, she told me that she focused on the kindness she received and not the hostilities. Her statement resonated with me and the indignities that I had faced while in uniform. She didn't dwell on the spit aimed at her and did not surrender her spirit to the negative attitudes. Ms. Bailey also requested that I dispel the social media myth of her service as an Army pilot. She reminded me to not believe everything I saw on the internet.

Working on the 6888th's recognition provided me insight into why my father had objected to my military service and why my Third Herd had felt marginalized. My father did not want me to experience the same hostilities that he faced while in the Army. Nor did he want me to become a victim to rumors and disrespect as a woman from those who believed that women, especially Black women, did not belong in uniform. The soldiers in my Third Herd were intelligent but may not have had the right educational opportunities before enlisting in the Army. As a result, many acknowledged and accepted society and the Army's labeling of them as inferior or less than. My Third Herd soldiers and many others became victims to the "mental spits."[14]

Along with other members of the WACs and Army Nurses, a small number of Black Code Girls, or cryptographers, worked in the United States, including Ethel Highwarden Just, who is presumed to have been a cryptographer. According to the National Archives, "the identities of most of Arlington's Black code breakers remain unknown," and Just "led a team of translators." Black WACs also served as cryptographers. One WAC, Annie Knight (Jordan), worked as a cryptographer code compiler deciphering Morse code at Camp Gruber, Oklahoma, before joining the 6888th.

One of the most fascinating stories I read about was the friendship formed between Black WAC nurses and German prisoners of war (POWs). Researching the 6888th led me to *Enemies in Love* author Alexis Clark. She describes how prisoner of war camps in the United States became an ongoing assignment for most Black nurses who were forbidden to treat White soldiers. A Black nurse and a German POW developed a romance and later married. In the ETO, German POWs worked alongside the 6888th. Ms. Indiana Hunt-Martin discusses how the Germans gave her a lot of "junk." A German POW in France gave her a jewelry box with the inscription, "1945 France To Hunt, From Gipson." When asked about the jewelry box, Ms. Hunt-Martin either refused to respond or rendered a dismissive, "mind your business" demeanor with her facial expressions.

Although it was uncommon for a Black woman to join the military, a few of 6888th married fellow service members, and many had brothers who also served in military. Researching the 6888th and speaking with families dispelled suggestions that Black men didn't respect Black military women or that Black families disapproved of their service. Charity Adams's brother, Sgt. 1st Class/Technical E. Avery Adams Jr., was assigned to the China Burma India Theater and visited her while she was assigned to Fort Des Moines.[15] After Adams's Army discharge, she married a World War II soldier, Stanley Earley, who worked with German POWs. After the war, he attended medical school in Switzerland.[16] The brother of Capt. Abbie Noel Campbell, the 6888th's Executive Officer, Capt. Thomas Campbell, was the 6888th's physician.[17] On August 19, 1945, Pfc. Florence A. Collins's marriage to Cpl. William A. Johnson of the 1696th Labor Supervision Co was the first African American marriage to be performed in the European Theater of Operations.[18] Vashti Murphy was married to a Robert Williams Matthews, a member of the Coast Guard.[19] Pvt. Romay Davis had two brothers, Purcell[20] and Stansbury,[21] who served in the Montford Point Marines and were Congressional Gold Medal recipients. Two sisters, Pvt. Marian Elzie and Lt. Vivian Elzie, served in the 6888th, Vivian married a Silver Star Recipient and member of the 761st Black Panther Tank Battalion.[22] Hester Givens married Samuel M. Massey, a member of 227th Port Battalion, one of the support units that landed at Normandy.[23]

According to the Army Heritage and Education Center, by the end of World War II, enlistments in the WACs declined. Like most WACs, many of the 6888th returned to their communities and didn't discuss their service. WAC schools and training centers closed in August 1945. In February 1946, then Army Chief of Staff General Eisenhower directed the preparation of legislation to make the WACs a permanent part of the Army. In September 1947, legislators combined the bill with the Women Accepted for Volunteer Emergency Service (Navy WAVES) and Women Marines. Legislators added a section to include women in the Air Force and renamed the bill the Women's Armed Services Integration Act, Public Law 80625.[24] President Truman signed the bill into law on June 12, 1948.[25] A month later, on July 26, Truman signed Executive Order 9981: Desegregation of the Armed Forces.

Although Truman included WACs as serving members of the military and desegregated the Armed Forces, the legislation but did not end racial and gender inequities. A 2020 Brookings Institution study asserts, "While the share of women in the military is higher than ever, the experiences of women in the military are often inequitable. Women in the military services continue to suffer high rates of sexual assaults from their male counterparts. That is unacceptable and one of the many issues that must be addressed if we are to eventually see equal shares of men and women in the Armed Forces."[26] The Truman Library states, "It took six years to desegregate America's Armed Forces."[27] However, integration did not guarantee fair and equitable treatment.

On May 22, 1950, the President's Committee on Equality of Treatment and Opportunity in the Armed Services issued its final report, entitled

Freedom to Serve.[28] "It was the judgment of the Committee that these recommendations, when put into actual practice, would bring an end to inequality of treatment and opportunity."

In 2020, the Department of Defense Diversity and Inclusion Board released a report aimed at identifying ways to improve racial and ethnic diversity in the US military. Among the report's findings: The enlisted ranks of the active and reserve military were "slightly more racially and ethnically diverse than its U.S. civilian counterparts." But not the officer corps. Furthermore, it found that the civilian population eligible to become commissioned officers was "less racially and ethnically diverse than the civilian population eligible for enlisted service."[29]

EO 9981, Pub. L. 80625, and subsequent defense policies such as the Notification and Federal Employee Antidiscrimination and Retaliation (FEAR) Act symbolize attempts to eliminate discriminatory behavior and attitudes.[30] Since World War II, gender and racial diversity has increased nearly two- to threefold. The Military One Source 2020 demographic profile shows that approximately 48 percent of the more than 1.3 million active-duty personnel are in a racial minority group (including Hispanic) and 17 percent identify as female. In the Selected Reserve, the percentages are 41 percent and 21 percent respectively. The same report states that "the lowest percentage of racial diversity is found among high-ranking officers in all service branches."[31]

Despite the inequalities that I've experienced and the challenges of today's military, I have no regrets about my military service, and neither do the 6888th veterans whom I've met. The 6888th families express one common statement about their veteran family members, "She never talked much about her military service." It remains unclear why these trailblazers seldom discussed their services. I attribute some of the quietness to the slanderous statements about military women that permeated the public and military ranks. Women of all races who served in the military were victims of these gender-based slur campaigns. When they reentered civilian life after the war, many employers refused to hire ex-WACs. Veteran status for women impeded their employment, while for men, military service was an asset. Another reason is humility.

Unless they are sharing experiences with other veterans, many veterans don't talk about their service.

I encourage readers to capture your family's history. In doing so, you may uncover their journey, update a family's history, and view life with a broader lens. When I read about World War II, the Korean War, and Vietnam, my father's service provides context and firsthand recollections. I listened differently to the history of these wars in an attempt to place his whereabouts during those times.

Janice Martin, daughter of 6888th veteran Indiana Hunt-Martin, thanked me for helping her learn about her mother. I thanked her for sharing her mother with the world and me. When this journey started in 2018, approximately thirteen 6888th veterans were known to be alive. Now there are four, ages 100 to 104. Another common theme these veterans express is that they wish the other members of the 6888th were alive to share the honors.

The 855 women of the 6888th were on a mission larger than mail. Their service represented opportunity and hope for others who wanted to serve.

FINAL THOUGHTS

Breaking Barriers and Cracking Armor

AS THE GUEST OF AUTHOR and Retired US Army Maj. Gen. Mari K. Eder in October 2021, I attended the American Valor Awards event in Washington, DC, hosted by the American Veterans Center (AVC). The American Valor Awards is an annual gala that shares stories of American heroes from World War II to the present. I was familiar with the format, having attended in October 2019, when the AVC honored six living 6888th members with the Audie Murphy Award.[1] Seated next to me at the 2021 awards ceremony was a regal, tall Black woman with short, wavy, silver hair who introduced herself as Carlotta Walls LaNier, an honoree. Carlotta was one of the Little Rock Nine, the nine students who, in 1957, integrated Little Rock Central High School. I knew that the Little Rock Nine had received the Congressional Gold Medal, and I shared information with her about my quest for the 6888th to receive that honor. Carlotta and I kept in touch afterward, and she sent me a congratulatory note when the 6888th's Gold Medal passed the House of Representatives. A few weeks later, I experienced a range of emotions from empathy to anger when I read her book, *A Mighty Long Way*. Her book is about how she overcame indignities as a fourteen-year-old enrolling in Little Rock High School in Arkansas.[2]

In 1956, President Eisenhower sent soldiers from the 101st Airborne to escort the Little Rock Nine into the school building. Eisenhower's actions on behalf of these Black students reminded me of his actions during World War II. Of the three theater commanders during World War II, then General Eisenhower eventually supported the 6888th's assignment to his command with the vital task of clearing the mail backlog and restoring reliable mail service. None of the other commanders wanted Black WACs. Upon the 6888th's arrival, they had to overcome the stigma of having social responsibilities for the Black soldiers. Major Adams ensured that the women learned martial arts to protect themselves against unwanted advances. After the 6888th's stellar performance in the ETO, some of its members including Major McClendon had orders to report to the China Burma India Theater. But the war ended, and the 6888th returned to a nation where Jim Crow laws were used to enforce segregation.

Post World War II, Black WACs reported overseas, made possible by the 6888th's stellar performance. With the Little Rock Nine, Eisenhower protected their freedom and right to learn, and in World War II, he had protected the 6888th's freedom to serve. In mid-2022, I located my father's 1957 military liberty pass dated January 21, 1957. He marched in President's Eisenhower's inaugural parade for his second term. This piece of history reshapes Eisenhower's legacy for me as a commander in chief who also protected my father's freedom to serve. My first memory of the military was at Fort Gordon, Georgia, now redesignated as Fort Eisenhower.

I empathized with Carlotta's bravery and journey when she returned to Little Rock High School fifty years later. She faced her tormentors, the ghosts from 1957. In her 2010 book, Carlotta wrote that President Bill Clinton cracked her armor when he talked about courage, gratitude, and the responsibility to contribute to the world. I called Carlotta and told her how powerful her story was for me. Her story reminded me of events in my life that cracked my armor and redirected my personal and professional trajectories. I also experienced ghosts returning to Fort Leavenworth in 2018 for the 6888th Monument Dedication. Coincidentally, my 1988 CGSC classes were held in Eisenhower Hall, where I made my decision to return to active duty.

After several of my armor cracks—potentially devastating circumstances—people forced me to listen and adopt a perspective that I had never considered before, which brought great rewards. At the suggestions of friends, I reentered the military after a bitter departure, completed CGSC during a family tragedy, and pursued the daunting task of securing a Six Triple Eight Congressional Gold Medal.

Being a Black woman in the Army in the 1970s had its own set of challenges. The WAC was not disbanded until five months after I entered the ranks in October 1978.[3] But despite decades of exemplary military service by uniformed women, the secretary of defense did not open all military occupations and positions to women until January 2016.[4] Women and minorities continue to prove themselves qualified for positions and yet lag behind their male counterparts.

The Department of Defense's latest recruitment reports present an even greater challenge to diversity in the ranks. In 2023, "Fewer than 25% of all young Americans between the ages of 17 and 24 qualify academically and physically to serve in the military. Many of them can't pass the Armed Services Vocational Aptitude Battery [ASVAB], a test that measures potential recruits' aptitude and fitness to serve."[5] Unfortunately, these statistics are reminiscent of World War II's draft eligibility challenges. To remedy the eligibility shortfalls, the Army developed a Future Soldier Program to develop meet the Army's body fat composition standard and improve ASVAB test scores.[6]

As of 2021, more than 90,000 African Americans serve in the Army's Active Component; more than 39,000 are in the Army Reserve and more than 52,000 in the Army National Guard.[7] As of June 2022, 32 percent of Army women on active duty identified as Black. But the numbers at senior levels are much lower. In 2018, the Service Women's Action Network reported that the services had sixty-three female admirals and generals on active duty in the five services, compared to thirty in fiscal year 2000.[8] The report further states senior enlisted women on active duty only comprise 11.8 percent of the E-7 to E-9 pay grades in the Army; 20.3 percent in the Air Force; 11.6 percent in the Navy; 5.6 percent in the Marine Corps; and 8.7 percent in the Coast Guard.

Celebrating the "first" for women and underrepresented populations acknowledges that the "first's" journey was harder than for others in similar positions. The secretary of defense did not lift the military's combat exclusion policy until April 28, 1993, but it only applied to aviation positions. In 2013, combat assignments opened for women, and in 2016, all positions in the military became unrestricted for women including attendance in specialty schools (Army Ranger, Special Operations, etc.) In April 2019, Sgt. 1st Class Janina Simmons became the first Black woman to complete the sixty-two-day Army Ranger school specializing in conducting raids and assaults.[9]

In 2008, Ann Elizabeth Dunwoody became the Army's first woman four-star general. In 2023, the highest rank achieved by a Black woman in the Army is lieutenant general (three-star), with Nadja West being the first (2016) and the second being Donna Martin, the Army's inspector general, who is still serving. Stacey Harris became the Air Force's first Black woman lieutenant general in 2016. In July 2014, Adm. Michelle J. Howard became the first female four-star admiral in the US Navy, and the first African American to be vice chief of naval operations.

Though we celebrate the firsts, I continue to look forward to the "next." Some 43 percent of the 1.3 million men and women on active duty in the United States military are people of color. African Americans make up only 9 percent of active-duty officers and 6.5 percent of generals.[10] The Armed Forces is much better for minorities and women than it was when my father and I served, but the work for fairness and equity never ceases.

I appreciate the opportunity to share my story and hope that it inspires others to step outside their comfort zone. I'm often asked, "Why do you think you were successful with the Six Triple Eight Congressional Medal campaign?" My usual response alludes to the hundreds of volunteers and organizations who donated their resources to advocate for the

Gold Medal. Professionally, I applied my forty-plus years of experience to the campaign. My personal connections to their history from my father's service and my own made me dig deeper into the 6888th's stories.

First and foremost, I had faith in myself and passion for the purpose. James 2:14 in the King James version of the Bible, reads, "What doth it profit, my brethren, though a man say he hath faith, and have not works? Can faith save him?" In 2018, Lizz and I prayed when we started the 6888th fundraising. We had faith. Afterward, we worked with an unrelenting passion.

Second, I ignored the naysayers among potential monument donors and Gold Medal supporters. I became deaf to their negative comments about me working with Republicans and White men (for example, Senator Moran and the documentarian Jim Theres). I reminded the naysayers that supporting unheralded veterans such as the 6888th is something most people are willing to move forward with a unified purpose. When a naysayer persisted with unsupportive comments, I asked, "Do you intend to contact your member of Congress?" I received one of three responses, "Yes," "No," or "I'll think about it." I also ignored claims that no one cares about older Black women veterans. I considered it my charge to *make* people care. One White man sent me an email cautioning me about going too far and getting swept up in the Black Lives Matter movement after the death of George Floyd. I ignored him.

I asked a friend about his view of my 6888th advocacy, and whether I was too aggressive or harsh. He reminded me that I exhibited tenacity and a laser focus—the attributes needed to find common ground with others and elevate public consciousness. A former coworker contacted me and likened me to a bulldog. Throughout my life, I've been called many names but never a bulldog. He told me, "Edna, when you sink your teeth into something, you don't release it until you are finished." I didn't respond to him, but I thought to myself, "Isn't that what I'm supposed to do?"

Third, I managed and mitigated risk and understood that events with the lowest probability of occurrence have the highest impact. With the 6888th, the probability of occurrence was low, but the impact was far-reaching and a catalyst for elevating their history. The low-probability, high-impact event was the amplification of the 6888th's history with the nation's highest civilian award, the Congressional Gold Medal. When the legislation was introduced in both sessions, it had less than a 3 percent chance of passing. To increase probability of its passing, I used the Strength, Weakness, Opportunities, and Threats model of strategic planning and assessed the Gold Medal campaign's operational framework:[11]

Strengths (Advantages): Bipartisan legislative sponsors gave the campaign a strong advantage over other bills under consideration. To eliminate administrative time, I used a decentralized model and did not form an ad hoc committee or a nonprofit organization. I provided supporters with talking points, templates, images, and other items to use at the local level. The *Six Triple Eight* documentary strengthened the Gold Medal campaign and brought the story to life. Instead of relying on articles and historians, audiences heard firsthand recollections from the 6888th veterans. The screenings were—and still are—emotional and heartfelt. The 6888th veterans and their families who attend events either in person or virtually enrich the conversation and share information and photographs that had not previously been available to the public.

Weaknesses (Challenges and Constraints): A decentralized model incurs the risk of limited funding and operational capacity. To mitigate the costs, I used vendors (for example, Vista Print, Zazzle, etc.) that offered coupons and discounts on giveaway items and sent the templates to supporters. I established email and telephone goals to contact LDs (for example, for states with low cosponsors, five emails a day, five phone calls a day, etc.).

Opportunities: Veterans' organizations, colleges and universities, churches, schools, and social media provided opportunities to educate the public and advocate for the Gold Medal. Media outlets gravitated to the story from social media and attended documentary screenings. I posted 6888th stories on social media with the intention of their becoming "click bait" for readers. Several organizations and media outlets advised me of their online statistics. Their 6888th stories performed the highest with the most views and interactions.

Threat (External Risks): The biggest risks to the Gold Medal campaign were the other bills under consideration and national events. Advocates and I mitigated these risks by remaining vigilant in contacting legislators and following up when we did not receive a response. We contacted state legislators and asked them to contact their congressional members for support. I elevated the narrative and focused more on the 6888th's performance and exemplary outcomes above and beyond those of their peers, the entire WAC. As evidence, *Afro American* articles and Department of Defense publications provided proof points of the 6888th's exceeding Army's goals.[12] The media helped us mitigate the risks by elevating the 6888th story and quest for the Gold Medal to the national and international levels. During interviews and presentations, I provided the legislation's countdown (for example, passing in the Senate, the number of cosponsors needed in the House). I shared these interview links with current and potential cosponsors. I had a clear and concise ask.

Using my military training of organizational hierarchy, I task-organized the 6888th supporters into three groups (military framework) and disseminated information to best suit their needs.

Strategic (Executive Level): The strategic level consisted of national organizations with legislative agendas and lobbyists. I asked organizations with lobbyists to add the Gold Medal to their legislative agenda and to write letters of support to legislators. Their lobbyists contacted legislators about the Gold Medal. I provided them with talking points and highlighted 6888th members from that state and district. These organizations published 6888th articles online and in print.

Operational (Midlevel): Operational level supporters consisted of nonprofits, media outlets, and academic institutions that did not have lobbyists or legislative agendas. These organizations held documentary screenings, wrote letters of support, and contacted state and local governmental agencies about the 6888th. I provided them with templates and images for their signage and websites.

Tactical (Basic Level): Families and individual citizens provided a basic level of support by writing letters as constituents and calling Congress. I provided them with templates, giveaway items, branding materials (postcards, bookmarks, posters) and other items for them to display as they talked about the 6888th.[13]

The 6888th journey impacted my life and caused me to reflect on how I became an advocate. Writing this autobiography has caused me to reflect on my life's trials and triumphs and embrace two basic philosophies:

Perfect is relative and not static. Perfect indicates that there is nothing else that can be done or that whatever is being evaluated is flawless and has met the absolute required conditions. The founding fathers of our nation realized that perfection is situational. The Constitution states its aim to form a "more perfect union" and allows for amendments that reflect changes in society.[14] Organizations have quality-control systems and change-management processes for ongoing process improvement and managing change. As individuals, we must be open to change and growth.

Scars represent healing. I hope this book provides readers insight into what it feels like to be unwanted, unwelcomed, and unappreciated, and yet manage to thrive. A scar is a reminder of something that has healed. Everyone has a reminder or scar (mental or physical) of something that they have overcome. Many people, including veterans and their families, neither heal nor survive; sometimes the scars become unbearable. A November 2024 article in the *Conversation* states that "America's military veterans make up about 6% of the adult population but account for about 20% of all suicides. That means that each day, about 18 veterans will die by suicide."[15] When least expected, personal friends and professional advocates appeared to support and guide me in the military and beyond. Whatever the journey, don't go it alone.

By either coincidence or destiny, I started my military career at Fort Lee, Virginia, redesignated to honor the former quartermaster general, Lt. Gen. Arthur Gregg, and the 6888th commander, Charity Adams.[16] A 700-square-foot 6888th exhibit now exists at the Army Women's Museum at Fort Lee. Along with my signing pen from Speaker Pelosi, my authentic signed presidential copy of the Six Triple Eight Gold Medal is in the exhibit. Appendix 6 contains additional 6888th recognitions since 2018.

I wondered if younger soldiers appreciated and understood the impact of the 6888th's service. An email from a West Point African American female cadet who read about the 6888th addressed my uncertainty. She wrote, "I am excited and comforted that I wasn't alone in the pursuit to recognize Black women and their contributions to the military."

I've navigated the intricacies and nuances of the military from several aspects as a military child, an Army officer, as a military spouse, a military widow, a military single mother, and, thankfully, a retiree. I am blessed with friends and family who coached and guided me through life's mazes. I learned to choose my battles and learn from my mistakes.

The military taught me never to go it alone. I'm not a gambler, but I know that with the help of family, friends, and perhaps celestial connections or covering, I overcame circumstances where odds were not in my favor. But I pushed through, ignored the naysayers, and achieved results beyond what I could have imagined.

Obviously, the higher the goal, the lower the odds of success. Regardless of the odds, I encourage everyone to at least try to fulfill their goals and aspirations. This soldier's life has been full of unexpected successes, twists, and turns. Through it all, I hope that I have created unforgettable experiences and made an impact, or at a least a difference, in a few lives.

ACKNOWLEDGMENTS

I am grateful to my family and friends and blessed by the hundreds of people, organizations, and 6888th families along with my own who supported the effort to obtain long-overdue recognition for the 6888th. A special thanks to Maj. Gen. Mari K. Eder, who encouraged me to step way outside of my comfort zone and write this autobiography. She has been a sincere mentor, supporter, and friend. I'm especially grateful to the University of Virginia Press for providing me with an opportunity to share my story, and to Dr. Le'Trice Donaldson, who opened the door for my initial dialogue with the Press. My thanks to all who are listed here and my deepest apologies to anyone I may have omitted: the 6888th families; 6888th Monument Committee, 9th and 10th Cavalry Horse; Retired US Army Brig. Gen. Clara Adams-Ender; Dr. LaTonya Afolayan, former vice chancellor of advancement, Winston-Salem State University; Tunde Afolayan, artist; Kaia Alderson, author; Dr. Renee Allen; American Veterans Center; Retired US Army Maj. Gen. Dorian Anderson; Archer-Ragsdale Arizona Chapter Tuskegee Airmen—Retired US Navy Senior Chief Christine Martinez (deceased), Retired US Navy Senior Chief Joseph Olano, and Retired Air Force Col. Richard Toliver; Army Women's Foundation; Army Women's Museum; Association for the Study of African American Life and History; Association of the United States Army; Brian Autry, interpretive park ranger, Chickamauga and Chattanooga National Military Park; US Army Maj. Gen. Maureen Birckhead; Retired US Army Maj. Edgar Brookins (deceased); Richard Brookshire, Black Veterans Project; Center for Women Veterans; Congressional Black Caucus, Veterans

Brain Trust, Ron Armstead; Congressional Black Caucus Foundation; Congressional Hispanic Caucus; Clarence "Tiger" Davis; Delta Sigma Theta (Baltimore County); Department of Veterans Affairs; Dr. Frances "Toni" Draper, CEO, Afro American Newspapers; First Baptist Church, Fayetteville, North Carolina; Foundation for Women Warriors; Retired US Army Col. Mike Freeman; Friends of the Army Women's Museum; Gloria White Gardner (deceased); Retired US Marine Corps Master Gunnery Sgt. Joe Geeter; George W. Bush Center Veteran Leadership Program; Walt Green, President, Norfolk Real Deal Track Club; Retired US Army Master Sgt. Elizabeth Helm-Frazier; Retired US Army Maj. Natasha Hinds, owner, Keep Your Hair Headgear; Cricket Holder, Vietnam veteran and curator, Virtual Graves; Mr. Kevin Hymel, historian; JDH Iron Designs (HGTV's Jimmy Don Holmes); Retired US Army Maj. Dominic Johnson; Carlotta Walls LaNier, Little Rock Nine; Robert Lewis, Van Aucker Group; Lincoln Penny Films, Jim Theres, executive producer; Los Angeles NAACP; Maryland State Legislature and the Women's Caucus; Christine McKeever, former executive director, 6th Cavalry Museum; Retired US Air Force Col. Eries Mentzer; Military Association Officers of America; Senator Jerry Moran's staff, including the four Defense Fellows (2018–21); Montford Point Marines; Montgomery County (Maryland) NAACP; Rep. Gwen Moore, her legislative director, Chris Goldson, and former Gold Star Fellow LaToya Bell; Helen Murdoch, Birmingham, England; Russell Myers, American Legion, Department of Maryland; National Association of Black Veterans; National Association of Black Women Veterans; National Coalition of Black Veteran Organizations; Retired US Army Maj. Frank Phillips; Ms. Debbie M. Ransom; Dr. Elwood Robinson, former chancellor, Winston-Salem State University; The Rocks, Inc.; Retired US Army Lt. Col. Suzanne Russell; Molly Sampson, former curator, 6th Cavalry Museum; Servicewomen's Action Network; Garry Stewart, President, Recognize, Birmingham, England; Steven Tedesco, director of education, Buffalo and Erie County Naval & Military Park; Edna Wagner, executive director, Richard Allen Museum and Cultural Center, Fort Leavenworth, Kansas; Retired US Army Maj. Ellsworth "Tony" Williams, President/CEO Veterans Counseling Veterans; Retired US Army Maj. Diedre Windsor, President and CEO, Windsor Group; Zeta Phi Beta Sorority, Inc.

APPENDICES

APPENDIX 1

PANMUNJOM, KOREA— SECURITY OFFICERS' MEETING 9 OCTOBER 1981— CAPTAIN WALTER CUMMINGS JR., JSA COMMANDER

I called this meeting for the following reasons:

First, to inform you [of] the results of my investigation of the charges you made at the last formal Security Officers' Meeting held on 23 September 1981. As I said I would. Second, to bring your attention to recent unprofessional conduct by your security guards in the JSA. Third, to propose once again that we conduct as much of our business as possible at informal Security Officers' Meetings. Fourth, to ask that you identify yourself, or that your side identify your side's security officer, so that I know who from your side has security officer authority in the JSA.

At the last formal meeting, you accused our side's security guards of exposing the lower parts of their body on numerous occasions. Such conduct is immature and irresponsible and will not be tolerated. However, we cannot substantiate your charges. It will help our future investigations if you provide photographic evidences of these alleged incidents. If any of our personnel are found guilty of such a misconduct, they will, of course, be disciplined.

We have investigated each of your allegations carefully and cannot find any basis in fact for them.

Your charge that our security guards threw rocks on 17 September 1981 is completely false. It was your security guards who threw the rocks, and it was my commander who immediately protested informally through the JDO phone. After our informal protest of this serious incident, you sent a formal message alleging that we investigated this incident, in an attempt to shift the blame.

The next day at an informal Security Officers' Meeting, I discussed this rock throwing incident with Captain [name withheld], who I thought was your side's Security Officer. I do not believe that it is proper to discuss my conversations with Captain [name withheld], but I felt that we had resolved this issue. Then you called a formal meeting and again falsely charged us with the rock throwing incident of 17 September 1981. I do not understand your conduct in this incident. I don't believe a formal meeting was necessary in this case. False charges only heighten tension.

Now, I have several charges to make concerning serious recent violations of the subsequent agreement to the AA. On 25 September, at 0341 hours, your security guards near MDL marker number 98, yelled profanity at our security guards in an attempt to provoke a fight. About 1510 hours on 27 September 1981, and about 0805 hours on 28 September 1981, and about 1600 hours on 30 September, your security guards crossed the MDL near marker number 099 in violation of the subsequent agreements to the AA. Most of these MDL crossings occurred because your security guards came over to our side to pick up chestnuts from under the trees on our side.

There have been other instances of unprofessional and provocative behavior on the part of your security guards, such as shining spotlights on our guard posts at night.

We have photographic evidences of some instances of unprofessional conduct on the part of your side's security guards. We have noted the nature of the incident on the back of each picture. I offer them to you so that you may take appropriate action.

I would have preferred to bring these incidents and photos to your attention at an informal meeting. Our side believes that we should attempt to handle most matters informally between the security officers. We believe that the procedures as agreed upon at the last informal meeting on 18 September 1981, should be used at future informal Security Officers' Meetings. We see no need to highlight incidents at either formal meetings or in messages, until we have first tried to resolve them informally. We believe that informal meetings will help us reduce tension. Let me repeat that—We believe that informal meetings will help to reduce tension in the JSA and thereby be more productive than formal meetings.

However, if you refuse to meet with us, as you have on three consecutive occasions, we will answer your charges and make our own charges by messages or through the formal Security Officers' Meetings.

To improve our formal meeting procedures, I suggest that the side proposing a formal Security Officers Meeting include in its message a statement of purpose. By doing so, the other side can come to the meeting better prepared to conduct meaningful dialogue and negotiations.

At the last formal Security Officers' Meeting, I asked that your side identify who your Security Officer is, so that my side knows who from your side has security officer authority in the JSA. I repeat that request. Our side should know for the official records, with whom I am meeting at these formal Security Officers' Meetings.

In closing, I request that you investigate and answer my charges, as I do yours and take the actions necessary to preclude future incidents.

I have nothing more and propose we recess this meeting.

From Captain Cummings's personal files. Copy provided to US Army Heritage and Education Center, Carlisle, Pennsylvania.

APPENDIX 2

CHARITY ADAMS EARLEY, POST WORLD WAR II, 1946–2002

On December 26, 1945, Major Adams received a promotion to lieutenant colonel. The Women's Army Corps had only one colonel's position, the WAC director, a position she believed was out of her reach. Adams departed the Army, completed her master's degree in vocational psychology at Ohio State, and became active in the civilian community. From 1946 to 1948, she worked as a registration officer with the Veterans Administration in Cleveland, the dean of student personnel services at Tennessee Agricultural and Industrial State College in Nashville, and the dean of Students at Georgia State College in Savannah.

In 1949, Adams married Stanley A. Earley Jr. They met while undergraduate students at Wilberforce. Earley was a former Army sergeant, trained as a French and German translator. He also served overseas in the ETO, and after the war, he helped German POWs reunite with their families. The Earleys moved to Switzerland while Stanley completed medical school. They returned to the United States in 1952 and settled in Dayton, Ohio, where they had two children, Stanley III and Judith.

During the 1950s, Adams Earley continued to break gender and racial barriers and sat on several boards, including the board of directors and the board of governors of the Dayton Chapter of the American Red Cross, the board of the Sinclair Community College, and the board of the Dayton Power and Light Company. In 1982, she founded the Black Leadership Development Program (BLDP) in Dayton, to educate and train African American community leaders. In 2000, Adams Earley helped create Parity, Inc., to facilitate the Leadership's training program. An elementary school in Dayton, Ohio, bears her married name, the Charity Earley Academy for Girls.

The Smithsonian Institution has included her in its listing of the historically most important Black women, and the Red Cross cites her as one of the women who helped shape the organization's history. In 1996, the Smithsonian's National Postal Museum honored Adams Earley for her wartime service. Before leaving Dayton for the ceremony in Washington, she offered these comments: "When I talk to students, they say, 'How did it feel to know you were making history?' But you don't know you're making history when it's happening. I just wanted to do my job."

Adams Earley died at the age of eighty-three on January 13, 2002, in Dayton, Ohio, and is buried at the Woodland Cemetery and Arboretum.

Note: In August 2022, James Theres and the author honored Charity Adams Earley in Dayton, Ohio, with screenings of the documentary *Six Triple Eight* at Sinclair College and Charity Adams Academy (pre-K–6th grade), and a wreath laying at her gravesite at the Woodland Cemetery and Arboretum.

APPENDIX 3

6888TH CHRONOLOGY WITH CITY AND STATE LIST OF THE FIRST 6888TH CONTINGENT (738 WACS)

The 6888th names are listed by state and alphabetical order by rank. The cities represent the location where they joined the Army and not their hometowns. Many of the women joined the Women's Army (or Auxiliary) Corps in cities outside of their hometowns.

CHRONOLOGY OF US DEPARTURE, ETO ARRIVAL, AND RETURN TO THE UNITED STATES

1945

Mid-January	The unit known as RT1051c trains at Fort Oglethorpe, Georgia.
January 25	Maj. Charity Adams receives secret military orders directing her to report to the British Isles (London).
January 28	Major Adams and Capt. Abbie Noel Campbell arrive in London and report to WAC Headquarters, 47 Grosvenor Square.

Late January	RT-10–51c arrives at Camp Shanks, New York, under the temporary command of Capt. Mildred Carter, Boston.
February 3	RT1051c departs Camp Shanks on the *Ile-de-France*, a commercial French ocean liner. German U-boats chase the ship while it is en route to Europe.
February 7	Maj. Charity Adams and Capt. Abbie N. Campbell are assigned to the BPO, Sutton, Coldfield, United Kingdom.
February 11	The first contingent of 6888th arrives in Glasgow, Scotland.[1]
February 12	The 6888th disembarks and boards a train to Birmingham, England. Charity Adams refers to them as an "unhappy looking lot." Brig. Gen. Benjamin O. Davis greets them when they disembark.
March 4	Major Adams assumes command of the 6888th by writing her own assumption of command orders, General Order No. 1.
April 12	President Roosevelt dies; the 6888th holds a memorial service; Harry S. Truman assumes office as the thirty-third president of the United States.
Mid-April	The second contingent arrives, bringing the total number to 855 (24 officers, 831 enlisted).
April 30	Adolf Hitler commits suicide.
May 7	German Col. Gen. (Generaloberst) Alfred Jodl signs Germany's surrender on all fronts in Reims, France.
May 8	Victory in Europe (V-E Day); Germany surrenders; German Field Marshal Wilhelm Keitel signs surrender documents in Berlin.
May 27	The 6888th marches in the Joan of Arc parade, Rouen, France.
July 8	Pfc. Mary J. Barlow, Pfc. Mary H. Bankston, and Sgt. Delores M. Browne are involved in a vehicle accident; Barlow and Bankston die immediately.
July 13	Sergeant Browne dies from her injuries.
August	Some 6888th members return to United States.

September 2	Japan surrenders onboard the USS *Missouri;* World War II Allied Victory.
Late October	400 6888th members relocate to Paris.
November 9	173 6888th members return to New York on the *Queen Mary.*

1946

December 12	Major Adams returns to United States, arriving in New York on the troop ship *George Washington.*
December 26	Major Adams is promoted to lieutenant colonel, making her one of highest-ranking women in the WAC, and the highest-ranking Black woman officer in the Armed Forces.
February 12	The last of the 6888th return to United States without recognition of their service.
March 9	The Six Triple Eight is deactivated at Camp Kilmer, New Jersey.
March 26	Lieutenant Colonel Adams is discharged from the Women's Army Corps.

MILITARY RANK ABBREVIATIONS (ARMY AND ARMY AIR CORPS/FORCES)

Note: Major was the highest officer rank in the 6888th highest officer rank; TSGT was the highest enlisted rank.

Officer Ranks: Major (MAJ), Captain (CPT), First Lieutenant (1LT), Second Lieutenant (2LT)

Enlisted Ranks:

    Private (PVT)

    Private First Class (PFC)

    Corporal or Technician Fifth Grade (CPL/T5)

    Sergeant or Technician Fourth Grade (SGT/T4)

    Staff Sergeant or Technician Third Grade (SSG/T3)

    First Sergeant or Technical Sergeant (1SG/TSGT)

    Master Sergeant (MSG)

Alabama

Alexander City: PVT Ophelia D. Thomas
Bessemer: PVT Felicia L. Johnson
Birmingham: T5 Christel S. George, PFC Dorothy E. Brown, PFC Willie M. House, PVT Eva Edwards, PVT Minnie B. Quarles, PVT Mary L. Walthall
Decatur: PFC Tessie M. Seymour
Dixiana: T4 Addie L. Campbell
Florence: T5 Jeanette L. Moorehead
Mobile: T4 Mercelene L. Fairgood, PFC Elizabeth M. Davis, PVT Willie L. Coleman, PVT Irene R. Greene, PVT Delores H. Smith
Montevallo: PFC Susie I. Middlebrook
Montgomery: T5 Mary F. Smith, PFC Mary R. Muncie
Muskogee: PVT Izona Brown
Prairie: PFC Hattie I. Steele
Selma: PFC Margaret L. Young
Tuskegee: CPT Abbie N. Campbell, PVT Lillian I. Battle

Arizona

Nogales: PVT Lydia E. Thornton

Arkansas

Chidester: PFC Lynia E. Tate
Cleveland: PVT Esteel B. Williams
Crossett: T5 Vernice E. Evans
[El Dorado]: PVT Ruby L. Ward
Hot Springs: T3 Emma J. Jacobs
Little Rock: T3 Bessie M. Willis, PFC Cora L. Richardson
Magnolia: PFC Terrine D. Pressley
Osceola: CPL Virgie L. Caywood, PVT Anna M. Wilson
Paraloma: PFC Mattie L. Griffing
Roland: PVT Ella M. Davis
Trumann: PVT Rose M. Anderson
Van Buren: PVT Rebecca O. Glass
Wynne: PVT Eveyln M. Young

California

Bakersfield: SGT Dorothy B. Tabb

Los Angeles: 2LT Alice Edwards, T4 Mattie M. Moorehead, T5 Ora E. Bragg, T5 Viola E. Suarez, PFC Polly C. Frazier, PVT Gladys L. Collier, PVT Frances A. Foster, PVT Jessie B. Hall, PVT LaMonthal L. Williams
Monterey: PFC Bettie E. McDonald
San Francisco: PVT Thelma P. Johnson
Stockton: PVT Dorothy E. Daniels

Colorado

Denver: PFC Beula T. Fant, PVT Jessie G. Hudson
Pueblo: PVT Erma P. Brady

Connecticut

Bloomfield: PFC Marian S. Jackson
Bridgeport: SGT Delores M. Browne (buried at Normandy American Cemetery)
Hartford: PVT Mary J. Barlow (buried at Normandy American Cemetery)
New Haven: PFC Audrey E. Harris, PFC Elizabeth M. McNair, PVT Margaret Powell
New London: PFC Burnardine E. Fraser
Stamford: PFC Margaret B. Janer

Delaware

Marshallton: PVT Mary Crawford
Wilmington: CPL Edith Carter, PVT Evelina R. Gryfin

District of Columbia

MAJ Virginia G. Hurley, 1LT Blanche L. Scott, SGT Gertrude V. Hall, SGT Cecelia H. Kelly, CPL Erma Campbell, CPL Susan V. Crabtree, CPL Christina Stone, PFC Alice [Alyce] L. Dixon, PFC Edith M. Ellison, PFC Lillie B. Harrison, PFC Elvie L. Holder, PFC Hattie M. Lee, PFC Hylda M. Miller, PFC Margaret P. Simmons, PFC Constance Wardell, PVT Alreatha S. Battle, PVT Jessie M. Bridgers, PVT Olive K. Dedeaux, PVT Sarah B. Gary, PVT Eleanor W. Gibson, PVT Emma E. Johnson, PVT Lucille V. M. Johnson, PVT Thelma C. Lofty, PVT Genevieve Marshall, PVT Marie A. McKinney, PVT Dona Primus, PVT Deloris L. Ruddock, PVT Alva C. Truatt, PVT Doris M. Ware, PVT Constance E. Webb, PVT Jessie M. Williams

Florida

Daytona Beach: PVT Erma L. Rodringer
Gainesville: PVT Thelma A. Duncan

Goulds: PVT Ruby L. Everett

Homestead: PVT Florida B. Jackson

Jacksonville: PFC Florida D. Smith

Miami: SSG Elaine O. Smith, SGT Gladys Clayton, CPL Marion Mackey, PFC Elizabeth O. Lamb

Monticello: T5 Essie M. Watts, PFC Ethel Wingo

[Palatka]: SSG Fannie B. Little

Pensacola: PFC Beatrice Casey

Sanford: T5 Edna C. Burton

St. Augustine: PVT Geneva L. Smith

Tampa: PVT Jennie L. Fayson

Tarpon Springs: CPL Dannie M. Singleton

Titusville: CPL Jessie L. Godbolte

West Palm Beach: PVT Josie M. Loine

Georgia

Atlanta: 1LT Corrie Sherard, SGT Gladys L. Brumfield, CPL Florene J. Hill, T5 Nellie R. Harmon, T5 Leola L. Whet, PFC Mary F. Dairs, PFC Bessie G. Truner, PVT Lola B. Davis, PVT Beulah H. Patten, PVT Clara E. Wilson

Augusta: T5 Essie D. O'Bryant, PFC Julia C. Harris, PVT Ardella C. Pitts

Brunswick: CPL Elouise H. Pinkey

Cartersville: SGT Maria S. Goode

Columbus: PFC Jessie K. Faulk

Dublin: PVT Eugenia A. Brown

Hillsboro: PFC Lilla C. Waters

Lyerly: PFC Elouise H. Rice

Macon: SSG Marseleana H. Goodwin, T5 Henrie M. Smith

Marietta: PFC Lettie R. Williams

Moultrie: PVT Willie B. Irvin

Newman: PVT Phyletus C. Greene

Rome: PVT Sarah F. Morgan

Savannah: PFC Herlene R. Bradsher, PFC Vernell Al Hannah, PFC Annie M. Mason, PVT Sylvia E. Armstrong, PVT Wilma E. Barnes

Shiloh: PVT Annie O. Crawl

Smithville: PVT Ozie B. Smothers

Waycross: CPL Martha L. Goodard

Wrens: PFC Susie B. Brown

Illinois

Alton: 1LT Dorothy H. Scott

Chicago: 2LT Gussye D. Stewart, SGT Erma L. Fifer, SGT Mattie L. Jackson, T4 Mamie A. Doss, T4 Lucia M. Pitts, CPL Eddye G. Maddox, T5 Betty F. Bowen, T5 Evelyn Eilared, T5 Cecilia D. Goldsby, T5 Elizabeth M. Patterson, PFC Ella K. Armstrong, PFC Johnnie M. Barton, PFC Arjean G. Conner, PFC Anna M. Couch, PFC Jacquelyn Fuller, PFC Winona Fuller, PFC Callie N. Grant, PFC Margaret E. Hampton, PFC Ruth S. Jacobs, PFC Juanita R. Lane, PFC Lethelma Moore, PFC Helen M. Norris, PFC Thelma L. O'Kelly, PFC Edna P. Samples, PFC Sammye L. Trail, PFC Willie M. Whiting, PVT Mamie L. Beard, PFC Geraldine Beaumont, PVT Lila V. Bush, PVE Pinkie Collier, PVT Ruthanna Cummings, PVT Helen N. English, PVT Annie L. Grimes, PVT Marian U. Horace, PVT Ruth E. Lewis, PVT Leatrice Lowe, PVT Rosa L. Marsaw, PVT Mary J. McBride, PVT DeLois G. Miller, PVT Sarah A. Parker, PVT Rhoda Phibbs, PVT Maude V. Porter, PVT Margaret G. Sales, PVT Grace Vairin, PVT Lois M. Washington, PVT Mildred J. Wilson, PVT Johnie E. Yerger

Danville: T5 Gloria H. Carr, PVT Willen S. Fly, PVT Evelyn McDougal

East St. Louis: PFC Willa Mae Perkins

La Grange: PVT Mary J. Smith

Paris: PFC Florence L. Radcliff

Peoria: T3 Lorraine Hinton

Quincy: T4 Greadell J. Haley

Indiana

Evansville: PFC Croella L. Tolliver, PVT Lulu M. Edmonson

Fort Wayne: PVT Dolly B. Woods

Gary: CPL Bennye B. Daniels, PVT Josephine Machlin

Indianapolis: CPL Blanche W. Dogan, CPL Clara M. Webb, PVT Bridget V. Bevens, PVT Hazel D. Moore, PVT Mary L. Whiting

Terre Haute: PVT Doris M. Maxwell

Iowa

Council Bluffs: PFC Geraldine L. Herndon

Des Moines: 2LT Hazel E. Craddock

Kansas

Chetopa: PVT Mintha Jones

Hutchinson: PVT Lavinia C. Lowery

Kansas City: SGT Bettie J. Smith, T5 Hazel L. Washington, PFC Bettie M. Albert, PFC Rosalie A. Simmons, PVT Bernice N. Underwood

Larned: PVT Dollie E. Jackson

Manhattan: PVT Cecil I. Wilson

Kentucky

Bardstown: PFC Minnie G. Cross

Corbin: CPL Alberta Coleman

Erlanger: PVT Evelyn E. Miller, PVT Nettie M. Saunders

Henderson: PVT Grant E. Marshall, PFC Carrie E. Nelson

Lewisburg: T4 Marilyn E. Gill

Lexington: PVT Venus B. Cox, PVT Julia M. Jackson

Louisville: T5 Henrietta G. Adams, CPL Ruth H. Hammond, PFC Emma H. Brock, PFC Adele Ricketts, PVT Effie Chambers

McAndrews: PFC Sara E. Longmire

Owensboro: PFC Vivian G. Hayden

Richmond: CPL Jenetta S. Blythe

Tribbey: SSG Norene Harris

Louisiana

Baton Rouge: CPL Theresa M. Bell, T5 Shirley K. Weareye

Chestnut: CPL Willie M. Jewett

Church Point: T5 Daro Charlot

Couchatte: SGT Widdie M. Duncan

Farmerville: PFC Annie L. Moses

Franklin: PFC Marion M. Moore, PFC Almeta P. Morrison

Franklinton: PVT Lucille M. Jones

Jeanerette: T5 Martha L. Johnson

Marrero: T4 Annetta A. Baptiste

Pioneer: PFC Normal Niblet

Shreveport: PVT Luchertha M. Alexander

South Mansfield: PVT Gladys B. O'Giluie

New Orleans: 1LT Catherine G. Landry, 2LT Elfreda St. Anne LeBeau, CPL Charlotte M. McCullum, CPL Frances E. Pickett, T5 Annette W. Simmons, T5 Velma L. White, PFC Aletha V. Dunn, PFC Mary McClain, PFC Menthee R. Talbert, PFC Malinda A. Washington, PVT Maggie A. Chestang, PVT Margaret G. Ellis

Washington: T5 Annie Mae Lawson

Maryland

Annapolis: CPL Ada L. Jennings
Baltimore: SGT Vivian W. Young, PFC Vashti M. Matthews, PFC Ethel B. Philyan,
   PVT Laura M. Jones, PVT Annie B. Moore, PVT Thelma A. Parker, PVT Glo-
   ria A. Sydnor, PVT Gloria P. Taylor, PVT Grace M. Whyte
Brooklyn: PFC Emily O. Noisette
Cambridge: CPL Mary R. Jackson
Centerville: PVT Eleanor Ana Wilson
Crisfield: 2LT Vivian N. Elize
Cumberland: PVT Mary C. Nailor
Fruitland: PVT Lucy G. Pollitt
St. Mary County: PVT Agnes E. Barnes

Massachusetts

Amherst: PFC Laura A. Bias
Boston: CPT Mildred D. Carter, PFC Enid E. Clark, PFC Dorothy S. Daily, PVT
   Eloise B. McNeeley
Cambridge: T5 Beverly W. Carrington
Chelsea: CPL Constance M. E. Her[n]andez
Pittsfield: T5 Mary E. Moody, PFC Elsie J. Oliver
Springfield: PVT Cora L. Hurston

Michigan

Detroit: 1LT Mildred V. Dupee, CPL Madelyn L. Hudgins, T5 Annie L. Braceful, T5
   Ruth V. Wade, PFC Philista Johnson, PFC Gladys O. Thomas, PVT Arthurine
   Collins, PVT Rosetta Gains, PVT Annie K. Grinter, PVT Maetoris Hairston,
   PVT Bernice Hester, PVT Adella King, PVT Celestine Mathis, PVT Betty J.
   Richardson, PVT Lucy J. Ussery
Flint: PVT Maude Taylor
Hamtramck: T5 Leoynia Woodward

Minnesota

Minneapolis: CPL Virginia M. Lane, PFC Bernice E. Huggar, PVT Ednora A.
   Wallace
St. Paul: SGT Vernie M. Smith

Mississippi

Greenwood: T5 Mildred Montgomery, PVT Olivia Johnson
Hub: PVT Leona Abram

Jackson: PFC Mable Haskin
Laurel: CPL Flora Grace
Learned: PVT Adlease Harding
Madison Station: PFC Girtie M. Saddler
Magnolia: PFC Edna A. Fletcher
Meridian: T4 Minne P. Lockey, PFC Annie L. Winnberty
Moss Point: PVT Isabel J. Griffin
Mt. Oline: PFC Sophia E. Easterlings
Natchez: PFC Louise R. Bruce
Nettleton: T5 Bessie A. Foster
Ocean Springs: T5 Doris L. Paige
Ofahoma: SGT Anne P. Reed
Pinola: PFC Minne S. Sibbie
Vicksburg: PVT Lola I. Cliggett

Missouri

Jefferson City: T5 Theada G. Weddle
Kansas City: T5 Dorothy Cox
Salisbury: PVT Georgia E. Kitchen
Sedalia: PFC Anna M. Jackson, PFC Hazel E. Threadgill
St. Joseph: T5 Georgia E. Tivis
St. Louis: 1LT Violet W. Hill, CPL Pearline McKell, T4 Florence V. Scales, T4
    Odessa Taylor, PFC Helen S. Simmons

Montana

Butte: PVT Genevieve H. Williamson

Nebraska

Lincoln: CPT Mary E. Miller
Omaha: CPL Alberta O. Bradley

Nevada

Beatrice: CPL Mable V. Nevels

New Hampshire

Portsmouth: PVT Doris Moore

New Jersey

Allentown: PVT Marion V. Orkey
Asbury Park: CPL Lauretta Wray
Bayonne: SGT Lillian Butterfield
Camden: PVT Catherine E. Turner
Cape May: PVT Willamae Boatright
East Orange: CPT Ellen B. Hayes, PFC Gladys Eva Debman
East Riverton: PVT Delores M. Johnson
Elizabeth: PFC Velma J. Arkward, PFC Gladys B. Avant
Englewood: PVT Caroline E. Smith
Jersey City: PFC Verdell E. McMillian, PFC Beatrice Withers
Lawnside: PVT Breda V. Williams
Linden: PFC Hester Givens
Long Branch: 2LT Mercedes Jordan
Neptune: PVT Ada W. Holley
Newark: T5 Georgiana Morton, T4 Edith M. Linzey, PVT Doretha Miller,
Passaic: PVT Bernice S. Axam
Paterson: CPL Willene Johnson
Plainfield: PVT Johnita Alyse Johnson
[Roselle]: PVT Sylvia Gillis
Woodbridge: CPL Daisy B. Dinkins

New York

Bronx: T3 Mattie E. Garrett, SGT Bernice Thomas, CPL Callie K. Smith, T5
   Myrtle A. Rhoden, T5 Velma A. Riddick, T5 Beulah E. Robinson, T5 Fannie
   Talbert, PFC Evelyn L. Fray, PFC Crescencia Garcia, PFC Theodora P. Palmer,
   PFC Helen M. Wood, PVT Rebecca B. Ferguson, PVT Emantrude Finch, PVT
   Elverna E. Issac, PVT Sybil M. King, PVT Josephine Powell, PVT Edna Tookie
Brooklyn: CPL Bernice A. Augstine, PFC Margaret Anderson, PFC Phyllis L.
   Branch, PFC Lillian Cabble, PFC Ruth E. Daniel, PVT Joyce G. Anderson, PVT
   Pearl E. Cumberbatch, PVT Lular P. Downing
Buffalo: T4 Evelyn C. Martin, PFC Lillian V. Showell
Corona: CPL Marjorie Brown, PFC Mary E. Greene, PFC Lillian V. Jones
Flushing: PVT Henrietta Lee
Hillburn: PFC Norma D. Moore
Jamaica: PVT Edith J. Armistead
New York City: 2LT Frances E. Flatts, SSG Gertrude L. Rose SGT Cleopatra V.
   Daniels, T4 Ethel C. Loving, CPL Theodora D. Bryant, CPL Louise S. Heyward,
   CPL Lucie C. Owens, CPL Louise A. Reid, T5 Adelina H. Bell, T5 Madeline A.
   Coleman, T5 Geneve McRae, T5 Doris E. Stewart, T5 Mary E. Walker, T5

Edna B. Sanders, PFC Margi L. Amis, PFC Mary H. Bankston (buried at Normandy American Cemetery), PFC Marcella L. Canty, PFC Harriet E. Douglas, PFC Marie B. Gillisslee, PFC Bernice M. Grant, PFC Dolly F. Hall, PFC Aleese E. Johnson, PFC Emily C. Mays, PFC Beatrice R. Morris, PFC Earlene C. Reeves, PFC Blanch V. Swantner, PVT Dorothy A. Bartlett, PVT Clarice E. Blackett, PVT Virginia S. Blake, PVT Carmew I. H. Colliers, PVT Gwendolyn C. Deane, PVT Emma S. De Freese, PVT Izetta M. Douglas, PVT Amy M. Fairweather, PVT Indiana Hunt, PVT Ruth E. James, PVT Evangeline Jeffrey, PVT Lauretta Johnson, PVT Louise B. Jones, PVT Ruth M. Mays, PVT Rose Stone, PVT Benita F. Shuster, PVT Nepsa V. Tankard, PVT Dorothy G. Young, PVT Norma L. Watts
Port Washington: PFC Evelyn B. Lozi
Salt Point: CPL Dorie E. Braddock
Staten Island: PFC Harriet E. Douglas
Utica: SGT Mary A. Edo
White Plains: PVT Dorothy E. Lounds

North Carolina

Battleboro: PVT Odessa A. Brake
Charlotte: PFC Theopia L. Ledbetter
Cofield: Fannie C. Smith
Concord: PVT Frances M. Gray
Durham: T4 Maggie A. Latta
Elkin: PFC Elizabeth B. Barker
Goldsboro: CPL Esther D. Hall
High Point: SGT Anne L. Johnson
New Bern: PVT Emma L. M. Jenkins
Raleigh: T5 Mille L. Dunn
Stantonsburg: PFC Artelza Whitley
Statesville: PVT Virginia L. Glenn
Tarboro: PVT Nannie P. Jones
Uree: T5 Lottie S. Mills
Warrenton: PFC Sallie B. Alexander
Weldon: PFC Vemise C. Hayes, PFC Effie C. Sutton
Wilson: PFC Sarah Taylor
Winston Salem: PFC Lucile M. Houston

Ohio

Addyston: T5 Gertrude E. Cruse
Akron: PVT Dorothy Queen

Canton: CPL Elizabeth J. DeWitt

Cincinnati: T4 Alma G. Minter, T4 Essie L. Robinson, T5 Novella Auls, T5 Mary M. Daniels, PFC Effie V. Dawson, PFC Duray M. Prestwood, PFC Mary E. Rozier

Cleveland: SGT Bernyce Q. Scott, SGT Ruth L. Wyatt, T5 Velma P. Hayes, T5 Catherine C. Johnson, PFC Hettie Boyce, PFC Vivian Fitzsimmons, PFC Hazel Norman, PFC Virginia A. Singleton, PFC Dorothy E. Turner, PFC Alberta D. Washington, PVT Anna L. Bybee, PVT Moniesah Petway, PVT Tommie L. Rookard, PVT Louise R. Usher, PVT Laura F. Warder

Columbus: T5 Hazel M. Russell, PFC Dorothy M. Ringer, PVT Tommie M. Crockett, PVT Katherine S. Metoyer, PVT Darnela B. Smith, PVT Bertha M. Solomon

Dayton: PVT Carroll M. Edwards

Freemont: PFC Vivian M. Brown

Hamilton: CPT Vera A. Harrison

Massilon: PVT Doris J. Smith

Middleton: PFC Mildred R. Gates

Oberlin: 1LT Margaret Ellen Barnes

Piqua: CPL Ruth E. Jefferson

Sandusky: PVT Pearl L. Bennett

Toledo: PVT Dorothy M. Gatliff, PVT Eunice L. Johnson

Warren: PVT Claudia Braxton

Xenia: 1LT Bernice G. Henderson

Youngstown: T5 Ruth L. Lottier

Oklahoma

Ardmore: PFC Maggie M. McClenton

Colbert: T5 Allie E. Williams

Eufaula: PFC Guthrie H. Rowland

Hugo: PVT Irene Morrow

McAlester: CPL Jewell L. Jackson

Muskogee: PVT Izon Brown

Oklahoma City: SSG Birdie Tillman, T5 Leona M. Ziegler, PFC Opal D. Brown, PFC Elizabeth J. Colbert, PVT Leath M. Loggins, PVT Mabel F. Sneed

Payson: PFC Theodisa E. Lee

Tulsa: PVT Anjenettie Smith, PVT Trenna J. Stokenberry

Wagoner: PVT Balance Albreton

Pennsylvania

Belle Vernon: PFC Bebe C. Johnson

Bethlehem: PVT Alice H. Smith

Bridgeville: PVT Freda Md. Dean

Chester: PVT Isofine Jacobs, PVT Carolyn M. Berry

Clairton: PVT Bernice F. Lewis

Darby: SGT Rhoda A. Daniel

Donora: PVT Catherine J. Crump

Harrisburg: PFC Naomi Davenport, PFC Grace E. Lucal, PVT Wilma H. Lucas, PVT Elizabeth Moraney, PVT Ruby M. Wilson

Hollidaysburg: PFC Elise A. Dannals

Homestead: PVT Adele Evans

Jeannette: PFC Julia McNeal

Johnston: PFC Ophelia Mae Ewings

Lancaster: PVT Catherine Wright

Moylan: PVT Eleanor F. Sullivan

Philadelphia: TSGT Mary E. Baster, SGT Delores C. Cray, SGT Rosa M. Harris, SGT Catherine A. King, SGT Stella E. Pattila, CPL Love P. Anderson, CPL Lena D. Bell, CPL Lucile M. Brooks, CPL Alma M. Philpot, PFC Mary A. Artis, PFC Elizabeth H. Cornwell, PFC Violet Dabney, PFC Ursula V. Davis, PFC Addie M. Demby, PFC Marian M. Elzie, PFC Marian R. Grundy, PFC Willie M. Jackson, PFC Hessie Johnson, PFC Evelyn C. LeSueuer, PFC Thelma E. Purdy, PFC Juanita G. Rodgers, PFC Janyce L. Stovall, PFC Sarah L. Tabb, PFC Romma B. Wilson, PFC Hilda E. Wood, PVT Louisa Balls, PVT Edna Bastin, PVT Lillie Berry, PVT Gladys W. Brown, PVT Charlotte C. Cartwright, PVT Florence A. Collins, PVT Alvia Ferguson, PVT Alice O. Ford, PVT Thelma V. Green, PVT Hilda P. Griggs, PVT Berenice E. Massett, PVT Helen L. Pinkett, PFC Aleese J. Robinson, PVT Naomi V. Steward, PVT Harriet E. Warfield, PVT Dora M. Williams, PVT Alberta B. Willis, PVT Mary P. Young

Pittsburgh: T5 Mary P. Monroe, T5 Dorothy E. William, PFC Alice S. Charles, PFC Frances C. Jordan, PFC Dorothy C. Reid, PVT Frances Crews, PVT Ruth N. Dean, PVT Cornelia D. Warfield

Reading: PVT Phyllis G. Long

Sewickley: T5 Helen V. Gould

Titusville: PFC Vyvyonne E. Bugg

Washington: CPL Helen D. Stribbling

West Chester: PVT Margoit M. Townsend

Willow Grove: T5 Elaine V. Jones

Rhode Island

Providence: PVT Annie M. Ruse

South Carolina

Anderson: CPL Jennie R. Turner, PVT Wilhelmina L. Holmes
Charleston: PFC Ermane E. Taylor
Columbia: MAJ Charity Adams (Commander)
Darlington: PVT Alva B. Bacote
Hartsville: PFC Hazel S. Jackson
Kingstree: SGT Vivian A. Nazyck
Mullins: PVT Lucile M. Balloon
Saluda: PVT Carolyn B. Poole
Trenton: PFC Novella E. Jackson

Tennessee

Gallatin: PFC Myrtle Baker
Knoxville: PVT Ruth E. Boggues
Mason: T5 Luvenia Allen
Memphis: PFC Annie E. Burrell, PFC Cleopatra Evans, PFC Mary L. Ross, PVT
    Cova [Cora] D. Madison
Milan: PFC Crinia M. Barksdale
Nashville: PVT Gladys Dailey, PVT Ilda R. League, PVT Mary M. Martin
Paris: PVT Lima J. Howard

Texas

Arthur City: PVT Erma Boyd
Athens: PFC Mary L. Hill
Beaumont: TSGT Ruby M. O'Brien, T5 Ruth V. Brown, PFC Ella M. Jackson, PVT
    Mable J. Zenon
Berclair: PFC Essie O. O'Riley
Corpus Christie: PFC Hazel Allen, PVT Bessie Booker
Dallas: T5 Ernestine E. Hughes, PFC Maggie M. McClenton, PVT Marth A. McKnight,
Denison: PVT Mildred E. Peterson
El Dorado: 1LT Ella Tatum
Fort Worth: SGT Lucille Lewis, T5 Florence Cole, PFC Helen B. Minor,
Galveston: PFC Marguerite Ellis
Greenville: PFC Catherine Lee
Hankamer: PFC Willie R. Richardson
Hempstead: CPL Johnnie M. Walton, PVT Eddie T. Richards
Houston: 2LT Caloni Powell, T4 Rose Stuary, CPL Dorothy L. Howard, CPL Flor-
    ida E. Robey, PFC Ophalia Mills, PFC Erma L. Smith, PVT Essie L. Penn
Longview: PFC Mildred L. Hooper
Marshall: PVT Millie M. Taylor

Naples: PVT Minerva L. Kevernal
Port Arthur: PFC Kate Pate
Taylor: PFC Myrtle E. Wright
Timpson: T5 Mablyne Ortiz, PFC Onnie Roberts
Waco: SSG Juanita Goodloe
Wichita Falls: SGT Ruby L. McCluing, PFC Freddie W. Chinn

Virginia

Alexandria: CPL Gertrude Sessoms
Amonate: T5 Marie M. Hairston
Arlington: SGT Catherine G. Brown, PFC Edith F. Gaskill
Ashton: 1LT Vashti Tonkins
Bristol: PFC Dorothy M. Jackson
Capahosic: CPL Jennie D. Moton
Charlottesville: T5 Frances G. Jeerson
Cullen: PFC Maime L. Lewis
Dahlgren: PVT Romay C. Johnson
Danville: 2LT Bertie M. Edwards, T5 Mary N. Medley
Floyd: T5 Amelia Akers
Gloucester: 2LT Aubrey A. Stokes
Hampton: PFC Kitty C. Bowden
Hanover: PVT Mary M. Coleman
Hollins: T5 Helen R. Holmes
Hornsbyville: PFC Margaret F. Barbour
Lexington: PVT Annie L. Pleasants, PVT Louise V. Ross
Norfolk: SGT Marian E. Lawrence, CPL Ruth V. Reddick, CPL Elizabeth C.
    Moore, T5 Dorothy Mayfield Hutchins, PFC Lillie G. Bratcher, PFC Helen E.
    Henderson
Orange: PVT Phyllis I. Galloway
Petersburg: SGT Louise T. Penny, PVT Anne Garrison
Portsmouth: PVT Leona Virginia Jones
Richmond: SGT Marcell B. Wilson, CPL Martha A. Drummond, T5 Katherine Lee,
    PVT Ernestine A. Allen, PVT Eula G. Davis, PVT Antoinette L. Scott
South Boston: PVT Frances Chappell
South Richmond: PFC Dorothy E. Allen
Staunton: CPL Irene V. Carr
Suffolk: PFC Rosa G. Diggs, PFC Grace L. Ruffin
Winchester: PFC Annie T. Finley
Victoria: CPL Hazel C. Jennings
Wytheville: T4 Alice M. Allison

West Virginia

Berboursvile (perhaps Barboursville): PVT Mamie Gammon
Bluefield: SGT Sallie M. Smith, T4 Albert M. Smith, PFC Anletha M. Cawthorne, PFC Virginia P. Watkins
Crumpler: TSGT Lerohn N. Saunders
Gary: PVT Clara B. Simon
Handley: PFC Lucille A. Poindexter
Institute: PFC Ester R. Wells, PVT Jane E. Ferguson
Kimball: T5 Lelia M. Watkins, PVT Phoebe E. Miller
Sutton: T5 Jeanette B. Martin, PVT Frances Martin,
Ward: CPL Lovener F. Ford
Wheeling: PVT Dorothy D. Jackson

Wisconsin

SGT Alice G. Woodson, T4 Evelyn Ross

Permission to use content granted by the *Afro American* (Savannah Wood), January 5, 2023.

APPENDIX 4

BLACK TROOPS BURIED AND MISSING AT NORMANDY AMERICAN CEMETERY, COLLEVILLE-SUR-MUR, FRANCE

Of the 9,387 graves at Normandy, three are those of Black women from the 6888th Central Postal Directory Battalion who lost their lives in a vehicle accident: Sgt. Delores Browne, Pfc. Mary Bankston, and Pfc. Mary Barlow. The remaining graves are those of Black men whose ages ranged from nineteen to thirty-eight. Five Black men were declared missing.

Of the estimated 73,000 US forces who landed on this strip of beaches on D-Day, 2,501 Americans lost their lives. Only one Black combat unit, the 621-member 320th Barrage Balloon Battalion (Very Low Altitude), landed on D-Day at Omaha and Utah Beaches. Three soldiers from that unit died on June 6, or D-Day: Cpl. Brooks Stith from North Carolina; Cpl. Henry Harris, originally from Pennsylvania; and Pvt. James L. Simmons, from Upper Marlboro, Maryland. Brooks and Stith are buried at Normandy, and Simmons is buried at Mt. Carmel Cemetery, Upper Marlboro.

Thousands of African Americans served in segregated engineer general service regiments to construct and repair roads, airfields, and bridges. The 364th Engineer Service Regiment has five members buried at Normandy who died from July to August 1944.

NO.	RANK	LAST	FIRST, MI	*STATE	UNIT	EST. AGE	DATE OF DEATH (M/DD/YYYY)	PLOT	ROW	GRAVE NO.
Women										
1	PFC	Bankston	Mary H.	NY	6888th Central Postal Directory BN	23	7/8/1945	D	20	46
2	PFC	Barlow	Mary J.	CT	6888th Central Postal Directory BN	21	7/8/1945	A	19	30
3	SGT	Browne	Delores M.	CT	6888th Central Postal Directory BN	23	7/13/1945	F	13	19
Men										
4	PFC	Adams	William D.	AL	1323 ENGR GEN SVC REGT	31	9/20/1944	J	13	24
5	PVT	Littleton	Edmon	AL	131 QM BN	23	4/30/1945	B	17	11
6	PVT	Lyles	Lindsay	AL	511 PORT BN	21	3/4/1945	E	14	31
7	T4	Daniels Jr.	Hoyt N.	AR	414 PORT CO		6/19/1945	C	9	15
8	T5	Elliot	Cyrus S.	AR	514 PORT BN	23	11/5/1944	A	12	11
9	PVT	Hester	William	MS	306 RHD CO	23	9/10/1944	C	18	21
10	PVT	Hubbard	Harrison	AR	3867 QM TRK CO		9/4/1944	B	23	41
11	T5	Watson	Lee H.	AR	494 PORT BN		5/12/1945	B	19	11
12	PVT	Harris	John H.	DC	1323 ENG SVC REGT	30	8/20/1944	I	6	6
13	T5	Boyd Sr.	Rochester	FL	3398 QM TRK CO	24	8/1/1944	B	11	14
14	PFC	Mayes	Earl	FL	501 PORT BN	22	5/31/1945	D	10	40
15	CPL	Walker	General U.	FL	364 ENG SVC REGT	24	7/7/1944	E	12	33

NO.	RANK	LAST	FIRST, MI	*STATE	UNIT	EST. AGE	DATE OF DEATH (M/DD/YYYY)	PLOT	ROW	GRAVE NO.
16	PVT	Bouie Jr.	Dan	GA	821 AMPH TRK CO	20	4/21/1945	C	5	8
17	T5	Bridges	Clyde	GA	3519 QM TRK CO	36	5/24/1945	B	10	23
18	PFC	Brown	Otis	GA	388 ENG BN	24	10/12/1944	J	16	17
19	PVT	Clevland	Len	GA	501 PORT BN	23	1/1/1945	B	21	34
20	SGT	Collins	Willie L.	GA	491 PORT BN	22	6/6/1944	F	28	31
21	T5	Culpepper Jr.	Eddie B.	GA	17 SP SV CO	23	8/21/1945	D	10	33
22	CPL	Hicks	Jimmie	GA	1323 ENG SVC REGT	22	9/6/1944	B	19	18
23	SGT	Jones	Melvin	GA	364 ENGR REGT	22	7/8/1944	G	5	37
24	SGT	Purser	Curry	GA	389 GEN SVC REGT	21	8/6/1944	J	10	35
25	PVT	Scott	Logan S.	GA	951 QM SVC CO	22	11/18/1944	F	17	12
26	CK3C	Slaughter	Malcolm	MS	USNR	17	6/9/1944	G	20	35
27	T5	Williams	Albert B.	GA	470 TRK CO	23	8/20/1944	H	17	31
28	PFC	Cooper	Willie F.	IL	3999 QM LDRY CO	33	8/8/1944	G	18	26
29	PVT	Harvey	Charlie G.	IL	3275 QM SVC CO	22	6/27/1944	I	16	10
30	PVT	Jones	Eugene	IL	3275 QM SVC CO	22	6/30/1944	G	24	17
31	PFC	Rose	Jesse	IL	1432 LABOR SUP CO	30	5/20/1945	B	8	23
32	PFC	Russell	Paul L.	IL	3219 QM SVC CO		4/11/1945	E	4	5
33	CPL	Walker	Ernest J.	IL	4048 QM SVC CO	28	7/28/1944	G	14	30
34	PVT	Wilson	William A.	IL	485 PORT BN	19	3/3/1945	B	11	24

NO.	RANK	LAST	FIRST, MI	*STATE	UNIT	EST. AGE	DATE OF DEATH (M/DD/YYYY)	PLOT	ROW	GRAVE NO.
35	PVT	Anderson	James R.	IN	513 PORT BN	21	10/9/1944	C	6	41
36	SGT	Irvin Jr.	Luther J.	IN	237 QM SALV CO	29	7/29/1944	G	19	31
37	PVT	Kendrick	Selmer	IN	4083 QMSV CO	23	7/12/1944	E	15	12
38	PVT	Troop	Alexander	IN	165 CML GENRATOR CO	34	3/25/1945	E	1	15
39	PVT	Chambers	Harold K	KS	452 AA AW BN	20	8/6/1944	C	28	34
40	CPL	Drasdell	Edward L.	KY	4270 QM TRK CO	29	11/5/44	F	2	45
41	CPL	Herndon	Charlie L.	KY	4083 QM V CO	22	7/12/1944	F	11	21
42	CPL	Jackson	Jinse C.	OH	549 ENGR L PON CO	27	7/8/1945	A	8	39
43	PVT	Jarber	Pete L.	KY	74 CML GENERATOR CO	21	12/2/1944	E	20	14
44	SGT	Carey	Robert	LA	3399 QM TRK CO	20	8/11/1944	H	21	26
45	PFC	Jefferson	Henry	LA	988th QM SV CO	28	9/20/1944	C	14	28
46	PVT	Payton	Lawrence	LA	388 ENG REGT	31	3/18/1945	B	12	24
47	PVT	Brannon	John S.	MA	502 PORT BN	29	6/7/1944	H	25	3
48	CPL	Harris	Henry J.	PA	320th VLA	37	6/6/1944	I	16	21
49	PFC	Baltimore	Elihue E.	IN	963 QM SVC CO	27	4/28/1945	B	3	20
50	PVT	Carter	William	MI	3862 QM TRK CO	38	11/8/1944	A	9	23
51	PVT	Suber	Albert	MI	1323 ENGR SVC REGT	30	8/21/1944	G	5	23
52	PFC	Thompson	Luther J.	MI	521 PORT BN	UNK	4/7/1945	B	23	11
53	PVT	Gambles	Victor H	MO	365 PORT BN	31	4/4/1945	D	8	40

NO.	RANK	LAST	FIRST, MI	*STATE	UNIT	EST. AGE	DATE OF DEATH (M/DD/YYYY)	PLOT	ROW	GRAVE NO.
54	PFC	Smith	Charles C.	MO	4371 QM BAKERY CO	32	1/1/1945	B	2	28
55	PVT	Willis	J.S.	MO	450 GAS SUP CO	22	12/27/1944	D	27	40
56	PFC	Allen	Joseph	MS	244 QM BN	25	2/3/1945	E	22	42
57	PFC	Carothers	Earlie	MS	364 ENG GEN SV REGT	25	7/7/1944	F	14	22
58	PVT	Fountain	Sidney B.	MS	3135 QM SVC CO	22	6/3/1945	A	3	31
59	TEC5	Gray	William	MS	3393 QM TRK CO	20	7/28/1944	C	9	16
60	CPL	Long	James A.	MS	4090 QM SVC CO	27	6/10/1944	A	18	37
61	T5	Roby	Mack	MS	514 PORT BN	22	8/15/1944	I	27	24
63	T5	Saddler	Orin D.	MS	485 PORT BN	26	5/21/1945	B	1	23
64	T5	Thompson	Edward J.	MS	388 ENGR GEN SVC REGT	28	3/6/1945	D	13	41
65	MS	Gabriel	Earlie J.	NC	USMM	35	12/14/1944	B	1	24
66	PVT	Goode	Jessie	NC	3556th QM TRK CO	22	11/7/1945	J	24	26
67	PFC	Goodman	Levester	NC	3193rd QM SV CO	24	9/16/1944	B	8	7
68	T5	Hammonds	Thomas	NC	392 ENGR GEN SVC REGT	31	11/20/1944	B	20	11
69	PFC	Horton	Horace	NC	499 PORT BN	30	6/3/1945	C	10	23
70	PFC	Kelly	Leroy	NC	516 PORT BN	24	11/24/1945	A	4	19
71	PFC	McLean	James M.	NC	320th VLA	22	7/17/1944	E	5	6
72	1SG	Peele	Willis G.	NC	4454 QM SVC CO	29	3/21/1945	D	1	24
73	PVT	Platt	William A.	NC	388 ENGR GEN SVC REGT	30	2/7/1945	B	15	13

NO.	RANK	LAST	FIRST, MI	*STATE	UNIT	EST. AGE	DATE OF DEATH (M/DD/YYYY)	PLOT	ROW	GRAVE NO.
74	PVT	Tucker	James	NC	973 QM SVC CO	25	7/19/1945	D	17	33
75	T4	Anderson	Florzell	NJ	3116 QM SVC CO	23	1/19/1945	F	7	16
76	CPL	Brown	Henry	NJ	999 FA BN	27	7/18/1944	C	13	21
77	CPL	Headd	Joseph N.	NJ	3912 QM TRK CO		8/16/1944	J	26	28
78	T5	Jenkins	Albert	NJ	485 PORT BN		9/30/1944	E	15	35
79	PVT	Webster	David	NJ	3871 QM TRK CO	39	6/15/1945	A	8	31
80	PVT	Campbell	Vernon F.	NY	237 QM SAL CO	24	7/29/1944	J	6	35
81	PFC	Campbell	William L	NY	435 ENG DUMP TRK CO	34	8/4/1945	D	27	34
82	STM2C	Copeland	Clarence N.	NY	USNR		6/8/1944	I	16	25
83	PVT	Dorset	Cecil	NY	815 TRK CO	34	8/24/1944	C	23	42
84	CPL	Easter	Randolph	NY	3867 QM TRK CO	33	1/21/1945	B	14	23
85	PFC	Foster	Harold	NY	816 TRK CO	28	8/12/1944	E	6	3
86	PFC	Mayo	Vincent A.	NY	4059 QM SVC CO	26	8/26/1945	D	26	26
87	PFC	Ryerson	William L.	NY	364 ENG REGT	24	7/7/1944	G	8	38
88	T5	Griggs	Tom	OH	3682 WM TRK CO		9/24/1944	H	8	17
89	PVT	Jackson	George	OH	624 PORT CO	28	1/23/1945	J	25	28
90	PVT	Showes	John H.	OH	954 QM SVC CO	39	11/19/1944	G	7	19
91	T5	Hill	Roy	OK	483 PORT BN	22	2/3/1945	F	16	44

NO.	RANK	LAST	FIRST, MI	*STATE	UNIT	EST. AGE	DATE OF DEATH (M/DD/YYYY)	PLOT	ROW	GRAVE NO.
92	T5	Potts	Ernest R.	OK	3497 QM TRK CO	24	3/11/1945	B	5	24
93	CPL	Bell	Roy	PA	237 QM SALV CO	20	7/29/1944	G	13	12
94	PVT	Branson Jr.	Samuel	PA	4190 QM SVC SO	23	7/12/1944	B	11	32
95	PFC	Davis Jr	William E	PA	515 PORT BN	20	5/26/1945	A	20	41
96	T4	Dennis	Dawson E	PA	658 PORT CO	31	9/20/1945	B	11	33
97	MSGT	Greene	Zylphus L.	PA	237 QM SALV CO	27	7/29/1944	B	8	44
98	1SG	Jefferson	Gelain J	PA	4335 QM SV CO	22	3/14/1945	B	20	35
99	PVT	Jeffries	James H.	PA	509th PORT BN	20	4/23/1945	A	21	40
100	CPL	Martin	Lloyd A.	PA	236 QM BN	32	11/5/1944	D	13	18
101	PFC	Parker	George M.	PA	1323 ENGR SVC REGT	31	9/9/1944	C	1	16
102	PVT	Phillips	John D.	PA	502 PORT BN	21	5/29/1945	D	4	40
103	PVT	Pickens	James H.	PA	511 PORT BN	21	4/19/1945	G	7	16
104	T5	Weston	Willie R.	PA	663 QM TRK CO	20	9/18/1944	D	23	45
105	PVT	Anderson Jr.	Issac R.	SC	4148 QM SVC CO	20	12/31/1944	E	14	15
106	PVT	Blair	James M.	SC	4090 QM SVC CO	22	6/10/1944	A	1	37
107	SGT	Boyd	Bennie	SC	516 PORT BN	24	5/31/1945	B	13	14
108	PVT	Fair	Leo	SC	4083 QM SV CO	21	7/12/1944	I	27	21
109	T5	Graham	Ross	SC	3138 QM SVC CO	23	8/29/1944	F	23	39
110	T5	Nathaniel	Samuel G.	SC	3132 QM SVC CO	35	3/5/1945	D	23	41

NO.	RANK	LAST	FIRST, MI	*STATE	UNIT	EST. AGE	DATE OF DEATH (M/DD/YYYY)	PLOT	ROW	GRAVE NO.
111	PFC	Smith	Frank W.	SC	1697 ENGR COMBAT BN	25	7/16/1945	B	20	6
112	PVT	Bolton	E.L.	TN	3453 QM TRK CO	24	3/15/1945	B	19	8
113	MSG	Kersh	James W.	TN	364 ENG SVC REGT	30	8/11/1944	D	21	19
114	T4	Middlebrook	Oscar L.	TN	513 PORT BN	20	4/7/1945	B	20	25
115	PVT	Nash	Chester	TN	505 PORT BN	26	5/8/1945	A	19	3
116	SSG	Perry	Hiawatha L. E.	TN	652 QM TRK CO	33	10/19/1944	A	18	21
117	PFC	Woods	Clifford	TN	4057 QM SVC CO	23	12/28/1944	B	9	39
118	T5	Austin	Alvin T.	TX	549 ENG L PON CO	23	12/9/1945	A	3	39
119	T4	Davis	Oscar W.	TX	815 TRK CO	UNK	6/10/1944	D	11	25
120	T5	Glenn	Frank	TX	1310 ENGR BN	30	5/22/1945	B	6	34
121	SGT	Hansboro	Alex	TX	434 PORT CO	22	1/22/1945	D	10	34
122	PVT	Lewis	Nollie G.	TX	317 QM SVC CO	34	3/7/1945	A	6	23
123	T5	Richardson	James G.	TX	237 QM SALV CO	34	8/29/1944	H	5	19
125	PVT	Roberta	Hawkins	TX	3869 QM TRK CO	23	4/9/1945	D	1	26
125	PFC	Anderson	Howard	VA	3878 QM GAS SPT CO	32	7/6/1944	B	6	43
126	T5	Batts	Daniel	VA	485 PORT BN	37	4/20/1945	A	4	31
127	PVT	Beadle	William E	VA	511 PORT BN	20	2/29/1945	J	8	19
128	T5	Ellis	Howard F.	VA	237 QM SALV CO	38	7/29/1945	E	13	14
129	PVT	Johnson	William H.	VA	306 RHD CO	22	9/7/1944	D	28	8

NO.	RANK	LAST	FIRST, MI	*STATE	UNIT	EST. AGE	DATE OF DEATH (M/DD/YYYY)	PLOT	ROW	GRAVE NO.
130	T5	Jones	John T.	VA	502 PORT BN	21	9/19/1944	H	22	24
131	PFC	Moore	Raymond T.	VA	1310 ENG SVC REGT	20	9/21/1944	E	15	26
132	PVT	Myers	James E.	VA	3962 QM TRK CO	26	12/16/1944	D	11	18
133	T5	Self	Robert J.	VA	237 QM SALV CO	29	7/29/1944	E	9	14
134	CPL	Stith	Brooks	VA	320th VLA	22	6/6/1944	I	3	35
135	T5	Sykes	Rufus	VA	549 ENG L PON CO	25	7/16/1945	J	14	28
136	PFC	Toye	Vandyke S.	VA	388 ENGR GEN SVC REGT	26	6/10/1945	B	13	18
137	PVT	Collins Jr.	Andrews	WI	237 QM SAL CO	19	6/6/1944	J	12	35
138	2LT	May	Eddie	WI	1349 ENGR GEN SVC REGT	26	5/26/1945	B	9	23
Wall of the Missing										
1	PFC	Homer	Mack	GA	364 ENGR SVC REGT	20	7/7/1944			
2	T5	Wyatt	Daniel	LA	364 ENGR SVC REGT	39	7/7/1944			
3	PFC	Haggins	Sylvester D.	NY	364 ENG SVC REGT	33	7/7/1944			
4	T5	Boone	Reese G.	NC	514 PORT BN	19	8/15/1944			
5	TSGT	Heads	Raymond	TX	3688 QM TRK CO.	31	8/3/1945			

*State: State as listed on headstone, enlistment record, or Congressional Record.

Sources: Normandy American Cemetery, American Battlefield Monuments Commission (ABMC), https://www.abmc.gov/normandy; Congressional Record, vol. 163, no. 28 (February 16, 2017) [House] Pages H1251–H1255; https://www.govinfo.gov/content/pkg/CREC-2017-02-16/html/CREC-2017-02-16-pt1-PgH1251-3.htm; Find a Grave—Millions of Cemetery Records, https://www.findagrave.com/.

PUBLIC LAW 117–97 (03/14/2022) "SIX TRIPLE EIGHT" CONGRESSIONAL GOLD MEDAL ACT OF 2021

[117th Congress Public Law 97]

[From the US Government Publishing Office]

Public Law 117–97

117th Congress

An Act

To award a Congressional Gold Medal to the members of the Women's Army

Corps who were assigned to the 6888th Central Postal Directory Battalion, known as the "Six Triple Eight".

Be it enacted by the Senate and House of Representatives of the United States of America in Congress assembled,

SECTION 1. SHORT TITLE.

This Act may be cited as the "'Six Triple Eight' Congressional Gold Medal Act of 2021".

SEC. 2. FINDINGS.

Congress finds the following:

(1) On July 1, 1943, President Franklin D. Roosevelt signed into law legislation that established the Women's Army Corps (referred to in this

section as the "WAC") as a component in the Army. The WAC was converted from the Women's Army Auxiliary Corps (referred to in this
section as the "WAAC"), which had been created in 1942 without official
military status. First Lady Eleanor Roosevelt and Mary McLeod Bethune,
the founder of the National Council of Negro Women, advocated for the
admittance of African-American women into the newly formed WAC to
serve as officers and enlisted personnel.

(2) Dubbed "10 percenters", the recruitment of African-American
women to the WAAC was limited to 10 percent of the population of the
WAAC to match the proportion of African-Americans in the national
population. Despite an Executive Order issued by President Franklin D.
Roosevelt in 1941 banning racial discrimination in civilian defense indus-
tries, the Armed Forces remained segregated. Enlisted women served
in segregated units, participated in segregated training, lived in separate quarters, ate at separate tables in mess halls, and used segregated
recreational facilities. Officers received their officer candidate training
in integrated units but lived under segregated conditions. Specialist
and technical training schools were integrated in 1943. During World
War II, a total of 6,520 African-American women served in the WAAC
and the WAC.

(3) After several units of White women were sent to serve in the European Theater of Operations (referred to in this section as the "ETO")
during World War II, African-American organizations advocated for
the War Department to extend the opportunity to serve overseas to
African-American WAC units.

(4) In November 1944, the War Department approved sending African-
American women to serve in Europe. A battalion of all African-American
women drawn from the WAC, the Army Service Forces, and the Army
Air Forces was created and designated as the 6888th Central Postal
Directory Battalion (referred to in this section as the "6888th"), which
was nicknamed the "Six Triple Eight".

(5) Army officials reported a shortage of qualified postal officers within
the ETO, which resulted in a backlog of undelivered mail. As Allied forces
drove across Europe, the ever-changing locations of servicemembers
hampered the delivery of mail to those servicemembers. Because

7,000,000 civilians and military personnel from the United States served in the ETO, many of those individuals had identical names. For example, 7,500 such individuals were named Robert Smith. One general predicted that the backlog in Birmingham, England, would take 6 months to process and the lack of reliable mail service was hurting morale.

(6) In February 1945, the 6888th arrived in Birmingham. Upon their arrival, the 6888th found warehouses filled with millions of pieces of mail intended for members of the Armed Forces, United States Government personnel, and Red Cross workers serving in the ETO.

(7) The 6888th created effective processes and filing systems to track individual servicemembers, organize "undeliverable" mail, determine the intended recipient for insufficiently addressed mail, and handle mail addressed to servicemembers who had died. Adhering to their motto of "No mail, low morale", the women processed an average of 65,000 pieces of mail per shift and cleared the 6-month backlog of mail within 3 months.

(8) The 6888th traveled to Rouen, France, in May 1945 and worked through a separate backlog of undelivered mail dating back as far as 3 years.

(9) At the completion of their mission, the unit returned to the United States. The 6888th was discontinued on March 9, 1946, at Camp Kilmer, New Jersey.

(10) The accomplishments of the 6888th in Europe encouraged the General Board, United States Forces, European Theater of Operations to adopt the following premise in their study of the WAC issued in December 1945: "[T]he national security program is the joint responsibility of all Americans irrespective of color or sex" and "the continued use of colored, along with White, female military personnel is required in such strength as is proportionately appropriate to the relative population distribution between colored and white races".

(11) With the exception of smaller units of African-American nurses who served in Africa, Australia, and England, the 6888th was the only African-American Women's Army Corps unit to serve overseas during World War II.

(12) The members of the "Six Triple Eight" received the European African Middle Eastern Campaign Medal, the Women's Army Corps Service Medal, and the World War II Victory Medal for their service.

(13) In 2019, the Army awarded the 6888th the Meritorious Unit Commendation.

SEC. 3. CONGRESSIONAL GOLD MEDAL.

(a) Award Authorized.—The Speaker of the House of Representatives and the President pro tempore of the Senate shall make appropriate arrangements for the award, on behalf of Congress, of a single gold medal of appropriate design in honor of the women of the 6888th Central Postal Directory Battalion (commonly known as the "Six Triple Eight") in recognition of—

(1) the pioneering military service of those women;

(2) the devotion to duty of those women; and

(3) the contributions made by those women to increase the morale of all United States personnel stationed in the European Theater of Operations during World War II.

(b) Design and Striking.—For the purposes of the award described in subsection (a), the Secretary of the Treasury (referred to in this Act as the "Secretary") shall strike the Gold Medal with suitable emblems, devices, and inscriptions, to be determined by the Secretary.

(c) Smithsonian Institution.—

(1) In general.—After the award of the gold medal under subsection (a), the medal shall be given to the Smithsonian Institution, where the medal shall be available for display, as appropriate, and made available for research.

(2) Sense of Congress.—It is the sense of Congress that the Smithsonian Institution should make the gold medal received under paragraph (1) available elsewhere, particularly at—

(A) appropriate locations associated with the 6888th Central Postal Directory Battalion;

(B) the Women in Military Service for America Memorial;

(C) the United States Army Women's Museum;

(D) the National World War II Museum and Memorial;

(E) the National Museum of the United States Army; and

(F) any other location determined appropriate by the Smithsonian Institution.

SEC. 4. DUPLICATE MEDALS.

Under such regulations as the Secretary may prescribe, the Secretary may strike and sell duplicates in bronze of the gold medal struck under section 3 at a price sufficient to cover the costs of the medals, including labor, materials, dies, use of machinery, and overhead expenses.

SEC. 5. NATIONAL MEDALS.

(a) National Medals.—Medals struck under this Act are national medals for purposes of chapter 51 of title 31, United States Code.

(b) Numismatic Items.—For purposes of section 5134 of title 31, United States Code, all medals struck under this Act shall be considered to be numismatic items.

SEC. 6. AUTHORITY TO USE FUND AMOUNTS; PROCEEDS OF SALE.

(a) Authority To Use Fund Amounts.—There is authorized to be charged against the United States Mint Public Enterprise Fund such amounts as may be necessary to pay for the costs of the medals struck under this Act.

(b) Proceeds of Sale.—Amounts received from the sale of duplicate bronze medals authorized under section 4 shall be deposited into the United States Mint Public Enterprise Fund.

Approved March 14, 2022.

LEGISLATIVE HISTORY—S. 321:

———————————

CONGRESSIONAL RECORD:

Vol. 167 (2021):

Apr. 29, considered and passed Senate.

Vol. 168 (2022):

Feb. 28, considered and passed House.

APPENDIX **6**

6888TH RECOGNITIONS AND HONORS SINCE 2018 (HIGHLIGHTS)

2018

February 13   The Congressional Black Caucus Foundation presents the Avoice award to one-hundred-year-old 6888th veteran Millie Dunn Veasey, along with Gen. Colin Powell. Ms. Veasey dies in March 2018.

October 4   Congress unanimously passes Senate Resolution 412, honoring the Six Triple Eight.

November 30   The 9th and 10th Calvary (Horse) 6888th Monument Committee dedicates a monument to the Six Triple Eight. Along with Senator Moran, five of the unit's veterans attend.

2019

February 20   The secretary of the Army awards the 6888th the Meritorious Unit Commendation (MUC), the unit's only performance award.

March 26–28   The US Embassy (London) premieres the *Six Triple Eight* documentary at the embassy and consulates via teleconference. On March 28, the *Six Triple Eight* documentary premieres at the Women in Military Service for America Memorial (WIMSA). On behalf of Senator Moran, Lt. Gen. Nadja West presents the MUC to two Six Triple Eight veterans and family members of deceased veterans at the WIMSA documentary screening.

May 13–17   US embassy (London) sponsors *Six Triple Eight* documentary screenings and press junket throughout the United Kingdom with production team members, and the US ambassador dedicates a 6888th blue plaque at the King Edwards School, where the women were stationed. The junket commemorates the 1981 6888th reunion with the lord mayor of Birmingham and supported the D-Day seventy-fifth anniversary activities. Three 6888th veterans participate in the National Memorial Day Parade, Washington, DC.

October 26   The American Veterans Center honors the Six Triple Eight with the Audie Murphy Award at its annual conference in Washington, DC.

2020

December 10   S. 633, "Six Triple Eight" Congressional Gold Medal Act of 2020 passes the Senate.

2021

March 23   Congressman Brian Higgins, District 14, New York, introduces legislation to rename the Buffalo, New York, Post Office after 6888th veteran Ms. Indiana Hunt-Martin.

April 29   S. 321, "Six Triple Eight" Congressional Gold Medal Act passes the Senate.

November 10   6888th veteran Ms. Crescencia Garcia honored at Carnegie Hall during its Veterans Day Celebration during John Monsky's *Eyes of the World* concert.

December 13   The 6888th receives the Citizens Patriot Award from the Reserve Forces Policy Board Fellows Society.

2022

February 28	H.R. 1012, "Six Triple Eight" Congressional Gold Medal Act passes 422–0.
March 3	Actor Blair Underwood announces a Broadway-bound musical about the 6888th. Speaker of the House Nancy Pelosi hosts the Congressional Gold Medal signing ceremony in her office for 6888th families.
March 14	President Biden signs the "Six Triple Eight" Congressional Gold Medal Act into Public Law 117–97.
April–June	"Six Triple Eight" Congressional Gold Medal events in the five 6888th veterans' communities (signed copy presented).
	US Postal Service notifies the Army Women's Foundation of a Charity Adams postage stamp proposal under review.
	Army Women's Foundation establishes the "Six Triple Eight" Legacy Scholarship
	May Naming commission recommends Fort Lee be renamed Fort Gregg-Adams after Lt. Gen. Arthur S. Gregg and Lt. Col. Charity Adams.
June 4	6888th veteran Ms. Crescencia Garcia and families honored at Kennedy Center during John Monsky's *Eyes of the World* immersive concert.
June 15	Six Triple Eight Day, Military Women's Memorial, Arlington, Virginia.
December	Netflix announces a movie planned about the 6888th.

2023

April 27	Fort Lee, Virginia, is rededicated as Fort Gregg-Adams after Retired US Army Quartermaster General Lt. Gen. Arthur Gregg and Lt. Col. Charity Adams.
May 3	Gov. Wes Moore, Maryland, signs HB0370 proclaiming March 9 as 6888th Day.
June 20–30	Author leads 6888th descendants' tour to Europe to retrace the 6888th's journey (hosted by Steven Ambrose Tours).

2024

| April 26 | Army Women's Museum 6888th exhibit opens, Fort Gregg-Adams |

2025

| January 4 | President Biden signs H.R. 9580 into Public Law 118-266 to designate the facility of the US Postal Service located at 2777 Brentwood Road in Raleigh, North Carolina, as the "Millie Dunn Veasey Post Office." |
| TBD | Congressional Gold Medal Presentation at the Capitol |

NOTES

INTRODUCTION

1. "40 Months since the Jan. 6 Attack on the Capitol," Department of Justice, United States Attorney's Office, District of Columbia, https://www.justice .gov/usao-dc/39-months-since-the-jan-6-attack-on-the-capitol.
2. "Pelosi Appoints First Black House Sergeant-at-Arms, William J. Walker," CNN Politics, March 26, 2021, https://www.cnn.com/2021/03/26/politics /nancy-pelosi-sergeant-at-arms-pick-william-walker/index.html.
3. Ryan J. Reilly and Danier Barnes, "Capitol Officer Harry Dunn Testifies Oath Keepers Weren't Helping Him on Jan. 6," NBC News, October 31, 2022, https://www.nbcnews.com/politics/justice-department/capitol-officer -harry-dunn-testifies-oath-keepers-werent-helping-jan-6-rcna53924.
4. Retired US Army Sgt. 1st Class Willie R. Cummings, Enlistment records 1946–72.
5. Nigel Thompson, "Puerto Rico's Harlem Hellfighters," The United States World War I Centennial Commission, https://www.worldwar1centennial.org /index.php/communicate/press-media/wwi-centennial-news/5923-puerto -rico-s-harlem-hellfighters.html.
6. Susan Ellis, "V.I. Pilots Helped Make Aviation History during World War II," The St. Thomas Source, March 3, 2021, https://stthomassource.com/content /2021/03/03/v-i-pilots-helped-make-aviation-history-during-world-war-ii/.
7. Bryon Greenwald, "Absent from the Front: What the Case of the Missing World War II Black Combat Soldier Can Teach Us about Diversity and Inclusion," National Defense University, *Joint Force Quarterly* 111 (October 2023), https://ndupress.ndu.edu/JFQ/Joint-Force-Quarterly-111/Article/Article /3571057/absent-from-the-front-what-the-case-of-the-missing-world-war-ii -black-combat-so/.

8. "Los Veteranos—Latinos in WWII," National World War II Museum, https://www.nationalww2museum.org/sites/default/files/201707/los-veteranos-fact-sheet.pdf.

9. Society and the military used the terms "Negro" or "colored" to refer to African Americans during World War II and immediately afterward. Throughout my autobiography, I use the terms "Black" and "African American" interchangeably, depending on the context.

10. "African Americans Fought for Freedom at Home and Abroad during World War II," February 1, 2020, National WWII Museum, New Orleans, https://www.nationalww2museum.org/war/articles/african-americans-fought-freedom-home-and-abroad-during-world-war-ii.

11. Barbara Maranzani, "The Unlikely Friendship of Eleanor Roosevelt and Mary McLeod Bethune," January 29, 2021, https://www.biography.com/news/eleanor-roosevelt-mary-mcleod-bethune-friendship.

12. Katherine Schaeffer, "The Changing Face of America's Veteran Population, April 4, 2021," Pew Research, https://www.pewresearch.org/short-reads/2023/11/08/the-changing-face-of-americas-veteran-population/.

13. "Percentage of U.S. Population Who Are Veterans in 2021, by Age and Gender," Statista, https://www.statista.com/statistics/250366/percentage-of-us-population-who-are-veterans/.

14. The Rocks, Inc., https://www.rocksinc.org/, copyright 2023.

15. Buffalo Soldier Monument, Fort Leavenworth, KS, https://home.army.mil/leavenworth/index.php/about/visitor-information/attractions/buffalo-soldier-commemorative-area.

16. Judith A. Bellafaire, "The Women's Army Corps: A Commemoration of World War II Service," CMH Publication 7215, https://history.army.mil/brochures/wac/wac.htm.

1. THEM "COTTON PICKING" WARS

1. Brent Staples, "Confederate Tributes Are Losing Their Patron Saint," *New York Times,* April 27, 2023, https://www.nytimes.com/2023/04/27/opinion/fort-lee-renaming.html.

2. "Robert E. Lee," Biographies, The Civil War in America, Library of Congress, https://loc.gov/exhibits/civil-war-in-america/biographies/robert-e-lee.html.

3. Steven Baker, "Fort Lee to Be Redesignated as Fort Gregg-Adams," *Army,* March 23, 2023, https://www.army.mil/article/265098/fort_lee_to_be_redesignated_as_fort_gregg_adams.

4. "Naming of U.S. Army Posts," U.S. Army Center of Military History, https://history.army.mil/faq/naming-of-us-army-posts.htm.

5. David Vergun, "Naming Commission Chair Details Progress, Way Ahead," May 21, 2021, US Department of Defense, https://www.defense.gov/News/News-Stories/Article/Article/2627802/naming-commission-chair-details-progress-way-ahead/.

6. Jim Garamone, "DOD Begins Implementing Naming Commission Recommendations," January 5, 2023, US Department of Defense, https://www.defense.gov/News/News-Stories/Article/Article/3260434/dod-begins-implementing-naming-commission-recommendations/.

7. T. Anthony Bell, USAG Fort Lee Public Affairs Office, "Celebrating the Career of Retired Lt. Gen. Arthur J. Gregg," February 14, 2023, US Army, https://www.army.mil/article/263852/celebrating_the_career_of_retired_lt_gen_arthur_j_gregg.

8. "On This Day: Sonny Liston Hammers Floyd Patterson to Win World Heavyweight Title," *Boxing News,* September 25, 2019, https://www.boxingnewsonline.net/on-this-day-sonny-liston-hammers-floyd-patterson-to-win-world-heavyweight-title/.

2. HIPPIE MURDERERS AND STRAWBERRY MILKSHAKES

1. Drew Brooks, "Fort Bragg's JFK Special Warfare Center Honors 12 Veterans, 3 Active-Duty Soldiers," *Fayetteville Observer,* May 29, 2015, https://www.fayobserver.com/story/news/military/2015/05/29/fort-bragg-s-jfk-special/22244004007/.

2. Carrie Cutchens, Special Warfare Museum (https://specialwarfaremuseum.org/), phone conversation with author, January 25, 2023: On May 29, 1965 Senator Robert Kennedy visited Fort Bragg, North Carolina, to dedicate Kennedy Hall of Heroes, JFK Special Operations Center for Special Forces.

3. Colonel Brendan J. O'Shea, "Operation Power Pack—U.S. Military Intervention in the Dominican Republic," US Army, https://www.army.mil/article/37660/operation_power_pack_u_s_military_intervention_in_the_dominican_republic.

4. Harry McKown, "January 1716: North Carolina 'Blue Laws,'" January 1, 2010, NC Miscellany, UNC University Libraries, https://blogs.lib.unc.edu/ncm/2010/01/01/this_month_jan_1716/.

5. Shane Hall, "Who Was Arabella Kennedy?," *Irish Central,* October 22, 2022, https://www.irishcentral.com/roots/history/who-was-arabella-kennedy.

6. "Vietnam War U.S. Military Fatal Casualty Statistics," National Archives, last updated August 23, 2022, https://www.archives.gov/research/military /vietnam-war/casualty-statistics.

7. Paul Wolverton, "Jeffrey MacDonald, NC 'Fatal Vision' Killer, Drops Bid for Freedom in Wife and Children's Deaths," *Fayetteville Observer,* September 17, 2021, https://www.fayobserver.com/story/news/2021/09/17/nc-fatal -vision-killer-jeffery-macdonald-drops-request-freed/8379040002/.

8. Steve Devane, "Ruby Murchison's Influence as an Educator Reached beyond Fayetteville," *Fayetteville Observer,* updated January 17, 2021, https://www.fayobserver.com/story/news/2021/01/15/educator-ruby -murchison-influenced-two-cumberland-county-commissioners /6646910002/.

9. Springbreak Watches, "SPGBK Watches Honors E. E. Smith Educators and Staff with Free Watches," https://www.springbreakwatches.com/pages /eesmithwatchdonation.

10. "E. E. Smith (Fayetteville, NC) Alumni Pro Stats," Pro Football Reference, https://www.pro-football-reference.com/schools/high_schools.cgi?id= 93ba391f.

11. Jennifer Brookland, "Called to Serve," *Our State,* April 27, 2021, https://www .ourstate.com/called-to-serve/.

12. "Marva Collins," The HistoryMakers: The Digital Repository for the Black Experience, February 2, 2000, https://www.thehistorymakers.org /biography/marva-collins-40.

13. Retired US Army Sgt. 1st Class Willie R. Cummings, Enlistment records 1946–1972.

14. Town of Boone, North Carolina, "Historical Population Information," http:// www.townofboone.net/163/Historical-Population-Information.

15. Boone, North Carolina, Data, USA, https://datausa.io/profile/geo/boone-nc.

16. Chuck McShane, "City Portrait: Fayetteville," *Our State,* February 18, 2016, https://www.ourstate.com/city-portrait-fayetteville/.

3. FROM A STUDENT ON THE MOUNTAINTOP TO A SOLDIER IN LOWER ALABAMA

1. Factbook Archives, Appalachian State University, Page II4, 1974–75, https:// analytics.appstate.edu/info_factbook_archives.

2. Rebecca Onion, "The Snake-Eaters and the Yards," *Slate,* November 27, 2013, https://slate.com/news-and-politics/2013/11/the-green-berets-and

-the-montagnards-how-an-indigenous-tribe-won-the-admiration-of-green
-berets-and-lost-everything.html.

3. Appalachian State University Mountaineers, https://appstatesports.com/.

4. "Appalachian State Demographics & Diversity Report," College Factual, https://www.collegefactual.com/colleges/appalachian-state-university /student-life/diversity/.

5. Alabama Heritage, "The WAC Is a Soldier Too," August 23, 2016, Alabama and the Women's Army Corps, https://www.alabamaheritage.com/from-the -vault/the-wac-is-a-soldier-too-alabama-and-the-womens-army-corps.

6. "Populations Characteristics," series P-20, no. 335, April 1979, US Bureau of the Census, US Department of Commerce, https://www.census.gov/content /dam/Census/library/publications/1979/demo/p20-335.pdf.

7. Jan Todd, "US Army Women's Foundation Honors Edna Cummings—App State Alumna and Military Trailblazer," *Appalachian Today,* March 20, 2020, https://today.appstate.edu/2020/03/20/cummings.

8. Andy Staples, "The Greatest Upset of Them All," *Sports Illustrated,* https:// www.si.com/longform/appstate/index.html.

9. Angelique S. Chengelis, "Sept. 1, 2007: The Day the Big House Shuddered," *Detroit News,* August 28, 2014, https://www.detroitnews.com/story/sports /college/university-michigan/2014/08/28/sept-1-2007-the-day-the-big-house -shuddered/14723113/.

10. "Edna W. Cummings: Maryland Ambassador," Army Reserve, https://www .usar.army.mil/Featured/Ambassador-Program/Find-an-Ambassador /Article-View/Article/2575850/edna-w-cummings/.

11. "History of the WAC and Army Women," Women's Army Corps Veterans' As- sociation–Army Women United (WACVA–AWU), https://www.armywomen .org/wacHistory.shtml.

12. Chapter 6, "Supply and Field Services," GlobalSecurity.org, https://www .globalsecurity.org/military/library/policy/army/fm/100-16/appe.pdf.

13. Justice Wright, "More Than 'The Peanut Man,'" February 2, 2021, US De- partment of Agriculture, https://www.usda.gov/media/blog/2014/02/25 /more-peanut-man#:~:text=Dr.,National%20Archives%20and%20Records %20Administration.

14. "#VeteranOfTheDay Army Veteran Marcella Hayes Ng," *VA News,* February 9, 2022, https://news.va.gov/98854/veteranoftheday-army-veteran-marcella -hayes-ng/.

15. "Col. Christine Knighton," The HistoryMakers: The Digital Repository for the Black Experience, July 26, 2013, https://www.thehistorymakers.org /biography/col-christine-knighton.

4. THE LAND OF THE MORNING CALM

1. Martin Limon, "Let's Not Forget U.S. Complicity in Korean Sex Trade," *Korea Times,* October 10, 2022.
2. Katarzyna Szpargala, "The U.S. Troops and Military Prostitution in South Korea," *Conflict, Justice, Decolonization: Critical Studies of Inter-Asian Societies* (2020), https://cjdproject.web.nycu.edu.tw/wp-content/uploads/sites/167/2020/12/Szpargala_2020_The-U.S.-Troops-and-Military-Prostitution-in-South-Korea.pdf.
3. "Around the World; South Korea Lifts Its 36-Year-Old Curfew," *New York Times,* January 6, 1982, https://www.nytimes.com/1982/01/06/world/around-the-world-south-korea-lifts-its-36-year-old-curfew.html.
4. Jamie Christopher Morris, "The Black Experience in Postwar Germany," Honors Scholar Theses, University of Connecticut Library, May 6, 2012, p. 1, https://opencommons.uconn.edu/cgi/viewcontent.cgi?referer=https://www.google.com/&httpsredir=1&article=1235&context=srhonors_theses.
5. "Uijeongbu, Location of M*A*S*H," New Zealand History, https://nzhistory.govt.nz/media/photo/uijeongbu-home-mash.
6. "Korean War," Dwight D. Eisenhower Presidential Library, https://www.eisenhowerlibrary.gov/research/online-documents/korean-war.
7. "Shopping with a Ration Control Card," USAG–Yongsan Public Affairs, June 26, 2008, https://www.army.mil/article/10406/shopping_with_a_ration_control_card.
8. Toby Luckhurst, "The DMZ 'Gardening Job' That Almost Sparked a War," BBC, August 21, 2019, https://www.bbc.com/news/world-asia-49394758.
9. "1st Theater Sustainment Command," US Army, https://www.1tsc.army.mil/About/History/.
10. "Capt. Cummings," *V.M.I. Cadet,* VMI Archives Digital Collections, Virginia Military Institute, February 18, 1983, http://digitalcollections.vmi.edu/digital/collection/p15821coll8/id/17531.

5. MELTED BANANA POPSICLE

1. Oak Grove Cemetery, Lexington, VA, https://lexingtonvirginia.com/directory/attractions/oak-grove-cemetery.
2. "Army to Consider Changes to Uniform for Expecting, New Mothers," US Army, November 13, 2020, https://www.army.mil/article/240816/army_to_consider_changes_to_uniform_for_expecting_new_mothers.

3. "Command and General Staff Officers' Course Summary," Combined Arms Center, US Army, https://usacac.army.mil/organizations/cace/cgsc/courses.

4. "Dante's Inferno | Summary, Characters & Analysis—Video & Lesson Transcript," Study.com, https://study.com/academy/lesson/dantes-inferno -summary-characters.html.

5. "Light-Chain Deposition Disease: Practice Essentials, Pathophysiology, Epidemiology," Medscape, updated January 31, 2023, https://emedicine .medscape.com/article/202585-overview.

6. Sidney Sheldon, *Windmills of the Gods* (London: HarperCollins, 1994).

7. Harold Kushner, *When Bad Things Happen to Good People* (New York: Schocken, 1981).

8. Patricia Kime, "Troops Get New Bereavement Leave for Loss of Spouse or Child," March 31, 2023, https://www.military.com/daily-news/2023/03/30 /troops-get-new-bereavement-leave-loss-of-spouse-or-child.html.

6. BRINGING DOWN THE GAVEL

1. "Congress, Civilian Control of the Military, and Nonpartisanship," Congressional Research Service, updated June 11, 2020, https://crsreports.congress .gov/product/pdf/IF/IF11566.

2. "The Gulf War, 1991," Office of the Historian, Department of State, https:// history.state.gov/milestones/1989-1992/gulf-war.

3. Office of Army Reserve History, US Army Reserve, https://www.usar.army .mil/OurHistory/DesertShield-DesertStorm/.

4. "Sexual Trauma in the Military," A Train Education: Continuing Education for Health Care Professionals, https://www.atrainceu.com/content/4 -military-sexual-trauma.

5. "Operation Desert Storm," US Army Center of Military History, https:// history.army.mil/html/bookshelves/resmat/desert-storm/index.html.

6. Retired US Marine Corps Reserve Col. W. Hays Parks, "Tailhook: What Happened, Why and What's to Be Learned," |*Proceedings* 120, no. 9. U.S. Naval Institute September 1994, https://www.usni.org/magazines/proceedings /1994/september/tailhook-what-happened-why-whats-be-learned.

7. Maureen Dowd, "Navy Defines Sexual Harassment with the Colors of Traffic Lights," *New York Times,* June 19, 1993, https://www.nytimes.com/1993/06/19 /us/navy-defines-sexual-harassment-with-the-colors-of-traffic-lights.html.

8. "Capital Traction Company Union Station—Exorcist Steps," National Park Service, https://www.nps.gov/places/capital-traction-company-union -station-exorcist-steps.htm.

9. MSCA is now Defense Support to Civil Authorities. See Department of Defense (DoD) Directive 3025.18, December 29, 2010, Incorporating Change 2 on March 19, 2018, p. 9; DoD Directive 3025.1, "Military Support to Civil Authorities (MSCA)," January 15, 1993 (hereby cancelled); and DoD Directive 3025.18, December 29, 2010, Incorporating Change 1 on March 19, 2018, https://www.esd.whs.mil/Portals/54/Documents/DD/issuances/dodd/302518p.pdf.

10. "Historic Timeline," National Counterterrorism Center, Office of the Director of National Intelligence https://www.dni.gov/nctc/timeline.html; "Eric Rudolph," Famous Cases and Criminals, History, Federal Bureau of Investigation, https://www.fbi.gov/history/famous-cases/eric-rudolph.

11. "Stafford Act," Federal Emergency Management Agency, Department of Homeland Security, https://www.fema.gov/disaster/stafford-act.

12. "Weapons of Mass Destruction," Department of Homeland Security, https://www.dhs.gov/topics/weapons-mass-destruction#:~:text=A%20weapon%20of%20mass%20destruction,these%20weapons%20to%20harm%20Americans.

13. Roger C. Schultz, Jay Steinmetz, Chuck Winn, Tim Madere, Dutch Thomas, Alicia Tate-Nadeau, Keith McCullough, and Bill McCoy, "Department of Defense Plan for Integrating National Guard and Reserve Component Support for Response to Attack Using Weapons of Mass Destruction," January 1998, Office of Justice Programs, US Department of Justice, https://www.ojp.gov/ncjrs/virtual-library/abstracts/department-defense-plan-integrating-national-gaurd-and-reserve.

14. Department of Defense, "Joint Pub 3–07: Joint Doctrine for Military Operations Other Than War," June 16, 1995, p. ix, https://www.bits.de/NRANEU/others/jp-doctrine/jp3_07.pdf.

15. "Statement of Robert J. Lieberman Deputy Inspector General Department of Defense to the Subcommittee on Emerging Threats and Capabilities Senate Armed Services Committee on National Guard Weapons of Mass Destruction—Civil Support Teams." May 2001, Office of the Inspector General, Department of Defense, https://media.defense.gov/2017/Apr/18/2001734112/-1/-1/1/01-113.PDF.

16. Megan Locke Simpson, "Fort Campbell Monument to Honor Black Paratroopers," August 29, 20014, https://www.army.mil/article/132860/fort_campbell_monument_to_honor_black_paratroopers.

17. US Department of Defense, "Unified Command Plan," April 2002, https://irp.fas.org/news/2002/04/dod041702.html.

18. US Department of Defense, *A Short History of United States Northern Command,* August 3, 2011, p. 5, https://www.northcom.mil/Portals/28/Documents/Supporting%20documents/Historical/NORTHCOM%20History.pdf.

7. A BLACK BEAN AND THE PARKWAY PATRIOT

1. "5 Lesser-Known Colorado Springs Mountains to Summit," Visit Colorado Springs, November 11, 2022, https://www.colorado.com/articles/5-lesser-known-colorado-springs-mountains-summit.
2. Meaghan Mobbs, "What You Think about Veterans Is Likely Wrong," January 24, 2018, https://www.psychologytoday.com/us/blog/the-debrief/201801/what-you-think-about-veterans-is-likely-wrong.
3. "Federal Acquisition Regulation" (FAR), US General Services Administration, last updated May 22, 2024, https://www.acquisition.gov/far/7.105.
4. Kathleen Fargey, "The 6888th Central Postal Directory Battalion (Women's Army Corps)," February 14, 2014, US Army Center of Military History, https://history.army.mil/html/topics/afam/6888thPBn/index.html.
5. "Buffalo Soldier Monument," Visit Leavenworth, Kansas, https://www.visitleavenworthks.com/search/site/Buffalo%20Soldier%20Monument?f%5B0%5D=im_field_microsite%3A291.

8. COLONEL "EDNA" MEETS MAJOR CHARITY "EDNA" ADAMS AND THE 6888TH

1. Women of the 6888th Central Postal Directory Battalion, https://www.womenofthe6888th.org/the-6888th-monument.
2. "All Who Want to Serve: Charity Adams Earl[e]y," February 5, 2016, George C. Marshall Foundation, https://www.marshallfoundation.org/articles-and-features/charity-adams-early/.
3. Jan Todd, "US Army Women's Foundation Honors Edna Cummings—App State Alumna and Military Trailblazer," *Appalachian Today,* March 20, 2020, https://today.appstate.edu/2020/03/20/cummings.
4. Charity Adams Earley, *One Woman's Army: A Black Officer Remembers the WAC* (College Station: Texas A&M University, 1995), 23.
5. Meritorious Unit Commendation, Department of the Army, February 20, 2019.
6. "23 Officers in 738 WACs to England as First All-Woman Army Postal Unit Afro-American," *Afro American,* February 24, 1945, 1.
7. "World War II in Europe," *National Geographic,* https://education.nationalgeographic.org/resource/world-war-ii-europe/.
8. Elaine M. Smith, Mary McLeod Bethune and the National Council of Negro Women, *Pursuing a True and Unfettered Democracy,* Historic Resource

Study (Alabama State University, for the Mary McLeod Bethune Council House, National Historic Site, National Park Service, 2003), 192.

9. "The 6888th Central Postal Directory Battalion," Mary McLeod Bethune Council House, National Historic Site, District of Columbia, National Park Service, https://www.nps.gov/mamc/the-6888th-central-postal-directory -battalion.htm.

10. "Interactive Timeline," Battle of the Bulge, World War II Military Situation Maps, Library of Congress, https://www.loc.gov/collections/world-war-ii -maps-military-situation-maps-from-1944-to-1945/articles-and-essays/the -battle-of-the-bulge/interactive-timeline/.

11. *The 6888th: Women Who Managed the Military Mail and Racism* (Elizabeth Barker Johnson interview), BBC Midlands, Birmingham, YouTube video, July 16, 2018, https://www.youtube.com/watch?v=yHnvzIZ9sAQ.

12. Martin Collins and Frances Collins, *Letters for Victory: History of the First Base Post Office in Sutton Coldfield, Warwickshire, during World War Two* (Studley, Warwickshire: Brewin, 1993), 33–34 and 137–38.

13. James William Theres and Retired US Army Col. Edna W. Cummings, "The Six Triple Eight: No Mail, Low Morale," February 10, 2021, https://www .nationalww2museum.org/war/articles/the-sixtripleeight-6888th-battalion.

14. Kathleen Fargey, "The 6888th Central Postal Directory Battalion," February 14, 2014, US Army Center of Military History, https://history.army.mil /html/topics/afam/6888thPBn/index.html.

15. Library of Congress, Research Guides, "6888th Central Postal Directory Battalion: A Guide to First-Person Narratives in the Veterans History Project," Research Guides, Library of Congress, https://guides.loc.gov/6888th-central -postal-directory-battalion.

16. "WACs Win Theatre Basketball Championship," *New Journal and Guide,* March 23, 1945.

17. Ollie Stewart, "Discharged WACs Working in Paris," *Afro American* (1893– 1988), December 29, 1945.

18. *Afro American,* "WACs Appear in US-Anglo Show," May 26, 1945.

19. Benjamin Brands, email message to author, July 31, 2023.

20. Scott Maucione, "Biden Signs Order Making Sexual Harassment a Punishable Offense in Military," Federal News Network, January 27, 2022, https:// federalnewsnetwork.com/defense-main/2022/01/biden-signs-order -making-sexual-harassment-a-punishable-offense-in-military/.

21. Ameer Rosic, "What Is Hashing? [Step-by-Step Guide—Under Hood of Block-chain]," May 4, 2020, https://blockgeeks.com/guides/what-is-hashing/.

22. "CBCF to Honor Gen. Colin Powell and African American Veterans during Avoice Heritage Celebration," February 2, 2018, Congressional Black Caucus

Foundation, https://www.cbcfinc.org/cbcf-to-honor-gen-colin-powell-and
-african-american-veterans-during-avoicc-heritage-celebration/.

23. "2 WAC's Get Labor Sentences," *Afro American,* April 1, 1944; "Fort Jackson
Wac Slapped for Drinking at Columbia Fountain," *Afro American,* December 22, 1945.

24. Sandra Bolzenius, "The 1945 Black Wac Strike at Ft. Devens" (Ph.D. diss.,
Ohio State University, 2013), 417, https://etd.ohiolink.edu/apexprod/rws_etd
/send_file/send?accession=osu1385398294&disposition=inline.

25. *The Hello Girls,* dir. James Theres (Lincoln Penny Films, 2018), https://
lincolnpennyfilms.com/index.php/the-hello-girls-documentary-a-wwi
-story/.

26. Elizabeth Cobbs, "How the Identity of the Only Black Woman to Serve in
the U.S. Army in World War I Was Just Discovered," Made by History, *Time,*
June 19, 2024, https://time.com/6989875/only-black-woman-in-us-army-wwi/.

9. FROM A MOMENT TO A MOVEMENT

1. Beth Warrington, "No Mail, Low Morale: The 6888th Central Postal Directory Battalion," *Military Review,* January–February 2019, https://www
.armyupress.army.mil/Journals/Military-Review/English-Edition-Archives
/Jan-Feb-2019/Warrington-Mail/.

2. "S.Res.412—A Resolution Expressing the Sense of the Senate Regarding the
6888th Central Postal Directory Battalion and Celebrating Black History
Month," Congress.gov, October 3, 2018, https://www.congress.gov/bill/115th
-congress/senate-resolution/412.

3. "S.3136—'Hello Girls' Congressional Gold Medal Act of 2018," Congress.gov,
June 26, 2018, https://www.congress.gov/bill/115th-congress/senate-bill
/3136/text?r=23&s=1.

4. Kevin M. Hymel, "6888th Central Postal Directory Battalion," Army Historical Foundation, https://armyhistory.org/6888th-central-postal-directory
-battalion/.

5. Edna Cummings, "Overlooked World War II Veterans: Hispanic Women of
the 6888th Postal," *Medium,* October 10, 2021, https://ccllc2008.medium
.com/overlooked-World War II-veterans-hispanic-women-of-the-6888th
-postal-battalion-65e7b5e3bea2.

6. Access to Archival Databases (AAD), "Display Full Records [Lydia Thornton]," National Archives, https://aad.archives.gov/aad/record-detail.jsp?dt=
893&mtch=1&cat=WR26&tf=F&q=lydia+thornton&bc=sl&rpp=10&pg=1&rid
=130734.

7. Afro Staff, "AFRO's Murphy-Matthews among Those Honored for World War II Service," *Afro,* December 20, 2018, https://afro.com/afros-murphy -matthews-among-those-honored-for-wwii-service/.

8. "Study, Employment of Negro Man Power in War," US Army War College, November 10, 1925, https://www.fdrlibrary.org/documents/356632/390886 /tusk_doc_a.pdf/4693156a-8844-4361-ae17-03407e7a3dee.

9. *The Hello Girls,* dir. James Theres (Lincoln Penny Films, 2018), https://www .amazon.com/Hello-Girls-Cokie-Roberts/dp/B07V4TP7G2/.

10. "Hands across the Water Give a Warm Shake," *Detroit Free Press,* May 19, 1981.

11. "US Ambassador Presents Plaque to Commemorate 6888th Battalion," May 16, 2019, King Edwards School, Birmingham, England, https://kes.org.uk/us -ambassador-presents-plaque-to-commemorate-6888th-battalion/.

12. "About Blue Plaques," English Heritage, https://www.english-heritage.org .uk/visit/blue-plaques/about-blue-plaques/.

13. "6888th Legacy Tour: The Only African American WAC Unit of WWII," Stephen Ambrose Historical Tours, https://stephenambrosetours.com/tour /6888th-legacy-tour/.

14. "Six Triple Eight Congressional Gold Medal Campaign," American Veterans Center, https://www.americanveteranscenter.org/2019/07/six-triple-eight -congressional-gold-medal-campaign/.

15. "AVC Events," American Veterans Center, https://www.americanveterans center.org/.

16. S. 633—"Six Triple Eight" Congressional Gold Medal Act of 2020, Febru- ary 28, 2019, Congress.gov, https://www.congress.gov/bill/116th-congress /senate-bill/633.

17. H.R.3138—"Six Triple Eight" Congressional Gold Medal Act of 2019, June 5, 2019, Congress.gov, https://www.congress.gov/bill/116th-congress/house -bill/3138.

18. "Statistics and Historical Comparison," govtrack.us, https://www.govtrack .us/congress/bills/statistics.

19. Reginald F. Lewis Museum of Maryland African American History and Cul- ture, "Past Events, Sundays @2 Films," June 30, 2019.

20. "Montford Point Marines Awarded Congressional Gold Medal," June 27, 2012, United States Mint, https://www.usmint.gov/news/press-releases/20120627 -montford-point-marines-awarded-congressional-gold-medal.

21. Saatchi Art, "Tunde Afolayan Famous," https://www.saatchiart.com /tundevisualart.

22. "The Six Triple Eight," Twitter, October 15, 2020, 2:37 p.m., https://mobile .twitter.com/SixTripleEight/status/1316810438785597440.

23. "Indiana Hunt-Martin," Stars and Stripes, October 15, 2019, Facebook, https://m.facebook.com/stripesmedia/posts/10158574767752316.

24. Jim Axelrod, "An All-Black Women's Army Corps Unit from World War II Is Still Fighting for Recognition," November 14, 2019, CBS News, https://www.cbsnews.com/news/how-an-all-black-womens-army-corps-unit-still-fighting-for-recognition/; Channon Hodge and Tawanda Scott Sambou, "These Black Female Soldiers Brought Order to Chaos and Delivered a Blow against Inequality," updated October 9, 2020, https://www.cnn.com/2020/07/20/us/6888th-battalion-african-american-women-world-war-ii/index.html.

25. "University of Phoenix and the National Society of Leadership and Success Foundation Have Announced the Winner of the 2020 Major Fannie Griffin-McClendon Scholarship," January 14, 2021, University of Phoenix, https://www.businesswire.com/news/home/20210114005196/en/University-of-Phoenix-and-The-National-Society-of-Leadership-and-Success-Foundation-Have-Announced-the-Winner-of-the-2020-Major-Fannie-Griffin-McClendon-Scholarship.

26. "'The Six Triple Eight' Premieres in Chattanooga Feb. 13," Walker County Mesenger, 6th Cavalry Museum, https://www.northwestgeorgianews.com/catoosa_walker_news/lifestyles/the-six-triple-eight-premieres-in-chattanooga-feb-13/article_8e24c3b2-3646-11ea-8b46-e331403f024c.html.

27. "Chickamauga and Chattanooga: National Military Park, GA, TN," National Park Service. https://www.nps.gov/chch/learn/historyculture/people.htm.

28. The Triple Victory of the 6888th, exhibition, 6th Cavalry Museum, Fort Oglethorpe, Georgia (now closed), https://risingrock.net/2021/04/28/the-triple-victory-of-the-6888th/.

29. Aimee Custis, DC Policy Center, "A Timeline of the D.C. Region's COVID-19 Pandemic," March 24, 2020, https://www.dcpolicycenter.org/publications/covid-19-timeline/.

10. ADVOCACY DURING LOCKDOWN

1. "23 Officers in [and] 738 WACs to England as First All-Woman Postal Unit," Afro American, February 24, 1945.

2. Edna Cummings and Elizabeth Helm-Frazier, "The Silent Six Triple Eight," Afro American, May 19, 2020, https://afro.com/World War II-ve-day75-tribute-the-silent-six-triple-eight/.

3. Christina Brown Fisher, "The Black Female Battalion That Stood Up to a White Male Army," New York Times, June 17, 2020, updated September 2,

2020, https://www.nytimes.com/2020/06/17/magazine/6888th-battalion
-charity-adams.html.

4. Jerry Moran, United States Senator for Kansas, "Sen. Moran's Bill to Honor
Women of the 'Six-Triple-Eight' Passes Senate," December 11, 2020, https://
www.moran.senate.gov/public/index.cfm/2020/12/sen-moran-s-bill-to
-honor-women-of-the-six-triple-eight-passes-senate.

5. Drew DeSilver, "Nothing Lame about This Lame Duck: 116th Congress Had
Busiest Post-Election Session in Recent History," January 21, 2021, Pew Research Center, https://www.pewresearch.org/fact-tank/2021/01/21/nothing
-lame-about-this-lame-duck-116th-congress-had-busiest-post-election
-session-in-recent-history/.

6. "Gold Star Family Fellowship Program," Chief Administrative Officer,
https://cao.house.gov/gold-star.

7. "First Sgt. Russell Ryan Bell, January 20, 1975–August 2, 2012," memorial
page, LaFayette Funeral Home, Fayetteville, NC, https://www.lafayettefh
.com/obituary/FirstSgtRussell-Bell.

8. *Afro American*, "GI's Unload 3,600 Tons of Yuletide Mail in 5 Days," January 13, 1945.

9. "Only WAC Postal Unit Re-routes Soldiers' Letters from E.T.O.," *Cleveland
Call and Post*, June 30, 1945.

10. "How Much Does a Letter Weigh?," What Things Weigh, https://
whatthingsweigh.com/how-much-does-a-letter-weigh/.

11. "Domestic Mail Manual, M033 Sacks and Trays," United States Postal Service, https://pe.usps.com/archive/html/dmmarchive20030810/M033.htm#:
~:text=The%20maximum%20weight%20of%20any,must%20not%20exceed
%2070%20pounds.

12. "Legislative Activity, Floor Summary: February 28, 2022," Clerk, United
States House of Representatives, https://clerk.house.gov/FloorSummary
?date=02/28/2022.

13. Congressman Brian Higgins, "Bill Introduced by Congressman Higgins, Honoring World War II Veteran Indiana Hunt-Martin, Signed into
Law," October 14, 2022, https://higgins.house.gov/media-center/press
-releases/bill-introduced-by-congressman-higgins-honoring-World War
II-veteran-indiana.

14. "Medals," United States Mint, https://www.usmint.gov/learn/coin-and
-medal-programs/medals.

15. "CCAC Meeting Images," Citizen Coinage Advisory Committee (CCAC),
https://www.usmint.gov/news/ccac-meetings.

16. "Congressional Gold Medal Event Honoring Legendary WWII Unit Six-
Triple Eight," May 26, 2022, Commemorative Air Force, https://www

.commemorativeairforce.org/news/congressional-gold-medal-event
-honoring-legendary-wwii-unit-six-triple-eight.

17. "Barrier Breaker: Anna Mae Robertson Played Key Role in Stabilizing Soldiers' Morale during World War II," *Milwaukee Journal Sentinel,* July 1, 2022, https://www.jsonline.com/story/news/2022/07/01/anna-mae-robertson
-connected-soldiers-loved-ones-during-wwii/7719458001/.

18. Arlington National Cemetery, "6888th Central Postal Directory Battalion (Women's Army Corps)," https://www.arlingtoncemetery.mil/Explore
/Notable-Graves/African-Americans/6888th-Central-Postal-Directory
-Battalion.

19. "6888th Central Postal Directory Battalion (Women's Army Corps)," African American History, Arlington National Cemetery, https://www
.arlingtoncemetery.mil/Explore/Notable-Graves/African-Americans
/6888th-Central-Postal-Directory-Battalion.

20. "For Unsung Black Military Women, a Gold-Medal Day with Broadway Pizzazz," *Washington Post,* June 16, 2022, https://www.washingtonpost.com
/arts-entertainment/2022/06/16/black-women-6888-gold-medal/.

21. "102-Year-Old World War II Veteran from Segregated Mail Unit Honored, July 26, 2022," NBC News, https://www.nbcnews.com/news/us-news
/102-year-old-world-war-ii-veteran-segregated-mail-unit-honored
-rcna39971.

22. "The Unsung Story of the Six Triple Eight," February 14, 2022, George W. Bush Presidential Center, https://www.bushcenter.org/publications/the
-unsung-story-of-the-six-triple-eight.

23. Adam Reiss and Rehema Ellis, "At Long Last, 101-Year-Old Black World War II Veteran Gets Overdue Recognition, Honor," November 11, 2021, NBC News, https://www.nbcnews.com/news/veterans/long-last-black-101-year-old
-wwii-veteran-receives-overdue-n1283751.

24. Whitchurch Hospital, Cardiff, December 14, 2018, Blurred Boundaries, https://www.blurredboundaries.co.uk/2018/12/14/whitchurch-hospital
-cardiff/.

11. WORLD WAR II BLACK WOMEN

1. "Cathay Williams," Santa Fe National Historic Trail, National Park Service, https://www.nps.gov/people/cwilliams.htm.

2. Shay Dawson, "Harriet Tubman (1822–1913)," National Women's History Museum, https://www.womenshistory.org/education-resources/biographies
/harriet-tubman. Olatunji Osho-Williams, "Harriet Tubman Just Became a

One-Star General, More Than 150 Years after Serving with the Union Army," *Smithsonian Magazine*, November 13, 2024, https://www.smithsonianmag.com/smart-news/harriet-tubman-just-became-a-one-star-general-more-than-150-years-after-serving-with-the-union-army-180985458/.

3. Cara Moore Lebonick, "Mustering Out: The Navy's First Black Yeowomen," November 9, 2020, Rediscovering Black History, National Archives, https://rediscovering-black-history.blogs.archives.gov/2020/11/09/golden-14/.

4. "African American Nurses," Fort McHenry National Monument and Historic Shrine, Maryland, National Park Service, https://www.nps.gov/fomc/learn/historyculture/african-american-nurses.htm.

5. Aaron Randle, "'Black Rosies': The Forgotten African American Heroines of the WWII Homefront," November 10, 2020, updated September 12, 2023, Black History, History.com, https://www.history.com/news/black-rosie-the-riveters-wwii-homefront-great-migration.

6. "African American Army Nurses in World War II," Charles Young Buffalo Soldiers National Monument, National Park Service, https://www.nps.gov/articles/000/ww2armynursecorps.htm.

7. "Highest Level of Educational Attainment for 25 to 34 Year Olds in the United States, from 1940 to 2009," September 30, 2010, Statista, https://www.statista.com/statistics/234586/educational-attainment-rates-in-the-us/.

8. "U.S. Service Member Deaths by Race, War/Conflict and 1980–Present, as of April 20, 2022," Defense Manpower Data Systems, https://dcas.dmdc.osd.mil/dcas/assets/Documents/RACE-OMB-WC-2022.pdf.

9. "Soldiers' Solace: Clubmobile Women during World War II," December 30, 2013, Moment of Indiana History, *Indiana Magazine of History*, https://indianapublicmedia.org/momentofindianahistory/soldiers-solace-clubmobile-women-world-war-ii/; Gordon Williams, "The Wartime Tales of Red Cross Donut Dollies," June 3, 2021, American Red Cross NW Region, https://redcrossnw.org/2021/06/03/the-wartime-tales-of-red-cross-donut-dollies/.

10. "23 Officers in 738 Wacs to England as First All-Woman Army Postal Unit," *Afro American*, February 24, 1945, https://mgaleg.maryland.gov/cmte_testimony/2023/hg0/1dNNRXB4l7NupG9v5JKpU79VQKMVOcb3p.pdf.

11. Defense Acquisition University (DAU), https://www.dau.edu/cop/se/resources/systems-engineering.

12. "WACs' Crossing Fair; Find English Hospitable, Entertainments Plentiful, Exchange Confusing," *Afro American*, March 10, 1945, National Association of Black Military Women.

13. Martin Collins and Frances Collins, *Letters for Victory: History of the First Base Post Office in Sutton Coldfield, Warwickshire, during World War Two* (Studley, Warwickshire: Brewin, 1993), 80.

14. Kat Stafford, James LaPorta, Aaron Morrison, and Helen Wieffering, "Deep-Rooted Racism, Discrimination Permeate US Military," Associated Press, May 27, 2021, https://apnews.com/article/us-military-racism-discrimination-4e840e0acc7ef07fd635a312d9375413.

15. Charity Adams Earley, *One Woman's Army: A Black Officer Remembers the WAC* (College Station: Texas A&M University, 1995), 106.

16. "Earley Couple's Post-Military Lives Built on Giving Back," April 20, 2023, Defense Visual Information Service, https://www.dvidshub.net/news/443018/earley-couples-post-military-lives-built-giving-back.

17. Earley, *One Woman's Army*, 185.

18. Margie Bedell-Burke, "Chaplain Reads Benediction at WAC Wedding," Women of World War II, US Army Signal Corps, https://www.womenofwwii.com/army/army-wacs/chaplain-reads-benediction-at-wac-wedding/.

19. "AFRO'S Murphy-Matthews among Those Honored for WWII Service," *Afro American,* December 18, 2023, https://afro.com/afros-murphy-matthews-among-those-honored-for-wwii-service/.

20. David N. Young, "Former Marine, 97, Presented with Congressional Medal in La Palma," *News Enterprise,* February 29, 2024, https://event-newsenterprise.com/former-marine-97-presented-with-congressional-medal-in-la-palma/.

21. Jonathan Grass, "Montgomery Centenarian's Brother to Posthumously Get Congressional Gold Medal," January 17, 2024, WFSA, https://www.wsfa.com/2024/01/18/montgomery-centenarians-brother-posthumously-get-congressional-gold-medal/.

22. Retired US Army Col. Edna W. Cummings, "The Untold Story of a 761st Black Panther and the 6888th Elzie Sisters," *Afro American,* August 26, 2023, https://afro.com/the-untold-story-of-a-761st-black-panther-and-the-6888th-elzie-sisters/.

23. "The Normandy Invasion: The Assault Force," US Army Center for Military History, https://www.history.army.mil/html/reference/Normandy/asltforce.html.

24. Melissa Ziobro, "'Skirted Soldiers': The Women's Army Corps and Gender Integration of the U.S. Army during World War II," National Museum of the United States Army, https://armyhistory.org/skirted-soldiers-the-womens-army-corps-and-gender-integration-of-the-u-s-army-during-world-war-ii/.

25. "S.1641, A Bill to Establish the Women's Army Corps . . . [and] to Authorize the Enlistment and Appointment of Women in the . . . Navy and Marine Corps . . . (Women's Armed Services Integration Act), July 16, 1947," US Capitol Visitor Center, Artifact Explorer, https://www.visitthecapitol.gov/artifact

/s-1641-bill-establish-womens-army-corps-and-authorize-enlistment-and
-appointment-women.

26. Lori Robinson and Michael E. O'Hanlon, "Women Warriors: The Ongoing
Story of Integrating and Diversifying the American Armed Forces," May
2020, Brookings, https://www.brookings.edu/essay/women-warriors-the
-ongoing-story-of-integrating-and-diversifying-the-armed-forces/.

27. Farrell Evans, "Why Harry Truman Ended Segregation in the US Military
in 1948," History.com, November 5, 2020, updated May 6, 2024, https://
www.history.com/news/harry-truman-executive-order-9981-desegration
-military-1948.

28. President's Committee on Equality of Treatment and Opportunity, *Freedom to Serve: Equality of Treatment and Opportunity in the Armed Services*,
May 22, 1950, Harry S. Truman Library, National Archives, https://www
.trumanlibrary.gov/library/freedom-to-serve.

29. "AP Report: Deep-Rooted Racism and Discrimination Permeate U.S.
Military," PBS News, May 27, 2021, https://www.pbs.org/newshour/nation
/ap-report-deep-rooted-racism-and-discrimination-permeate-u-s
-military.

30. Office of the Under Secretary of Defense for Personnel & Readiness, "No
Fear Act," https://prhome.defense.gov/NoFear/.

31. Department of Defense, 2020 *Demographics Profile of the Military Community*, https://download.militaryonesource.mil/12038/MOS/Reports/2020
-demographics-report.pdf.

FINAL THOUGHTS

1. "American Valor Awards 2019 Honoring the 6888th Narrated by Terry
Crews," American Veterans Center, YouTube video, https://www.youtube
.com/watch?v=NmLH1dlh7RE.

2. Carlotta Walls LaNier, Lisa Frazier, and Bill Clinton, prologue to *A Mighty
Long Way: My Journey to Justice at Little Rock Central High School* (New York:
Random House, 2009).

3. Cheryl Pellerin, "Carter Opens All Military Occupations, Positions to
Women," December 3, 2015, US Department of Defense, https://www
.defense.gov/News/News-Stories/Article/Article/632536/carter-opens-all
-military-occupations-positions-to-women/.

4. Chucik, "Female Fighter Pilots and the Combat Exclusion Policy," *The Un-
written Record* (blog), October 3, 2019, National Archives, https://unwritten

-record.blogs.archives.gov/2019/10/03/the-sky-no-longer-has-limits-female
-fighter-pilots-and-the-combat-exclusion-policy/.

5. "National Security Snapshot: DOD Active-Duty Recruitment and Retention
Challenges," GAO-23–106551, March 28, 2023, US Government Accountability
Office, https://www.gao.gov/products/gao-23-106551.

6. Brig. Gen. Patrick R. Michaelis, Fort Jackson Commanding General, "Fort
Jackson's Future Soldier Preparatory Course," August 4, 2022, https://
www.army.mil/article/259078/fort_jacksons_future_soldier_preparatory
_course.

7. "Black Americans in the U.S. Army (1941–45 and 2021-Present Day)," US
Army, https://www.army.mil/blackamericans/timeline.html.

8. "Number of Female Generals and Admirals Doubles since 2000," http://
www.nawrb.com/womenadmiralsandgeneralsdoubles/.

9. #TeamEbony, "First Black Woman Graduates from U.S. Army Ranger
School," May 14, 2019 https://www.ebony.com/first-black-woman-graduates
-us-army-ranger-school/; "Army Rangers Lead the Way, No Matter the
Mission," US Army, https://www.goarmy.com/careers-and-jobs/specialty
-careers/special-ops/army-rangers.html.

10. Christopher S. Chivvis and Sahil Lauji, "Diversity in the High Brass,"
September 6, 2022, Carnegie Endowment for International Peace, https://
carnegieendowment.org/2022/09/06/diversity-in-high-brass-pub-87694.

11. Noah Parsons, "What Is a SWOT Analysis and How to Do It Right (with Examples)," LivePlan, February 2, 2021, https://www.liveplan.com/blog/what-is-a
-swot-analysis-and-how-to-do-it-right-with-examples/.

12. "Only WAC Postal Unit Re-routes Soldiers' Letters from E.T.O.," *Cleveland
Call and Post,* June 30, 1945.

13. Andrew S. Harvey, PhD, "The Levels of War as Levels of Analysis," *Military
Review* (November-December 2021), https://www.armyupress.army.mil
/Journals/Military-Review/English-Edition-Archives/November-December
-2021/Harvey-Levels-of-War/.

14. "The U.S. Constitution: Preamble," United States Courts, https://www
.uscourts.gov/about-federal-courts/educational-resources/about
-educational-outreach/activity-resources/us#:~:text=%22We%20the
%20People%20of%20the,for%20the%20United%20States%20of.

15. Jordan Batchelor, Charles Max Katz, and Taylor Cox, "Military Veterans Are
Disproportionately Affected by Suicide, but Targeted Prevention Can Help
Reverse the Tide," *The Conversation,* November 7, 2024, https://the
conversation.com/military-veterans-are-disproportionately-affected-by
-suicide-but-targeted-prevention-can-help-reverse-the-tide-238975.

16. "Fort Gregg-Adams Redesignation," US Army Garrison, Fort Gregg-Adams, US Army, https://home.army.mil/greggadams/redesignation.

APPENDIX 3

1. Lucia M. Pitts, *One Negro WAC's Story* (Los Angeles: privately published, 1968; distributed by Pitts).

BIBLIOGRAPHY

BOOKS

Bolzenius, Sandra. *Glory in Their Spirit: How Four Black Women Took on the Army during World War II.* Urbana: University of Illinois Press, 2018.

Clark, Alexis. *Enemies in Love: A German POW, a Black Nurse, and an Unlikely Romance.* New York: New Press, 2018.

Collins, Martin, and Frances Collins. *Letters for Victory: History of the First Base Post Office in Sutton Coldfield, Warwickshire, during World War Two.* Studley, Warwickshire: Brewin, 1993.

Earley, Charity Adams. *One Woman's Army: A Black Officer Remembers the WAC.* College Station: Texas A&M University Press, 1989.

LaNier, Carlotta Walls, Lisa Frazier Page, and Bill Clinton *"A Mighty Long Way": My Journey to Justice at Little Rock Central High School.* New York: Random House, 2009.

Mullenbach, Cheryl. *Double Victory: How African American Women Broke Race and Gender Barriers to Help Win World War II.* Chicago: Chicago Review Press, 2013.

Mundy, Liza. *Code Girls: The Untold Story of the American Women Code Breakers of World War II.* New York: Hachette, 2017.

FILMS AND DOCUMENTARIES

The Six Triple Eight: No Mail, Low Morale. Directed by James Theres. Lincoln Penny Films. 2019.

The Hello Girls. Directed by James Theres. Lincoln Penny Films. 2018.

NEWSPAPERS

Afro American, 1939–50.

WEBSITES

"Interesting Facts about Victory in Europe Day (VE)." US Airborne and Special Army Special Operations. https://www.asomf.org/interesting-facts-about -victory-in-europe-day/.

CONVERSATIONS AND CORRESPONDENCE WITH AUTHOR (2018–2023)

Vivian "Millie" Bailey, World War II veteran
Benjamin Brands, historian, American Battle Monuments Commission
Carrie Cutchens. Fort Bragg Special Operations Museum, Fort Bragg, North Carolina
Carlotta LaNier, member of Little Rock Nine; author of *"A Mighty Long Way"*
6888th Central Postal Directory Battalion veterans and family members:
    Stanley Earley (son, 6888th veteran Charity Adams [Earley])
    Tara Garcia (granddaughter, 6888th veteran Crescencia Garcia)
    Ms. Indiana Hunt-Martin (688th veteran)
    Elizabeth "Bernice" Barker Johnson (6888th veteran)
    Dr. Carmen Jordan-Cox (daughter, 6888th veteran Annie Knight)
    Janice Martin (daughter, 6888th veteran Indiana Hunt-Martin)
    Betty Matthews Murphy (daughter, 6888th veteran Vashti Murphy)
    Roger Matthews (son, 6888th veteran Vashti Murphy)
    Retired US Air Force Maj. Fannie McClendon (6888th veteran)
    Dennis Miller (grandson, 6888th veteran Sylvia Armstrong)
    Rosenda Moore (daughter, 6888th veteran Lydia Thornton)
    Cynthia Scott (daughter, 6888th veteran Elizabeth "Bernice" Barker Johnson)
    Alva Stevenson (daughter, 6888th veteran Lydia Thornton)

INDEX

THE BLACK SOLDIER IN WAR AND SOCIETY

New Narratives and Critical Perspectives

This series is open to a wide array of scholarship on the ramifications of "soldiering" on the economic, social, cultural, or political lives of Black individuals, families, and communities. The editors seek projects that will highlight the long, and in many cases unending, fight for racial and social justice across time and space in the Black Atlantic.

Race, Politics, and Reconstruction: The First Cadets at Old West Point
Rory McGovern and Ronald G. Machoian, editors